Susie Boyt is the author of six ac..
Hope of Girls which was shortlisted for the John Llewellyn Rhys Prize
and *Only Human* which was shortlisted for the Mind Book of the
Year. Her latest novel, *Love & Fame*, is a highly strung comedy about
grief and show business. She has written columns and reviews for the
Financial Times Weekend for sixteen years and last year she edited
The Turn of the Screw and Other Ghost Stories by Henry James for
Penguin Classics. Susie is also a director at the Hampstead Theatre
in London and works part time as a bereavement counsellor.

My
Judy
Garland
Life

Susie Boyt

virago

VIRAGO

First published in Great Britain in 2008 by Virago Press
This paperback edition published in 2019 by Virago Press

10 9 8 7 6 5 4 3 2 1

A CIP catalogue record for this book
is available from the British Library.

ISBN 978-0-349-01338-1

Typeset in Garamond by M Rules
Printed and bound in Great Britain by Clays Ltd, Elcograf S.p.A.

Papers used by Virago are from well-managed forests
and other responsible sources.

MIX
Paper from
responsible sources
FSC® C104740

Virago Press
An imprint of
Little, Brown Book Group
50 Victoria Embankment
London EC4Y 0DZ

An Hachette UK Company
www.hachette.co.uk

www.virago.co.uk

For my mother and father

———————

I had, from my beginning, to adore heroes
& I elected that they witness to,
show forth, transfigure: life-suffering & pure heart
& hardly definable but central weakness

for which they were enthroned & forgiven by me.

John Berryman, 'The Heroes'

Contents

Preface

Is the art of consolation a life's work? It might be. There is always more to learn. Ten years ago in this book I described the way the world's greatest entertainer sang with pure undilute feeling straight into the heart of a little girl whose childhood hurt her pride.

Judy Garland suggested to me that the best moments always have an element of kill or cure. Days, weeks, years will be spent celebrating and mourning, but these things can be practised at the same time, if you dare. Little girls, women of all ages often fear they are too much, that they want too much, that there's an ugliness to our needs which are innately untoward. Judy Garland turned this inside out for me. Exterminate your feelings? Are you out of your mind? They'll be the making of you. They have been in their way.

When I listen to Judy Garland now I still get the enthralling sense of the arm of a record player being lowered onto life itself. It might interest her to hear that once this book brought a man out of a coma in his hospital bed, only not long afterwards the woman reading decided he wasn't right for her after all . . .

How do we best celebrate a difficult life? In writing about someone's triumphs, by navigating life in the eulogy gear can you do away with a tiny bit of the harm? Garland's gallantry in bringing joy to millions when her own life was sometimes impossible, or worse, is a sort of miracle. How do we reach back in time and compensate our loved ones, for things they endured before we were born? How do we protect them from damage once they've gone? I have suffered myself at the hands of scurrilous biographers and on a bad day it has felt as though they've dug up the dead only to murder them.

The trespasses her family has borne . . .

The modest mews house where Judy died in London fifty years ago has been razed and rebuilt. It's grand and luxurious now, the sort of place the second son of a billionaire might hustle and strut. It tells a lie about how she lived, a lie I wish were true. Is that wrong of me? It offends me when people are more drawn to Judy Garland's suffering than her magnificent achievements. I feel outraged that my mother's life was often tough. Do I betray anyone by having an easier time of it myself?

Although I think psychoanalysis an unrivalled method of human understanding, I occasionally wonder if its theories apply a little more to the Freud family than the population at large. Recently I dreamed an interviewer asked me about my father. 'I didn't always tell him what he wanted to hear and he didn't always like it, and that affected our relationship, but I think he respected me for it and I don't wish I had done things differently.'

'Sounds reasonable,' the interviewer said.

My mother and father are gone now, they're in the same cemetery although they never lived together. It's bright with birdsong, there are green and white feathery grasses and meadow flowers, strange ancient monuments bound with ivy, the scent of wild garlic in the breeze. There are ninety footsteps between them. I took her to see him at the end in a taxi. I wasn't sure that it would work. She was frail, he more so. I crept upstairs and he was sleeping but he opened one eye. 'I've got Mum in the kitchen. She's come to see you, to say . . . Hello.' I crossed my fingers.

'Mum?' he said. 'Here? God how lovely!'

Two years ago Judy Garland's children moved her from Ferncliffe Cemetery in New York to Hollywood, to be close to them.

I am writing this in the Cinderella Bar at the London Palladium where Judy's second act as a concert artist truly began in 1951.

I have much love in my heart.

London August 2019

How
It All
Began

I've been half or more in love with Judy Garland all my life. Since my earliest beginnings, when I was so sensitive that my heart went out to everything – strangers, ants, even that sad cluster of abandoned items in the supermarket next to the cashier's till – Judy Garland has inspired and enriched my inner world.

Her presence, through her films and her recordings, her concert footage and her television shows, has consoled and invigorated, educated and disturbed. The imperative intimacy I feel with Judy Garland is similar to that which I feel for my mother or my children. It is a sort of profound kinship, a peculiar personal connection, an emergency of friendship and sympathy that has the same passion to it as a crisis. This sense of attachment to Judy Garland allows me to sidestep others' ignoble concerns about the way she lived, the way she worked and her reputation in the world at large; it makes me feel I have a reasonable claim to call myself her friend.

And, although Judy Garland died five months after I was born, this has always seemed to me a two-sided affair that has suited us both. I've felt Judy Garland's acute need of me and this prolonged fantasy – you might call it – of intimacy has been both sustaining and exhilarating. It has been a central part of my development as a person, as real as meat, as tears. I know for certain that something at the heart of Judy Garland connects directly to something at the heart of me. I feel implicated in her myriad struggles and triumphant in the face of her success. There are flashes of understanding between us, almost supernatural shocks of intense recognition, which assail me when I hear her sing or speak, or watch her dance.

As a young child it seemed that all anyone ever said to me was: 'You must learn to toughen up. You mustn't take everything to heart so. You really ought to try to control your feelings more or you just won't have a happy life.' This then, I learned, was the job of

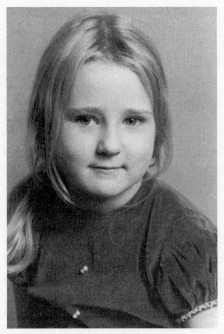

Me aged six

childhood, the work of adolescence. If you could only gain mastery of your emotional world, why, you would be set up for ever! But how to do it? Nobody said. Was I to arrange myself so that I had no feelings at all? Was I to turn everything I felt into a secret? Or was it more a question of keeping very still and quiet for a few years until my mental capabilities could match the intensity of my heart, which had simply outgrown its casings?

Into this fragile environment, one day, came the voice of Judy Garland. At the cinema for the first time with my mother, I listened, transfixed, to Dorothy singing 'Over the Rainbow'.

Dorothy and Toto relaxing between takes

3

I had never heard anything like it in my life. It was immediately clear to me that Garland's singing bypassed all the indignity of strong feelings that I was grappling with, and instead she capitalised on her struggles. She absolutely led with them, presenting them as the best things life contains. Since early childhood I have always entertained a lot of dark thoughts – I put out a welcome mat for them; I feed them and clothe them – but Judy Garland seemed miraculously to transform the harsher truths of life into something wonderful, where all feelings, however dark, are good and true because they're *yours*. There was an instant – and I felt it even then – *historic* meeting between us, a kind of tessellation of spirit accompanied by thick bolts of not just fellow feeling but of fellow being. I wanted to slip right then inside the screen.

From here, our life took off together in delightful ways. I had an LP of *The Wizard of Oz* – not just the songs, but the entire soundtrack – and I put it on whenever I was in my room. I mouthed the words alongside: 'That dog's a menace to the community. I'm taking him to the sheriff and make sure he's destroyed.' It was my wallpaper for several years. 'Put him in the basket, Henry,' I would murmur wryly in the face of any sort of defeat. I listened to Judy Garland's music continually, lying on my bedcover with the yellow moons and the pink stars. We cared about so many of the same things, chiefly the importance of making other people happy, a huge concern of mine, which no one else I knew seemed to speak of at all. I still believe one of the best ways to help the environment is to be 50 per cent kinder to all family, friends and strangers and then sit back and watch the world improve.

And although I did not begin to understand Judy Garland's sorrows, I saw that she had them and that they weighed heavily on her four foot eleven frame, and that she was a bigger person for them. Like thousands of others before me I felt that just by listening to her I could help. This made me immensely hopeful. The idea that uneasiness could be channelled into something beautiful, something triumphant that could somehow link us and transform us was a revelation. Even as a child I could see that Judy's courage was contagious; it was almost pneumatic. Everything she did seemed like a staggering act of human generosity, designed especially to appeal to me. She must have been the most conscientious unreliable person who ever lived.

I was a conscientious and reliable and helpful girl, chubby and intense, keen to stay a child for as long as possible – for ever, if I could manage it – because I knew the grown up world inhabited by my parents, by my much older siblings, was far more dangerous than I could bear. To emulate Judy's dance routines I started taking tap, ballet and modern classes, three days a week, in a local church hall presided over by a Miss Audrey. I loved it. It was a cruel joke that I might ever have a dancer's body but I was praised and encouraged endlessly, not for my talent but because of my sheer hard work and my excellent memory which, when you are a very young dancer, can take you quite far. I worked hard also at staying cheerful, with discipline and willpower, practising my dancing for hours at a time to a record called *The Young Judy Garland*, using the mantelpiece in my bedroom as a barre. I loved and learned a song called 'Friendship', in which Judy and Johnny Mercer make hysterical, competitive pledges of allegiance to each other, such as, 'If you ever lose your teeth when you're out to dine, borrow mine', and 'If you ever lose your mind, I'll be kind.' I loved the idea that there might one day be someone I'd do anything for.

I passed through a difficult year. My parents had parted before I was born and I missed my father so much it was a physical pain. Yet as my love for Judy Garland began to grow and deepen something hopeful stirred in me, and things to do with life and the outside world and the people in it gradually started to seem a little more possible, even slightly inviting. Practising my tap routines to Garland's

5

records, reciting the mesmerising chains of steps, the endless hop-shuffle-hop-brush-hop-pick-ups (repeat) I could see that it might be desirable to grow up one day and it would be awful sometimes, more painful than my darkest dreams, but it might also be, now and then, a bit lovely. My strength of feeling that I'd learned to view as an affliction, Judy seemed to think might be the making of me. She ennobled and forgave. It was the first time she had intervened. And so we began.

What does it say about this extraordinary performer that I've felt linked to her so powerfully all my life? What does it say about me? Whatever strange alchemy has been at work between us, the facts are these: I wasn't there at the moments of her greatest triumphs and her cruellest despair. But she has been at mine.

World's
Greatest
Entertainer

Of course Judy Garland was the greatest entertainer of the twentieth or any century. Her singing made a direct assault on the heart that no one else has ever matched. When Judy performs, every moment in life becomes a rite of passage, a disaster or epiphany so exhilarating that you need to raise the calibre of your personality in order to meet it.

Matters of life and death hang in the balance when Judy Garland sings. Everything is celebration or mourning. There's no prevarication. Her voice aims straight at our central nervous systems, to our red and white blood cells, inside our ventricles, auricles and valves. No other performer ever communicated so sincerely and with so much lustre that the truth actually dazzles.

Judy Garland changed the face of popular entertainment for ever. She created a whole new theatrical idiom in which glamour and frankness nudge and jostle unabashedly. The rapport Garland maintained with her audiences is unequalled in history. In Judy's presence our hopes and disappointments flee their straitjackets and dance before us wildly. Our emotions have their colour and brightness turned up to the highest pitch. We are uncurbed, all our self-censorship goes, our codes of practice and our ludicrous controls, and there's no place for anything artificial, or learned or resolved. Judy brings off impossible feats: to combine absolute candour and absolute valour is a moral impossibility – but not in Judy's hands. Her humour and intelligence comprise a brand of warmth that has a devastating grace. At least they do for me.

Garland's mature voice affected her concert audiences so deeply they unravelled before her. The sympathy she offered was visceral and hard. Her fans felt along the lines of her songs and found both the symptoms of life and their cures. 'Bedlam superimposed upon bedlam' describes a typical end-of-performance crowd who no longer knew their names or where they were or why or who, but just lay down madly in the theatre aisles or beneath the apron of the stage, *feeling*. Think of the wild sorrow of the white-gloved ushers at the Palace Theater as they applauded Judy into the stratosphere when she ended her triumphant nineteen-week run there on 24 February 1952. Picture the crazed despair of the star-struck usherettes as they serenaded Judy with 'Auld Lang Syne'! Judy frequently drew standing ovations from her orchestras. No singer is a hero to her accompanists – they play four times as many notes and earn a small fraction of the fee – but Judy was.

Judy Garland's admirers use extraordinary images to describe her effects. Critics take on disguises when analysing her magisterial sway. One moment they are scientists, acute and intrepid, investigating an inexplicable human phenomenon; the next they turn swooning suitors, love-torn sonneteers; then they are faithful guardians, staunch and perturbed, setting out for their adored charge a model for living, for staying alive. 'That girl should work two hours and then be taken home in an ambulance! How she gives of herself!' the actress Ina Claire said when she visited the set of *A Star Is Born*.

Judy leaves your levels of receptivity so high that after an hour in her company even dry London pavements look poignant and acute. Tall buildings take on that shimmering, provisional look they get when viewed through fumes. Her songs destroy your calluses while sandpapering your plumpest hopes. Judy sensitises and quickens and makes every aspect of life more extreme and affecting. Her voice undoes people, cutting through layers and layers of masks and defences until we can't help exclaiming at the thinness of our skin. Garland's performances leave us in a state of crisis, but it's a good crisis, like falling in love or having your stitches removed.

When Judy's in the house the unendurable and the delightful go hand in hand, hoisted and throbbing across the room, demanding your greatest respect. There's no need for alleviation when Judy sings, no room for dilution or pretence. Likewise courage and fear, by this point, are silly and cosmetic. When Judy sings your heart of hearts has no other home but her throat.

Garland was the most generous of artists. She went all-out, keeping nothing back from her fans, giving of herself to such a degree it was almost insane. Asked by a reporter in 1968 how she'd like to be thought of by people, she replied, 'I would like them to know that I have been in love with them all my life.' Judy Garland's talent had a Robin Hood quality to it. She reduced, in concert, the hardest, most cynical Hollywood figures to infants, all mucus and tears. She exalted the lowly, the broken-down clown in a fix, on its uppers, and was a huge respecter of the rejected and the uncared-for in love. But she triumphed equally in her more sophisticated drawing room register, witty, wistful and debonair. Her face was half imp, half cherub, but her constitution was that of an ox.

No two performances Garland gave were the same. The chances that she took! She shone as a child star, electric with hope and yearning, and dazzled as a young girl as ecstatic at the thought of life's promise as a line from Whitman's *Leaves of Grass*. Over her early performances there hovers a sort of permanent dew. No one can touch her for thoroughbred ardour. And her ardour is so powerful! In Oz it helps her thwart an evil regime, depose two cruel rulers and debunk then befriend – so characteristic that – a sham wizard. In *Presenting Lily Mars* her moral energy even wins her the lead in a Broadway show. Judy's version of longing was of the richest and most festive hue. Other esteemed performers faded in her presence. Who else could partner Astaire and eclipse him? Judy's face, full of ripe emotion, makes Fred seem lacklustre. You scarcely even think about his feet! 'The greatest entertainer who ever lived, or probably ever will' he called her, generously. Judy Garland was an impossible act to follow, her ease and her lavish sincerity utterly beguiling. 'If you did four flips in the air, cut your head off and sewed it on again it wouldn't mean a thing' Betty Hutton complained. 'Just stand there' Garland's audience begged when the encores were running out at Carnegie Hall.

At times a later Judy seems to sing against the grain of herself so that all the sincerity and theatricality, the effervescence, vulnerability, frustration, irony and passion are vying wildly for position. As

10

I hear her overture I sometimes imagine a person I love in the dark at a party, hovering half out of sight, with a face partly lit by a cake bearing many candles and suddenly the glare of flame is dancing a little too close to my flyaway hair and the thick scent of vanilla sugar ambushes my nostrils and then a hundred people are singing 'Happy Birthday' to me and a thin channel of icing drips from the rim of the plate threatening my toes that peep from high sandals in descending sizes, varnished in Dior's Rouge de Fête.

When I begin to listen to Judy Garland there is no joy or wound from the story of my life that isn't with me. Great flashes of past experience dazzle and dismay, the good and the bad, at the same time, in vivid layers. It is an unstable moment, one that cannot be too often indulged. Her central credo, and it always always comes to me as her voice begins to swell, is that to be the person with the strongest feelings in life is to be the best. This is an instinct I am quite sure I was born with. A notion that is right inside my bones. Yet I know it is something I am no longer meant to believe.

After this initial seizing and unhanding I feel the familiar unravelling too. It is a sensation filled with pleasure and alarm. They say once Judy has you she has got you for life, and it's true. My resistance to her is awfully low. And as I take her in through my pores the things that habitually seem important and vital to me fall away or shrivel and I feel new beliefs knitting together in their place. Then, before I know it, the following statements appear to be true:

*Things that are hard have more of life at their heart than things that are easy.
*The future must prove better and happier than the past.
*All feelings, however painful, are to be prized.
*The opposite of good feelings are not bad feelings but no feelings.
*Glamour is a moral stance.

*The world is crueller and more wonderful than anyone ever says.

*Loss, its memory and its anticipation, lies at the heart of human experience.

*Any human situation, however deadly, can be changed, turned around and improved beyond recognition on any given day, in one minute, in one hour.

*You must try to prepare and be ready for the moment that you're needed, for the call could come at any time.

*The fluctuations of the heart mark the trajectory of the human career, but you must try not to pay this too much heed.

*There are worse things in life than being taken for a ride.

*If you have a thin skin all aspects of life cost more and have more value.

*Loyalty to one other is the best kind of human system.

*Grief is no real match for the human heart, which is an infinitely resourceful organ.

To accompany my Garlandian truisms I experience startling rings of similarity. Judy's soaring, outstretched emphases and the things she hushes or omits seem, to the letter, my own. I want to ape the little drawn-out hesitancies that bridge her spoken words. 'Do you . . . do you like "A Foggy Day"? I do,' she asked at Carnegie Hall in 1961. I love it too. And then, before I know it, I can feel the impression of her on my person so acutely that the wildest claims start pouring from me and in my mind I am gazing at a whiteboard in a back corner of a hospital ward on which an X-ray of Garland's tiny frame is illuminated, the blank navy hollows and the white knot of bone and next to it is pinned an X-ray of me and the lines and the shadows, the order and the eternal human disarray are to a bone, to an artery, exactly the same.

Of course I can see this is not quite true. We have different strengths and our weaknesses are hardly the same. I love to sing and dance but no one else loves it very much.* I still retain my natural ardours and excesses, but not a soul has ever termed me 'something of the forest' or a 'wonderful splash of rain'.

Over me – sad to say – there hangs no dew. When I speak, now, people pay attention but I sure can't lay a claim to Judy's imperial sway. I have never been a person to whom it's hard to say, 'No'.

Stunned by life's hierarchies, I like a prominent position in the background or in the inner circle on a lowish rung. I have always, always longed for the stage but I am probably more the lady-in-waiting type or the facilitator, the dresser in the wings, the solid bridesmaid, the willing paid companion, the staunch librarian or the kindly nurse with armfuls of starched linen who knows when to avert her gaze. I am reasonably balanced and settled, people tell me, both driven and content, while Judy Garland lived out her days at the apex of excitement in such a maelstrom of lurching highs and bitter lows that by the end of her life she was circling the world, impossible, penniless, looking anywhere for a foothold or some moorings yet still stunning audiences with her consummate performing skills, right up to the last. I know all this. Of course I know it. Yet when I watch her, when I think about her and the choices that she made, it seems to me that Judy Garland proves something I've all my life believed, that nobody else in the world thinks is true.

I don't quite understand what happens at these moments, the avalanche of feelings, the rapid swell of kinship and concern. I know it's some kind of collusion and that matters of ownership are involved. And it isn't hard to pathologise – my story won't be un-familiar – you can match this lack with that lack and here a strength and there a need, if you are so inclined. But it is so much more than this.

*Apart from my parents.

Whole new departments of feeling are created when Judy's on my mind, and of living, too, and words like success and health and love seem faltering and inchoate. The communion between Judy and me is so heightened when I hear her singing that all misgivings disappear: everything is binding, definite, irrefutable and curiously exact, yet the landscape of feelings is vast. It's all there, the world and its opposites and all the gradations that lie in between: there's devastation, bravely worn, excitement, recovery and anxiety paired with wit and charm; there's hankering and satisfaction and relief and faith and a kind of familiarity that is startling. There are mistakes and humility and then full-voltage superstar quality thickly entwined. As I

ponder all this I'm beyond thought and feeling and wishes. Everything stands on its head, all distinctions petty and banal and good and bad and death and life are starkly realised before me and illuminated and exalted and mourned. It's a monumental moment, yet it's curiously intimate for all the lightning flashes. We're in a small room, alone together, seated at a side table. We're each other's everything. I'm completely in her hands.

I am a 'loss' person by nature, certainly, but I'm happy these days – you should hear my continual whistling and chirping. My grief is secure now and dwells far away in my past. So isn't it extraordinary that even the idea of a tiny woman singing, forty years after her death, should move a sane soul in this way?

When I was born in a tall thin house with no foundations, in an eerie Gothic London square, my mother already had four children; allegiances had been formed and strong characters established. It soon seemed to me quite clear that all the major personality types had been taken. There is a battle to make yourself heard when you are last on the production line. And I couldn't help wondering, what did my family want with another child? Part of the trouble was that I had no idea what I was like and my fear was that I simply lacked a personality. As a small person you can feel very unformed and there is a certain humiliation attached to this. I had my strong feelings, of course, for companions, but I couldn't see what they might add up to or where exactly they would lead.

Besides, my family had recently returned from its greatest adventure and I had played no part in it. When her mother died and left her a bit of money, my mother bought a ship called *Inge*, took my brothers and sisters out of school and set sail around the world. At one stage, the crew mutinied and my mother had to stand over them with a gun, or so the story went. At another point, one of my brothers, a babe in arms, fell overboard and two sailors nearly clanked heads with my mother as they all dived in to save him. I heard these stories as if they were fairy tales from a book and in my mind the sailors were pirates with gold hoop earrings and fearsome grins. The captain was a huge, red-faced, surly fellow and I imagined he was made of meat.

'Tell me about the ship,' I used to say. I knew the bare bones of the story, that *Inge* was a cargo ship and she had sailed to Trinidad, via Norway, where my family had eaten sugary salamis and learned the word for mashed potato, which was *kartoffelmos*. And I knew that in Trinidad, when the ship was declared unseaworthy and no longer viable as a means of support for my family, they were deported back to England, third class, so as not to be a burden on the West Indian state. But it was the specifics that enchanted me. I liked to hear of the shipmates' duties: swabbing the deck, looking over the rigging and painting the deck house, which was meant to be a little school room but was always getting blown away. I read the diaries my siblings had kept on board ship, which formed part of their education. My mother referred to mysterious tasks such as 'pumping out the bilges' and 'checking the charts'.

My narrow escape from this high drama, which I know I would have loathed, prompted me to view myself firmly outside the exciting world the rest of my family seemed to inhabit. My mother was a hero; my father, the painter Lucian Freud, lived five miles away and ate, slept and drank paint in his handsome top-floor flat. My brothers and sisters seemed so different from me, not tentative at all or fledgling or unsure; they were leaders and pioneers, daring, stylish and free. I felt my excessively emotional nature strike everyone as an embarrassment of the silliest order. My cautious personality was itself a caution. My flights of fancy mercilessly mild. 'May I possibly have a pineapple pina colada but without the rum?' I asked my father in a Soho restaurant, when I was twelve, because the sign above our table said Cocktails. To his credit, when the waiter came to take our order he *did* ask.

My sisters seemed so modern, with their cropped hair and fast talk, embracing the latest trends, even initiating and popularising them. There was always a small queue of their dashing yet nervous admirers round at our house. Sometimes they plied me with sweets in the mistaken belief that winning me over might further their romantic suits. Me! I had to laugh for I was quite without influence, in a quaint little world of my own making. I was an old-fashioned girl with olden-days habits and olden-days values. The codes I held dear championed outmoded social virtues such as smiling through tears.

My childhood was quite literally steeped in the past, for when I was about six my mother started to sell old-fashioned clothes on a stall in an antiques market and afterwards in a shop she named Susie's after me. Victorian nightgowns, nineteen-forties silk and crêpe dresses, peach rayon satin underclothes and beaded nineteen-fifties cardigans hung by padded hangers from every door-frame in our house and frequently fell on my head as I passed between rooms. There were sprigs of felt flowers, cards of buttons, bolts of millinery velvet, the odd hat and occasionally something exceptional like a Schiaparelli jacket covered in electric blue paillettes that friends of hers would be invited round to view. On the cooker, an aluminium cauldron of white cotton and soap and bleach continuously bubbled away, sending steam into the room and a scent similar to spaghetti.

'What's for supper?' I would ask. 'Smells delicious!'

'Oh, just some old bloomers. They came up a bit yellow so I'm giving them an extra boil.' I admired my mother hugely for her faith and industry, and her high spirits.

When I was eleven or so we moved to a smaller house and, as my older siblings came and went, in the main it was just the two of us. It was very cosy. Our afternoons passed in continual tea-times. The cargo of buns we must have put away! At weekends my mother made dawn raids on Brick and Petticoat Lanes to find her stock, bringing back hot bagels and platzels for my breakfast when it was still dark. Every other Thursday she went to a rag yard in east London where she bought special items picked out for her by a team of friendly female sorters, paying by the weight then giving tips on top to the women who unearthed incredible gems from among the items people threw away. In the school holidays or when I nursed a mild cold I went with her to a Stratford warehouse. We both liked the idea that rubbish could yield such beautiful things. The women there spoiled me with confectionery: 'She's such a good girl' they said. We would hold up an exquisite silk blouse or dress and all shake our heads as one as we imagined the crazy types who could discard such a prize. It was not an exaggeration to say that thoughts of rescue flashed through all our minds. At Christmas we bought perfume and talc for these women, and bottles of whisky which I wrapped for the men who worked the compressing machines.

It was always clear to me that my mother thought her work rather feminine and romantic, and it was in a way. This was a relief as I knew she would rather be painting: she had been a star student at art school and I respected the courage in her sacrifice. Occasionally when I came down in the morning my mother would still be sitting in a chair in dim light, asleep with her sewing on her lap, and once or twice I remember her cries of outrage when, through tiredness, she had sewn the garment she was mending on to her own skirt and the whole thing had to be unpicked with a little metal stitch-ripper that looked like a wishbone. Towards the end of the week, as the stock piled up in our small basement kitchen, there were buckets of starch containing lace curtains and plastic basins filled with stain remover, where small items of silk were put to soak, wherever you looked. It was the nineteen-eighties but you might not have known it in our house. As my mother sewed I brushed her hair for a penny a minute and sang her Judy songs.

I loved my mother so much I scarcely let her out of my sight, night or day. She took it very well. I helped her with her work sometimes, sitting at her feet doing what she did, only in miniature, clumsily embroidering lazy daisies very slowly on to a bright cashmere cardigan, undoing the hem of a coat or a dress, feeding satin ribbon through the slits of a lace camisole with the vague sensation these were the sorts of clothes that Judy wore. I knew very little about my mother's family. I sensed her mother had been highly strung and very glamorous, and when my mother visited her in London, shortly before she died, her mother wore a grand pink dress because she was about to go and see her psychiatrist.

'What sort of pink?' I asked her. It seemed very important suddenly, bright or pale? I imagined a crinoline squished and swishing through the heavy door of a Wimpole Street consulting room.

'It was subtle, you know, sort of ombré,' my mother said.

'Oh how beautiful!'

I knew that when my grandmother was young and if it was Saturday night and she didn't have a date or a party she would get into bed with her cousin Angela and gossip and share a bottle of champagne and fall asleep. My mother's mother died at fifty-seven, before I was born, from some sort of accidental overdose or build-up of prescription drugs, my mother said.

'Like Judy?' I asked. The pink dress made me think of Judy too, and the Saturday night sprees. I knew my mother had seen *The Wizard of Oz* with her mother and they had left the cinema doing the lilting yellow brick road double-skip all the way home.

'My mother was no Judy Garland,' my mother remarked to me, once firmly, once wistfully, but the connection in my head never quite went away.

Of course my parents and siblings have had more of an effect on my development, have moulded and shaped me more than Judy Garland could have done. They did things for me and to me and with and without me just as any family does and the results don't surprise. Yet Judy and I always had our own tight little circle. She was my life in purest form, encapsulating and refining all the things that interested me most: my mother's high spirited stoicism and her generous festive nature; my father's devotion to his work; the job of cheering; the value of glamour; the call of dark spirits and the lengths you have to go to to resist them. My head and heart then and now are always making paths to Judy in a way they have not quite done to anyone else. She calls to me frequently. It's part of the texture of my days. Lightning seeks the atmospheric courses it has carved out before and I am repeatedly drawn back to you-know-who. This occurs without my permission sometimes, as sighs do or dreams, and now and then it happens without my even noticing.

*

When you adore someone absolutely everything that pertains to that person is fascinating. Say you discover that Meinhardt Raabe, the actor who played the munchkin coroner in *The Wizard of Oz*, had a massive growth spurt at the age of thirty-five. Well, you feel like telephoning everyone you know. He was twenty-four and just four foot tall in the film. He's in his nineties and four foot seven now, only four inches shorter than Judy was herself. Can you believe it? Your good friends, at least your very best ones, express some interest. You don't need much to go on. Practically nothing is enough.

Another time you glance at an entry in your hero's old address book which says *Day, Lena (theatrical maid) 3046 11th Ave., Los Angeles, Calif* and there's a telephone number too and you wonder,

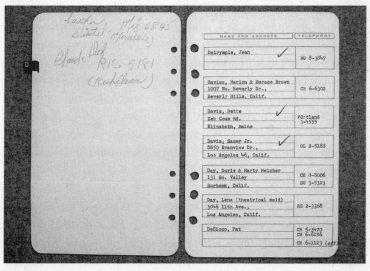

Bette Davis, Sammy Davis Jr., Doris Day and Lena Day (theatrical maid) in Judy's 1950s address book

absently, is that an actress who specialises in playing servant girls, or a helpmeet who's prone to histrionic gestures or is it simply a handy source of dressing room support? You muse on the skills involved in all these professions; you wonder if you have any of them yourself. You might, at a loose end one day, even try calling the number, just in case, but the rudeness of the woman who answers the phone, when you timidly attempt to explain your business, fifty or so years later – well!

It's also hard not to adopt your loved ones' viewpoints or to indulge their crackedest whims. Their likes and dislikes, if you're not careful, can become your own. Strange webs of inclinations and fidelities knit and tangle. Watch *Annie Get Your Gun*, from which Garland was ejected? I'd rather eat nails! Disliking the correct things is especially important, my parents taught me. It's nice to carry on the family feuds. I know I'll never rent a film starring Lana Turner, just as I'll never read a book by Jung. Leafing through Turner's memoirs (solely for references to Garland) I find her sentiments so starkly unJudyish that it makes me mad. However cast down Judy might have felt at times, it never made her bland or banal or even silly. Lana says, 'Shortly after I met him he asked to marry me, but for once I knew I really didn't want to. After I declined he left for Arizona to do his nightclub act. Clever man, he didn't call me for a few lonely days. Sensing my mood, he again asked me to marry him. This time I agreed. Our wedding took place in Las Vegas. Why oh why?'

Indeed.

(Judy's five husbands weren't, perhaps, immaculately chosen but I'm certain each marriage was entered into with a blazing heart and hopes that were sky high.)

Because Judy's always hovering one rung below my consciousness, the littlest things draw her to the forefront of my mind. If I watch an item on the news that dwells on a crime scene and I hear a description

David

Vincente

Sid

Mark

Mickey

of the wanted man, I immediately think of David Letterman's remark the night a pair of ruby slippers was stolen from the Judy Garland Museum. 'Police are looking for someone armed and fabulous!' was what he said.

Or I am in the kitchen baking a pear and almond tart or a pie and I find myself thinking of the 'pastry speech' from *I Could Go On Singing*. I put half a pound of plain flour in a large bowl, guess what two or three ounces of chilled butter look like, add one egg and one yolk for good measure, a tablespoon of caster sugar and a drop of vanilla extract or a squeeze of lemon, a glug of cold water, but I scarcely notice my actions because what I'm really concentrating on is not muddling the lines:

> I can't be spread so thin. I'm just one person. I don't want to be rolled out like pastry so everybody can get a nice big bite of me. I'm just me. I belong to myself. I can do whatever I damn well please with myself and nobody can ask any questions . . . Well, I'm not gonna do it anymore, and that's final. It's just not worth all the deaths I have to die . . .

The dialogue in this pivotal six-minute scene was written and revised by Judy and her co-star Dirk Bogarde over a three-day period, rehearsed for a day and then shot in

23

one take. Judy's character Jenny Bowman, a world-famous singing superstar, is propped up in a room in St George's Hospital, drunk and nursing a sprained ankle when she is meant to be on the stage at the London Palladium. Bowman is frightening in this scene, stimulated by a wounded defiance that eventually unravels into a sort of brittle despair. It is Bogarde's job to help her out of it. His view is that she will let herself down if she doesn't make it on to the stage and that would be a crime of gigantic proportions. He simply won't allow it. This infuriates her further.

Do you think that you can make me sing? Do you think you can . . . do you think George can make me sing or Ida? You can get me there, sure, but can you make me sing? I sing for myself. I sing when I want to, whenever I want to, just for me. I sing for my own pleasure. Whenever I want. Do you understand that? . . . I've hung on to every bit of rubbish there is to hang on to in life. And I've thrown all the good bits away. Now, can you tell me why I do that?

'Complete, unforgettable magic', Bogarde called Garland in this scene. One member of the crew termed the sequence a 'miracle'. It is very good. Almost all agree at this moment that Jenny Bowman *is* Judy. Bogarde thought so and so, by some accounts, did the Legend herself. Most fans and biographers believe that these scenes are as successful as they are because Judy Garland was speaking directly about her own experiences. Even the director described it as a 'catharsis for everything that was taking place in her own life', the ambivalence about performing that she had, the custody battles she was fighting with her husband Sid Luft, which were mirrored in part by Bowman's struggles with Bogarde's character. Am I the only person in the world who has never completely gone along with this? It seems to me it isn't how art goes. Judy is drawing on her own experiences, certainly, but it insults the extraordinary skill of her handling of the material to say she has gone into some semi-automatic self-revealing trance.

As I crimp the pastry's edges, trim and twist the narrow strips to make the lattice top, I sometimes think the feelings expressed by Bowman here are an infinitely less subtle version of Judy's complicated attitude towards performing. There's no humour or irreverence and the self-awareness is foggy and all of one tone. The scene misses the dark warmth of Garland's own professional misgivings. In 1959, hospitalised for hepatitis, critically ill and almost double her favourite weight, with a liver inflamed to nearly four times its normal size, twenty quarts of fluid were slowly drained from her body.

'For the rest of your life,' the doctor told her gravely, 'all your physical activity must be curtailed. You are a permanent semi invalid. It goes without saying that under no circumstance can you ever work again.'

'Whoopee!' came the Legend's delicate little cry.

That's Judy.

I often search for extra opportunities to feel close to Judy. When I wash dishes – it doesn't happen very often – I always sing 'Look for the Silver Lining' as Judy does in *Till the Clouds Roll By*. Radiant with a pregnancy the director tries to hide behind a mountain of unwashed plates, Judy is all Technicolor vivacity as she performs this household chore. This is the most charming and witty occurrence of dishwashing in cinematic history. Yet Judy is not washing dishes in the ordinary way, she is playing the part of a famous actress who finds herself in a production number that involves washing dishes on stage. The scene could not be more theatrical or more literary, for it has absolutely no truck with cleanliness or even basic hygiene. We see Garland's character arrive at the theatre in a glamorous gown of glossy emerald silk, whereupon a box of bright roses is handed to her. We see three or four attendants help her out of her star's attire and in to a sort of urchin deluxe costume of dark cotton, a highly becoming

25

but humble creation of checked fabric, with a severe, slightly gathered neck. We see her roll up her sleeves as if to get a feel for the part.

A make-up person applies a seagull-shaped smudge of soot on her face above her left eyebrow to imply quite how arduous the task she performs will be and she's ready to go on. On stage, she faces a great many dishes, several hundred or possibly more for it is a restaurant kitchen we are shown, or even someone's very mild version of hell. Judy washes her dishes in inverted commas, the plentiful suds and the perilous stacks of crockery that wobble and loom all around produce a scene of pure domestic whimsy. My father once said to me that good cleaning is all in the rinsing, and when I watch Garland's character in this setting I think, I bet her father never said as much to her.

Yet in this production number where cheer and courage are the only real detergents, Garland's unorthodox dishwashing technique isn't viewed as any sort of failure, for cheer and courage, it is shown, matter far more in life than the traditional domestic arts. Judy

Garland at this point is undeniably 'one of the loveliest human beings imaginable'. It is a mesmerising scene. Judy's character knows she's no good at her task – for quite a few bars of the song she even balances her head on a stack of plates in a little emotional reverie – and it is only when she is startled to see the dish-mop in her hands that she suddenly remembers what it is she is meant to be doing. Her dreaminess amuses her, and inwardly she rolls her eyes to herself and carries on with her work. Yet during this brief interlude, if you observe closely, it seems as though something, somehow, is fully or partially resolved. She's had a small idea that will help, or made an inward plan or perhaps the words of the song have situated some sort of solution within her grasp. Her technique may be a little slapdash, certainly, but the song's powerful message is that to be utterly lovely is more important than just about anything in life, and requires its own particular discipline and talents and routines.

I like to wash up at other people's houses, particularly at my mother's or my father's, where this dreary and inelegant task is strangely pleasurable. Tying a dishcloth at the waist of my dress – for I always dress up to see my parents – I roll up my sleeves in exaggerated fashion and somehow feel as though I am acting washing dishes on the stage or in a film. The priority is not high-calibre crockery cleansing, although I hope I always do a good job: it is all about appearances. Do I look a picture doing it? I just might. When I wash dishes in others' houses I certainly feel like a heroine. I can't help wondering if the larger plates flatter my small wrists or whether the electric light brings out the sheen in my hair. In my father's house, hunched and beaming at the sink, I wonder if I look a little like a Dutch painting, all shadows and delicate feminine instincts bathed in approval. In my fantasy my parents discuss their delight at my charming domestic humility on the telephone later in the evening. 'And do you know, she actually rolled up her sleeves. Without even being asked!'

The producers of Judy's CBS television series wanted her image to be deglamorised and made more human for the living rooms of America, so they inserted some oddly vicious and unflattering 'humor' into the show. It's painful to watch all the jokes at her expense; here she's called a 'little old lady', there she's told she's muddled or deluded or that the scenery is too costly and must be dispatched right away. 'I don't think I'm too glamorous or inhuman' was her dignified reproach. Well, my dishwashing life goes to show my own lack of airs and graces, just in case anyone thinks I have them, for I do in small measure.

Calls from Judy often add an extra layer of interest to my days. Whenever I am in a flower shop I make a little private nod of recognition to myself concerning the florist business that Judy started up in the early nineteen-forties – it was her mother's idea of a nice refined investment, no doubt. Was she plied with so many flowers that canny Ethel Gumm (by this time known as Mrs Gilmore) thought the legions of bouquets might be recycled for cash? In Judy Garland Flowers Inc the young star is photographed in an apron and sensible shoes wrestling with gladioli, the most unbiddable of flowers. The

caption reads, 'The young star enjoys trying her hand at an arrange-ment of flowers and is becoming quite an expert at the art.'

If I buy shampoo I remember one of the surprising opening lines in *Meet Me in St Louis* where the mother played by Mary Astor reminds Judy's character Esther Smith that she mustn't forget to buy shampoo as it's hair-washing night. This line is particularly remark-able because when you consider Esther and Rose Smith's colossal interest in their appearance, they are more likely to forget their own names.

When I am introduced to a new person, I remember my father's story of meeting Judy Garland. Brought over to her at a party in London some time after *A Star Is Born*, they shook hands but it didn't quite come out right: only three of her four fingers made it into the handshake. 'Hey, you missed one!' she cried out and they shook again and this time the wayward little finger *was* included. I've asked him to tell me this story time and time again in case any new details emerge. I feel for that finger sometimes.

Dorothy's impeccable manners are often on my mind in social situations. In Oz she is not just polite, she is staggeringly imaginative in her dealings with all others. When proclaimed a national heroine by the munchkins you can see her heart and mind deciding it would be a rudeness to deny or refute her new status, however accidental, and the way her confusion abates and the start of a smile begins is so charming and appropriate. Heroism carries with it a sense of duty, and this she shoulders squarely. After the Scarecrow's 'If I Only had a Brain' number she attests to him that the crows she knows in Kansas would be scared to pieces by such song and dance antics, knowing full well he has an anxiety about his ability to frighten birds. When some of the Scarecrow's stuffing falls out of him she asks, 'Does it hurt you?' I can't be sure it would have occurred to me to pose that question.

When the Tin Man is in the middle of singing 'If I Only Had a Heart' Dorothy further exhibits her capacity for lovely human dealings when she quickly checks with the scarecrow before inviting the metal one to join them on their trip to Oz. Another heroine would have been more imperious, but not Dorothy. Her journey is a joint mission now, undertaken by equals. Although she has become a liberator and leader of a new race of people, it is instantly clear that her little troupe in Oz is founded on democratic principles. For one so emotional, she's awfully fastidious. I like to position these two character traits side by side but few people agree with me about this.

I'm very interested in good manners. I've always thought the speech that Cordelia makes about the storm in *King Lear* shows them in their highest form:

Mine enemy's dog,
Though he had bit me, should have stood that night
Against my fire . . .

Sometimes when Judy arrives in Oz I wonder what it must have been like for my father to arrive in London after his family left Berlin and the Nazis in 1933. We've barely spoken of it and I only know the tiniest things. The family rented, for a spell, a home in the West End and one day my grandmother caused a small amount of consternation when out shopping for white fish. 'Cod, Madam? In Mayfair?' came the fishmonger's incredulous retort.

'Over the Rainbow', to most people, is a song about longing, but to some – and there were an awful lot of exiles in 1939, when the film was first released – it will always be a song about leaving. Many of Oz's more elderly fans have told me that *The Wizard of Oz* was the last good thing in their lives before the horror and anxiety of war set in, and this fact adds to their affection for the film. For me, though, at three or four *The Wizard of Oz* did not represent the sense of an ending in any way. It was the start of something wonderful.

At Christmas time I often think of the half-second interlude in *Meet Me in St Louis* where Judy's character Esther, on the brink of singing 'Have Yourself a Merry Little Christmas' to her younger sister, makes a subtle emotional gesture with her mouth, which is a third of a kiss crossed with a nod of encouragement and a small physical expression of hope.

At the same time, this little flutter of eye and infinitesimal lip movement is also a fleeting but deep expression of sisterly sympathy. It is a self-conscious gesture, weighted with both anxiety and (naturally) a sort of salve for that anxiety. Judy's flicker of lip and eye reveals her to be making all sorts of assessments; the child she is addressing is not a baby any more and this is both alarming and a cause for celebration; in fact, the child before her has an understanding that goes far beyond her years. In this realisation there is a sense both of time passing rapidly and of change both sought and unsought, not just the family's imminent move to New York but also Esther Smith's brand new engagement to John Truett. Tied up in all these registrations is the sense that all signs of progress also signify loss.

I experience at Christmas such an overwhelming sense of loss I scarcely know what to do with myself. I adore Christmas and would do absolutely anything for it, but I meet it now like a cherished past love. Christmas and I will never ever be to each other what we once were – almost everything – and we must restrict ourselves severely in each other's company for fear of coming undone. This makes the festive season almost excruciating for me. I feel disloyal for writing that, because when I was a child the electric anticipation of Christmas would power me through autumn and winter leannesses and the ecstatic, medicinal thrill of it remembered would take care of the rest of the year. I hero-worshipped Christmas and the Christmases I had were so wonderful that I thought Christmas, with its beguiling twin freight of comfort and consolation, *was* the religion.

Sometimes I almost confuse Judy Garland with Christmas, for Christmas to me, when properly handled, must be lavish, excessive and dazzling, so brimming with emotion, that it's almost more than you can stand. You aim to feel overwhelmed and you arrange things accordingly. You colour your home emerald and ruby, decorating even the cereal packets and the coat hangers; you situate chocolate bells and reindeer on every available surface and eat and drink as much as you dare. You melt assorted fruit-flavoured boiled sweets in separate batches to make stained glass windows for your ginger-bread cathedral; your comely tree, skirted and laden, pierces the ceiling; your secondary tree comes pretty close too; you shop from

1 September, only selecting gifts for friends and family that you feel will have a truly life-transforming potential, presents that declare you value their sacrifices and efforts and you salute all that your loved ones do and are; you spend almost everything you have, more sometimes, steeling yourself cheerfully for January frugality and then, giddy with all the losses and gains and indigestion pains, you slump afterwards with the kind of exhaustion that always leads to a few days' illness.

The Christmases of my childhood were so spectacular that my fidelity and gratitude to this festival is firm for ever. For twelve years running, we six descended on the family of my mother's best friend and, in a large modern house in Gloucestershire, ten children crashed about, wildly merry-making. This family dazzled us with the warmth of its welcome. I didn't know why they liked us quite as much as they did, but it could not be denied. There was no sense that we were lucky beneficiaries in any way, for all their actions indicated that we, too, made their Christmases come true. I was not used to such high treatment. Our normal lives were straitened, no-frills, occasionally austere. I was anxious and wary by nature but the glorious punctuation in my life that was Christmas seemed to prove important things about me. I loved these Christmases so much I almost envied myself. I think, as a family, these Christmases helped us to bloom. If people treat you extremely well in life, it changes your view of things. These Christmases weren't just luxurious and sustaining, they did a great deal for our family morale. And then there were the presents.

My mother packed five stockings that, in actual fact, were pairs of tights. Even today the sensation of parcel-stuffed limbs lying heavy across my legs on Christmas morning and the sound of the presents rustling and crackling in their bright wrappings as you move in your half-sleep feature regularly in my dreams. If I were a writer of symphonies I'd include that magical music in my works. My mother's

Christmas stockings were legendary, crammed with all manner of delights. Things I remember: a small pale blue set of attached cardboard wheels that named all the common barre exercises for ballet and then when you rotated the inner disc a little window revealed how to do the steps and an even smaller one indicated how to pronounce them; a grown-up hardback book my mother painted with bright flowers that was a specially designated place for me to write my poems; a film-starry pair of nineteen-thirties silk satin pyjamas with tiny polka dots and black piping at the collar and cuffs. After lunch it was time for the presents proper. They formed monumental banks in the room and each child was allocated a sofa or a window seat or a table at which to receive. Our hosts made continual trips to the top floor, bringing down suitcase after suitcase of gifts and distributing them to the eager crowd. Once a great towering pile had been amassed by each child the unwrapping would begin and it could take up to two hours. And what presents! There was nothing mindless about it, for the thought processes that had obviously gone into the selection were both thorough and recherché. Something cosy, something glamorous, something to expand your mind; something to make you see that a new and fledgling personal development you had barely noticed in yourself had been acknowledged and admired and was being championed in the best possible way.

The mother of this family couldn't have chosen better presents if she had spent a month or so observing in minute detail the exact nature of each of our lives. A great Christmas campaign, I learned from this example, consisted of a proper understanding of need, want and desire. It might have been humiliating as children from a poor background to be given to excessively, for it could signal that a lack one wished to hide had been inferred. Yet all this was handled with extreme delicacy. I learned that excess needn't be gross if it had its roots in intelligence and care. Is it any wonder that I grew to hold Christmas in the highest possible esteem? That I don't quite know how to position myself in relation to it now that I have no needs?

Judy's small, nervous mouth movement in *Meet Me in St Louis* carries a part of the weight of these feelings of mine. At least, I imagine that it does and that to me is something further between us. I've never had a little sister, but if I did I hope I would treat her with such respectful tenderness.

When you love somebody this much almost everything about her stimulates your approval. I love the conversation Judy and Noel Coward have about their theatrical childhoods shortly after the Boston premiere of *Sail Away* in 1961:

JUDY: We both started on stage at about the same age didn't we?
NOEL: Yes. How old were you when you started?
JUDY: I was two.
NOEL: Two? Oh you've beaten me. I was ten. But I was—
JUDY: What were you *doing* all that time?

Judy Garland in conversation with Noel Coward

I love the fact that Judy Garland got rid of pesky policemen after her for late revelry in her staid Boston apartment building by singing 'Over the Rainbow' to them. They left in an ecstasy of tears.

I love the thought of her, aged thirty months, performing five encores of 'Jingle Bells' until her father carried her off the stage.

I am moved by the fact that at the first meeting with her proposed official biographer Judy greeted him, for ballast, in her hotel suite in clown make-up, 'a scarlet dab on the tip of her nose, black lines drawn starfish-like from each eye, the furrowed, absurd cheeks, the hectic colouring. The black touch on the tip of her chin.'

I admire her childhood nickname in vaudeville circles, Little Miss Leatherlungs.

I like the incredible names of her childhood friends: Mugsy Ming, Laranna Blankenship and Vera Shrimp.

Sometimes when Judy's really on my mind I only have to see the curve of an eyebrow or the hooped lid of a smile and I think of rainbows.

These prompts that send my thoughts to and from Judy occur almost imperceptibly. But I'm always looking for her. When someone's in your thoughts, or you've lost someone, or you miss a person terribly it's easy to single out the back of a head in a crowd or to recognise a pair of shoulders in the distance, the slight, stirring unevenness of a gait, a familiar hand gesture, a scarf or a coat that no one else has, and you beat a path to that person and greet him or her joyfully and with enthusiasm and springy limbs, then you watch delight register in the other person's face until the smile slides a little and dissolves and the eyes look puzzled and it wasn't who you thought it was at all, how could you have even . . . and its all embarrassment and apologies and maybe the other person thinks you're trying to start something and maybe you are or maybe he or she is and suddenly it's far too complicated and as politely as you can you disappear. But with Judy it's always, always, always the right person. Can you imagine?

Stage
Struck

I was born for stardom.
The photos never turned out
As well as I'd hoped,
But my mother told me
Cheekbones came with age.

In 1981 a sophisticated girl in the year above me wrote this poem that was published in the school magazine. I looked at her differently after that. I didn't know it was allowed to think such things. I wouldn't have dared to admit it, but I nursed similar dreams. 'You know, "Deep below the glitter, it's all solid tinsel",' I almost confided in her, for that was what I'd heard.

I knew it was immodest – it was lunatic really – but I longed with all my heart for the stage. I wanted dressing room life: fringed wraps, mirrors studded with light bulbs and good luck cards, charm bracelet opening-night gifts from my bow-tied agent, banks of long-stemmed champagne roses, a nice lady dresser, severe, but with an indulgent heart and perhaps the merest hint of an avuncular moustache. And even if I couldn't be the star, perhaps I'd be safer in the chorus, a sensible presence amongst a gaggle of girls, all legs and frills and feathers against balding red velvet, with continual high kicks and high jinks, endlessly warming-up in bleak rehearsal studios, or courageous and united in our draughty backstage Degas heaven, half sick with coffee and cigarettes. Failing that, the understudy's job would do, patience on a monument, a little lonely, aloof some might say – but for my own protection – the blank sum of my job a curtailment of my wild urge to flick out an accidental limb, which would send the spoilt star soaring and me straight out under the pink and amber lights. But if that couldn't work might I be the dresser, rendered a little sardonic by thwarted theatrical ambitions and with a look of the star that had thickened with age? Or the make-up lady?

Judy Garland with a favourite make-up artist, Dottie Ponedel

I would spring to her aid, au fait with all her kinks and quirks, her reliable rock, her port in a storm with never-ending panstick and icy flannels. With hairdryer akimbo I would cater for all eventualities, warmly soothing and smoothing, a sort of faithful human iron. Or, at a pinch, there was always the guardian of the stage door, staunch but fair, instinctively knowing at a glance who's in and who's out, gruff, witty and irreproachable. Or the box office lady, spry and professional, herself a former child star; or an ice cream girl, with vanilla chilblains; or the programme woman, plagued by paper cuts, who sees the show each night clad in a maroon striped polyester tabard, hankering for sequins.

FOUR THEATRICAL PUT-DOWNS

1. 'What do you want to be when you grow up?' barked a maths teacher at my school, a severe woman who had a frightening way with a sharpened pencil. She had taught maths at the Royal Ballet School and now had her own dancing academy.

'I'd quite like to be a star of musical comedies,' I whispered.

'Speak up girl!'

'I'd like to go on the, er . . . on the stage.'

'You'll have to shift a heck of a lot of weight before that's a possibility.' [*Hilarious laughter*]

2. Twelve years later I am auditioning for a part in a university production of *Calamity Jane*. Unaccompanied, I sing Noel Coward's 'Poor Little Rich Girl' with Judy's phrasing. 'With fate it's no use competing/You'll wind up terribly beaten.' It is a pleasing performance, poignant and sincere. I stand and face the twenty-one-year-old director, who is swinging back in his chair, chewing a ballpoint and caressing his arrogant chin.

41

'Are you trying out for the chorus or a solo part?' he sets his trap.

'Either,' I shrug helpfully. 'I really don't mind. Whatever you think. I'd be happy with anything really . . . anything at all.'

'Because,' and here he pauses for effect, 'quite frankly there are people here who'd sing you off the stage.'

3. Ten years later a writer friend is talking about compiling an anthology of regrets. 'I would love to have been in musicals,' I say, 'stage or screen.'

'That won't quite do though, as a regret, will it Susie? Because to qualify as a regret something has to have been within the realms of possibility.'

4. Last year, a friend of mine tells me that his cousin puts on musicals in women's prisons. She's planning to stage *Chicago* in our local women's jail in the coming year! I had seen, that day, a beautiful and capacious red patent handbag in a department store window for eight hundred pounds and, next to it, a stunning navy blue silk faille evening trench coat for double that price. The two items combined would lend my lacklustre autumn an intrepid Parisian flair. I instantly hatch a plan to smash into the store that night and steal the goods, thus ensuring I either have a highly glamorous season or I land a plum role in the forthcoming prison production, perhaps the only way it could ever happen to me, I explain.

'Thing is,' my friend says, sucking in his breath with faux tact (why is the economy of sympathy so hard for most to master?), 'in the prisons, where my cousin works, the standard's usually really, really high so, you know . . .'

Sometimes when I'm sleeping I hatch far-fetched get-rich-quick schemes. I often dream that I am setting up a chain of luxury care homes for the elderly that caters specifically for those whose theatrical ambitions have so far been unrealised in life. It would be a little like *Fame*, but with more . . . experienced personnel. We would stage three productions a year, which would be chosen carefully – nothing macabre like *Annie* – and every day there would be improvisation, singing and voice and dance classes, gentle bending and stretching exercises at the barre. Mickey Rooney would be a visiting professor – he can be hired via his website to attend your event – and would bring some of his legendary 'Hey! Let's put on a show, right here in this barn' zeal to the proceedings. He would reminisce with us, at my instigation, about his Mickey and Judy days and regale us with some of his notable quips: 'Always get married in the morning. That way, if it doesn't work out, you haven't wasted a whole day.' 'Senility is great for romance – you wake up with a new woman every day.' That sort of thing.

We would be inundated with applicants, to be sure, but we'd have a very careful vetting policy. No erstwhile professionals would slip through our portals: former Bluebell girls, Pan's Persons, ex-stalwarts of Broadway or even ENSA would all be ejected at the audition stage. They have had their time and must be satisfied. We wouldn't perhaps take you if you're really rather good. Our motto, emblazoned in satin stitch on all roller towels and stencilled on chamberpots?

*Nemo homo vitam relinquat antequam primas partes in scaena egerit**

Between 1976 and 1983 I attended almost two thousand dancing classes. Tap, ballet, contemporary and a very old-fashioned sort of dance – with much saucy grinning and kneeling and fluttery jazz hands – called modern. We wore red leotards with an attached shallow red frill that formed a forgiving, abbreviated skirt at the hips,

*No one should depart this earth before they have starred in a show.

and red leather ballet shoes or black Oxfords with silver American teletone taps.

My teacher, Miss Audrey, was a large woman with soft features, cosy and intelligent in her patterned dresses and flesh-coloured sandals; she was the first person, perhaps the only one, to champion my theatrical ambitions. I have no idea why, but it touched me deeply, then and now, that she went out of her way to show me such encouragement when my ability was so limited. And she wasn't acting. I had a keen ear for false notes as a child, all children do. Did I remind her of herself as a girl? Did she spy in me a shaky soul who needed bolstering? 'Well, you worked like a dog,' my mother said. It's an oddly unflattering remark. It's something, I noted, Princess Diana once said of Princess Anne on national television.

Hard work, of course, does not always augur praise. For many people, natural flair will always hold more allure. Oh, the disappointment of the ultra-conscientious schoolgirl when the teacher prefers her easygoing, careless classmate! The swot's forced intensity (surprise surprise) doesn't automatically appeal to the very person it is designed to please, but this wasn't the case with Miss Audrey. She simply believed in me physically. With my awkward body, she taught me it *was* possible to please. To her it was a fact that one could be both large and graceful, in a way most people simply will not allow. It was very profound. 'You're light on your feet considering your size,' various adults had said to me, but Miss Audrey's praise of my dancing was unqualified. Perhaps I was actually good! The day I first mastered the step-ball-change-pick-up-toe-hop, a little side-to-side move which in itself is as perfect a form as the sonnet (and a good deal less worldly), she hauled me out of the relative obscurity of the third line in our dance class and positioned me in the middle of the front row. I was so moved.

Shortly after this I was cast as the lead in what was called *Troupe*, a story in song and dance designed to be shown at competitive dancing festivals. At this time, Miss Audrey had experienced some success with 'Sweetmeat Joe the Candy Man', the tale of an itinerant confectionery vendor whose legendary generosity enhanced the lives of all the children in the locale. Next came a number called 'Lollipops and Skipping Ropes (Children Roll Down Grassy Slopes)', which was a song sung nostalgically, in age, by those recalling their care-free youth. 'Life was so much simpler then/Life was full of fun/But as the years go rushing by/I think of the time I was young.' It was performed by six-year-olds. I once heard a boy of five crooning Judy's 'Last Night When We Were Young' and it was similarly unsettling. My number was called 'Mrs Bond'. It had nothing to do with the glamorous super-spy who made that name synonymous with fast living; it was based on a well-known nursery rhyme none of us had ever heard. I played the eponymous heroine.

> Oh what have you got for dinner, Mrs Bond?
> There's beef in the larder, and ducks in the pond.
> Then fetch us first the beef Mrs Bond
> And then dress the ducks that are swimming in the pond.
> Dilly, dilly, dilly, dilly, come to be killed,
> For you must be stuffed and my customers filled.

On stage at Stoke Newington town hall. I am seated on the far left. The number is 'On a Wonderful Day Like Today'

It was an elaborate staging. There were about twenty girls: villagers, courtiers, farm hands, fowl and a lake. I didn't know it then, but Mrs

Bond was a character part. It would always be thus: I was destined to play the headmistress (Dame Crammer in *School and Crossbones*); the dowager (Lady Lucre in *Temptation Sordid or Virtue Rewarded*); the nun (Mother Abbess in *The Sound of Music*); or the apologetic and bumbling (but never racy) uncle in Fair Isle and braces and flat cap (*The Monkey's Paw*).

For Mrs Bond, my mother made me a costume with a white broiderie anglaise apron, a striped grey bodice, leg-of-mutton sleeves, black-and-white striped panniers and a bonnet with a maroon velvet ribbon. It was lucky she had studied dressmaking as a secondary subject at art school, she murmured as she sewed late into the night.

Three girls stood out at Miss Audrey's. Emma Smith, a neat and careful dancer with a perfectionist streak. She never ever made mistakes. Tara, her best friend, was at seven very exuberant, a tiny girl with huge eyes and long arms and legs who moved in a deeply exhilarating way. Then there was Zany, whose every movement had a professional gloss. Her dancing had 'acting' in it. She was at the Italia Conti stage school.

I longed for stage school. I felt ready to begin my career. I had glimpsed the timetables of some of my fellow dancers: voice, jazz, chorus, tap and song. A slip of paper had fallen from Zany's school bag one day, which said *Schedule of Rehearsals*. At Conti's rival establishment, the Arts Educational, it was said, you had to wear a sky-blue headband in the morning for normal lessons and in the afternoon you had to change it to a turquoise one for dance. Oh, the glamour! The Arts Educational had a high-class image at Miss Audrey's; it was not so much show tunes and shuffle-hop steps as ballet, the grandest calling of all. I think having the word educational in its name added to its kudos. I had such a firm feeling that at Italia Conti I would be absolutely understood. It was my strongest belief that my inside was very poorly represented by my outside, and I had it in mind that at Conti's this might finally be understood. My mother blocked it. It was the only time in my entire life she had stopped me doing something I wanted, so I could tell it was serious. A hypersensitive girl of some considerable girth, it seemed to her, would not flourish in Conti's unforgiving environs. 'You're just too intelligent,' was what she said. There were shocking rumours (unfounded, I now know) that weekly weigh-ins took place and the figures were chalked up on a board, but I almost didn't care.

How I wished with all my heart for a stage mother, a sort of showbiz Jiminy Cricket figure who would insist that the chorus girl inside me took command at every turn. My inner stage mother was already quite powerful. Catching myself frowning in a bit of smeared chrome while descending an escalator, I'd hiss 'Smile!' at myself. 'For God's sake someone might see you.' I still feel, once I leave the house, that I am somehow 'on' and must make sure my best foot is firmly forward. My mother told me recently about a certain time in her life when she woke up every morning thinking, 'Isn't everything WONDERFUL!' Even standing at the bus stop, she said, and seeing a double-decker bus coming towards her seemed like the most beautiful, amazing thing in the world. Even if it wasn't the right number! I've often thought it's important to look as though I feel everything's WONDERFUL. I'm not quite sure why. It's pride, I expect.

My inner chorus girl has made sure I am fully equipped with a funny story or a song to suit any occasion. I know jokes about shandy, trifle, scones, strawberries, permanent waves, tractors, bell-ringing, new dresses, eyeballs, opticians, doctors and severed heads, and one of these subjects crops up in most of the conversations I have and can be interpreted as a cue. I have three or four tap routines in my repertoire and a character dance from my grade three ballet exam. I know the words to most of Judy's songs. So, if a miracle happens and I am called on at short notice to mount any sort of a show, it won't be an especially tall order.

If only my mother had had thwarted stage ambitions. It seemed to me this was the finest legacy you could bequeath a child. To have a joint project we embarked on for our mutual satisfaction, with preparation and goals and steep steps to climb together, and then if hard work was mirrored by luck then a tiny opening, then a bigger one and then (more work + more disappointments + hard work squared) who knows? A star on your door! The thorough intimacy of the theatrical mother and her protégée is very alluring. She wouldn't, like a long-married spouse, just finish your sentences; she'd recite them with you. She would know your every move and mouth the names of all your steps. We were very close, my mother and I. My favourite thing in the world was to lie in bed next to her with my bent knees pressing into the little zigzag alcove that her bent knees created and my arms folded round her middle, but I wanted closer still.

When I met Judy's middle daughter, Lorna Luft, in a New York hotel tearoom last year I told her that when it comes to my girls I have to wrestle daily with the Mrs Worthington who dwells inside me, for I long to implement my plans for their careers. 'I wish I had no conscience so I could force them on the stage,' sighed I.

Her eyes widened with alarm. 'You just have to let them be children,' came her reprimand. She is a very sensible sort.

My mother did not permit me to go to Conti's but she did do something rather wonderful though, as a concession. She bought me, at great expense, the pale blue and dark blue houndstooth-checked kilt with knife-edge pleats that formed part of that school's uniform. I wore it with pride.

Me in the Italia Conti skirt, trying to inject some cheer into a forlorn Santa in Trafalgar Square. Note my silver top hat.

Perhaps the most distinguished stage school in history was the one at MGM in the nineteen-thirties where Judy and Mickey Rooney perched restlessly at their desks, as well as Deanna Durbin and Lana Turner and Anne Rutherford. The schoolhouse on the MGM lot – 'a one-story white wooden school, with a gabled roof and chimney and a small front porch furnished with rocking chair, with three wooden steps leading up to it from a cobblestone pavement' – was very likely dreamed up by a set designer. This little country-cute schoolhouse was ranged among the looming three-storey warehouses that housed the MGM sound stages. I imagine it like Dorothy Gale's Kansas house that flies through the air in the twister, bound for Oz: a nod towards normality in an otherwise crazy world. Miss Macdonald, the schoolmarm, was tall and slender, with hair scraped back tightly in a bun.

It has been noted that Miss McDonald was impressed by Judy's sensitive responses to poetry, for she learned long stretches of it eagerly and easily, and by her enjoyment of classical music. 'But everyone says all the money's in jazz,' the small thirteen-year-old girl apparently remarked. During the music appreciations sessions, when Miss McDonald would play records on the Victrola, the children would daydream and Mickey Rooney's eyes would wander fervently over Miss Lana Turner's bust and other parts. 'Mr Rooney!' Miss McDonald would cry.

Lana would excuse herself, then sneak outside for a cigarette. Her screen image, by 1937, in her own words was 'of sexual promise', the 'object of desire'. What a person to have in your tiny classroom!

Judy   Mickey   Deanna Durbin

One by one, as Lana went out, the boys would excuse themselves too.

I sometimes wonder what life lessons Miss McDonald should have taught these children to prepare them for their blossoming careers. Did she lie awake at night wondering how the daily grind towards fame would affect her gifted little charges' mental health? I would have done. I would have seen it as my job to interject some sanity into the proceedings. Shakespeare could have been a useful tool in diffusing anxiety and shallow pride. When I met Mickey Rooney in the chocolate brown lounge of a five-star London hotel last autumn, I asked him if there was anything Miss McDonald could have taught the little gang of stars to prepare them for the lives they would lead. 'Nothing,' he boomed, so I asked his wife Jan instead. 'She could have spoken to the parents. Told them their children needed protecting,' she says softly and with affection. 'It was a hard life for them. Who knows the damage that was done.'

I would have tried to help these half-children locate the exotic allure in everyday life and insisted that normality was a state to be prized. I would have instilled in them some sort of fledgling artists' camaraderie, the shared pride that good parents teach their offspring. I would, very lightly, have encouraged some healthy contempt for authority: *You are the talented ones and without you there are no films. Have your parents and agents negotiate on your behalf with this in mind. To the studio you are the equivalent of diamond mines and you must be respected as such.* I would encourage them to develop the sides of themselves that weren't connected to showbusiness. I'd urge them to challenge the studio's received idea that the job of work to be achieved in adolescence isn't maturity, but fame. In my more anarchic moments – perhaps after I'd been unceremoniously sacked and was being escorted off the lot, flailing and shrieking like a wicked witch in fear of a flying house – I'd invite my pupils to question whether (and here I'd raise my voice so that all studio employees could hear it) the show *always, always, always has to go on*? Another thing – very important this – I would have taught healthy eating to the girls.

When I hear of Judy's food being severely rationed by studio executives (she was sometimes called 'Little Hunchback' or 'The Fat One'), or I consider the MGM chicken soup diet, which was a travesty of that wholesome broth's famous healing powers, I feel like cooking her something nutritious and delicious. I know food isn't love – it's taken me a good while to work this out – but when you love someone giving them food is often a big part of it.

I think, but then *I* would, that food with its forbidden allure and its threat of ruin played an even more central role in the more unstable aspects of Judy Garland's life than is generally claimed. Her weight yoyo-ed dangerously throughout her life and this is what happens when you're taught that your natural appetites are not to be trusted, that they are essentially treacherous and bad.

53

The child star Sybil Jason, who signed a contract with Warner's at five (five!), remembers taking part in a Christmas parade with Judy Garland in Hollywood one winter. Judy was to be on one side of Santa and Sybil was to be on the other as the float proceeded down Hollywood Boulevard, with the girls belting out 'Santa Claus is Coming to Town'.

> That evening when Judy and I were waiting to board the float, she asked me if I had eaten anything as yet. I told her that I had had a tiny sandwich before we left home because I understood that we were going to be fed after the parade and I didn't want to spoil my appetite. She looked at me very sadly and asked what kind of sandwich did I eat at home. I thought it was a rather strange question, but I answered it and before we could say another word it was time to board the float.

It's a question that stayed with Sybil Jason all her life. Judy was one of the biggest stars in the world at this point. The longed-for sandwich makes such a poignant picture. This anecdote gains some of its power from the fact that sandwiches, a humble enough food to be sure, are a good measure of people's attitude towards food. You have to be pretty easy about your body, as a woman, to eat a sandwich in public. For all its humility there's something flagrant about that everyday snack. The awful thing is that more than half the women I know wouldn't be seen dead eating a sandwich either. Do they think they don't deserve it? Wheat! Gluten! Dairy! And filling! Are you insane?

After the sandwich conversation the evening continued:

> As we headed down Hollywood Boulevard, Judy waved to her side of the street and I did the same on mine, while Santa was kept busy throwing tiny candy canes down to the public from the

enormous sack on his back. After a little while I looked at Judy and I couldn't believe what I was seeing. As fast as she could unwrap those tiny candy canes that she took from Santa's sack she would shove them in her mouth and devour them. This went on till the end of the parade.

Afterwards the girls were taken to the Hollywood Roosevelt Hotel for dinner, where a large buffet table groaning with delicious food awaited them. They were just about to take their piled-high plates to their tables when a man came over, and without a word, took Judy's away. That man, Sybil believes, was an executive from MGM.

I sometimes wonder whether not being allowed to eat was a sort of punishment meted out to Judy for not being Lana Turner. I think she's beautiful always, but even her staunch admirers admit she wasn't of traditional film star build. Mickey Rooney wrote:

Judy was no glamour girl. In the first place she had a bad bite and her teeth were out of alignment. This of course was something that MGM's dentists could fix. In fact, they fitted her with shell caps that slipped on and off her teeth like thimbles. But there were some things about her that the studio couldn't fix. She was a little too short, a half-inch less than five feet tall. Her legs were long but they seemed to be hitched to her shoulders, which were too broad for her body. She looked, well, different.

Compare this to Rooney's description of Lana Turner, who had been made to change her name to the glamorous-sounding Lana from – guess what? – Judy: 'Her body said it all, and I got the message, loud and clear. Her auburn locks, her deep green eyes, her long lashes, the tip of her nose, her pouty lips, her graceful throat, the curve of her shoulders, and, yes, the nicest knockers I had ever seen . . . I thought, Here is a woman.'

Judy and Lana in 1937

If I feel anxious or troubled at night I don't generally have the nerve to ring round for assistance or even to wake up the people in my house; I've no dawn patrol on stand by as Judy did – and even if I did I wouldn't *dream* of disturbing anyone – but I sometimes, to self-comfort, read a little pale green booklet published by Ladurée, the Parisian patisserie. I keep it on my bedside table. As I mouth the words of the descriptions, my sugar prayers, I imagine the cakes assembled in neat rows, voluptuous and quivering in their square pink-lidded boxes. Order and plenty combined have always appealed. The *Religieuse à la Violette* sounds especially good: choux pastry, crème patissiere scented with violet and topped with violet cream; the *Mac Pomme Caramel*: smooth caramel macaroon, caramel muslin cream, roasted apples. I don't know quite what muslin cream is but it makes me think of a standard of baby care designed to stun.

In my mind, I compile an order for 140 fresh petits fours, ten of each of the following:

Beignet au Citron: almond fritter stuffed with lemon cream
Caroline: small éclair stuffed with chocolate or coffee cream
Délice Café: coffee macaroon base, coffee cream
Délice Chocolat Amer: dark chocolate macaroon base, dark chocolate cream, cocoa nougat
Délice Pistache: pistachio macaroon base, pistachio cream
Délice Rose Framboise: rose petal macaroon base, rose cream, litchies fresh raspberry on the top
Délice Vanille: vanilla macaroon base, vanilla cream, orange zests
Salammbô Pistache: choux pastry cake filled with pistachio crème patissière, pistachio fondant
Tartelette Caraïbes: tartlet with coconut cream, exotic jelly and pineapple
Tartelette Chocolat: tartlet with chocolate cream, cocoa nougat
Tartelette Citron: tartlet with lemon cream
Tartelette Framboises: tartlet with raspberries
Tartelette Mangue-Papaye: tartlet with coconut cream, mango and papaya, topped with exotic jelly
Tartelette Kiwi: tartlet with almond cream and kiwi

For three years of my life I didn't eat any sugar. At the time I was attending a group for people with eating problems and this is what everyone else in the group did, so I followed suit. There was a concert pianist, red-headed and effusive; there was a middle-aged former maths prodigy, somehow both intense and aloof. Twice a week we sat and talked round a Formica-topped table, while in a neighbouring room a brass band played military tunes. I know sugar is basically a low-level poison, and perhaps it's just a coincidence, but those three years without it were the saddest of my life.

When you spend your teenage years on diets – mine were always self-imposed – all your desires become oddly contorted. You mourn losses that have not yet taken place. You pine for things that are well within your grasp. Instead of thinking, what would I like, you think, what lovely things are there that I can't have? Almost all your actions are motivated by your third or fourth choices. Although the taste of longing can be oddly satisfying on occasion, it's a nasty gear in which to navigate.

Being hungry feels dangerous, but being full is worse, because then you're sunk. Every time you put food in your mouth you taste defeat. If only one could do without it altogether, but it's everywhere, a vast cloud permanently hovering inches above your head, calling to you, sending out perfumed ambassadors to wear down your resolve. The humiliation of depending on it, you who vowed never to depend on anybody. A dim belief you daily nurse is that all the best people save themselves, but how to set about it? The days drag on and with them the constant negotiation, the drive to starve yourself and its pressing gluttonous reverse occupy about 90 per cent of your waking thoughts, and this is perhaps your most giant failure. You're young – you should be carefree! Enjoy life! Empty your head! But the subject of what not to eat dominates everything and the endless inexorable food calculations distort the history and geography and geometry of your days until everything has the same low, dry grey flavour. You teach yourself to disregard your hungers because you know the things you want are bad; but what then do you do with your desires? And the mad equations that seem to hold good sense! If you can't have the things your really want, you're damn well not going to be deprived of the things you don't much care for. Soon you forget what it is you like and what it is you don't. Sometimes these things appear to be indistinguishable.

Even now, I often choose the things I quite like over the things I love. It's less taxing somehow. The responsibility of pleasure can be too much of a burden. Having what you want, sometimes, seems so far fetched it's like a madcap fairground ride with funny mirrors and cobwebs brushing your shoulders and climbs and drops in fast carriages and skeletons and disappearing floors. Having what you want is high whimsy, too rich an experience for the average palate. It's madness. 'I couldn't possibly!' You're almost bashful. You feel like Laurel and Hardy in one of their fixes, sleeves rolled and arms deep in snow-white suds for there are seventeen hundred dishes to wash, to pay for the meal. Have what I want? Don't be silly!

The perfect snack

A book I read, years ago, set the following exercise. Hold out your arms in front of you, parallel to the ground, and reach forward as hard as you can towards the opposite wall; then reach harder still. Stretch out your fingers as far as they will go. Hold the position for two minutes. Do you feel comfortable? Is this how you intend to live the rest of your life?

It's not ideal.

Of course, had I been in MGM's employ I may not have been able to practise what I preached. I'm very torn about it all. I might have been lulled into the studio's style of doing things, believing in some sequin-skewed way that the punishments were worth the triumphs. Judy never made fame look easy, but I've never been drawn to easy things. The difficulties were attractive, all the hard work and dedication in a single captivating cause, a clear path, a defined job of work, something to reach towards. Judy's speech in *A Star Is Born*, to a wrapt Norman Maine, was a sort of rosary of fame. I tape-recorded it from the television and wrote it into one of my notebooks. The details mesmerised:

Washing out my gloves in crummy hotel rooms and winning a contest on the radio . . . I can remember my first job singing with the band and one night stands clear across country by bus, putting on nail polish in the ladies' room in gas stations, waiting on tables – wow that was a low point, I'll never forget it and I'll never never do that again. No matter what! But I had to sing – I somehow feel most alive when I'm singing, it's like . . . it's like – you don't want to hear all this, do you?

Do you mind?

But you see how long it's taken me to get this far. Now all I need is just a little luck.

What kind of luck?

Oh the kind of luck that every girl singer with a band dreams of. One night a talent scout from a big record company will come in and he'll let me make a record.

Yes, and then?

The record will become number one on the hit parade; be played on the juke boxes all over the country and I'll be made. End of dream.

There's only one thing wrong with that.

I know. It won't happen.

No it might happen very easily, only the dream isn't big enough . . . How long will you be playing at the Grove?

Tonight was our last night; we leave for San Francisco in the morning.

Don't go.

What?

Quit, leave the band and stay on here. Let me see what I can do for you at the Studio. I'll talk to Oliver Niles right away. It's just a chance, but I'll take it.

A chance? Do you realise I'd be giving up everything I ever worked for?

That's right, but it's served its purpose. Listen to me, Esther. A career's a curious thing. Talent isn't always enough. You need a sense of timing, an eye for seeing the turning point, recognising the big chance when it comes along and grabbing it. A career can rest on a trifle like, like us sitting here tonight, or it can turn on somebody saying to you, 'You're better than that, you're better than you know.' Don't settle for the little dream. Go on to the big one . . . Scared? Scared to take the plunge?

Yes! Say, what makes you so sure about me.

I heard you sing.

Yeah, but—

I know, just my word, but you know yourself, don't you? You just needed somebody to tell you.

61

Listening to this speech time and time again, its manifesto seemed so sharp and clear. It is your moral duty to nurture and display your abilities in the best possible way. To hide your light is a sort of spiritual failure. It was a new parable of the talents for me. In the 1937 David O. Selznick original, Esther's grandmother sends her off to Hollywood with a bracing outline of her duty: 'If you're my granddaughter, you'll go to your Hollywood . . . You've got the blood of pioneers in your veins . . . Your grandfather and I came across the prairies in wagons because we wanted to make something out of our lives . . . You go to your Hollywood . . . but remember Esther, for every dream of yours that comes true, you pay the price in heartbreak.' Ouch.

As a child I would wander round Green Park alone at weekends, hoping that a theatrical impresario would hear me singing 'How About You' (with the phrasing from *The Young Judy Garland* album) and yank me out of my routine existence to play the lead in his newest show. On these walks I mourned, very lightly, the life of obscurity I would soon have to leave behind. Change, even good change, is always hard for me to swallow. And with fame comes many losses: freedom, privacy and the ability to place one's trust without an elaborate set of calculations.

Some people are miserable un-famous and only feel completely themselves when success hits hard, but for most it's rather unsettling, I understand. When I met Liza Minnelli she told me that so many people practically kill themselves to become famous, but when they get there they can't stand it. It was easier, she said, as though it were a sort of *tip*, if, like her, you could be born famous, because then you didn't have to make that difficult transition. Oh!

It's important, I counselled, if fame happens not to surround yourself with 'yes' people who dazzle and distort. You probably needed a few straight talkers like Cordelia. And how disastrously success might impact on matters of the heart!

Does anyone really master love and fame?

INTERVIEWER, 1967: What would you have liked to have
been if you weren't an actress and singer?
JUDY GARLAND: Happily married.

It was all awfully worrying. Yet the recipe for fame seemed clear to
me. You take theatrical ambitions, their sinewy twists and frustra-
tions, add hard work and patience, discipline and drive and a
thorough constant dedicated flexing of your showbusiness muscles,
then bring in risk-taking, timing and luck and charm and courage
and a complete immersion in the history and traditions and
conventions and disasters of the business and then, finally, you may
glimpse success!

One song encapsulates the journey to fame like no other. It was
written for Judy's triumphant nineteen-week run at the Palace
Theater by Roger Edens, her lifelong friend and collaborator – a
record-breaking, theatre-saving, career-reviving venture lasting from
autumn 1951 until almost the spring of 1952. I don't believe anyone
else has ever really sung it very much, apart from her and me. I find
footage of Judy singing this song as affecting as any Garland performance I've seen. Judy wears a slim column gown on which pale
flame-shaped tigerish panels creep up the body against a dark ground
of shimmering sequins – was ever a dress and a theme more perfectly
matched?

> I played the State,
> The Capitol,
> And people said,
> Don't stop!
> Until you play the Palace,
> You haven't played the top.
> For years I had it preached to me,
> And drummed into my head,

Until you play the Palace
You might as well be dead.
A team of hoofers was the headline,
At the Majestic, down in Dallas.
But they cancelled the day,
Their agent called to say,
You can open the bill at the Palace.
So, it became the Hall of Fame,
The Mecca of the trade.
When you had played the Palace,
You knew that you were made.
So I hope you understand my wondrous thrill,
'Cause Vaudeville's back at the Palace,
And I'm on the bill.

You can hear the unfurling of theatrical ambition in the steep climbing melody of this song. You can almost feel the years of hard work, the disappointments big and small that come with each step forward, the clinging on to the belief that one day it will happen if you keep on working, keep on hoping, keep on believing. In the texture of this song you can sense the low points, the lack of funds, the waitressing, the rinsing-out of stockings (or gloves) in draughty motel bathrooms and the stoic endurance of the roving and humourless hands of the arrogant comedian in the next room, and that room's thin walls.

I envy the drumming in and the preaching of the advice in this world that is so thoroughly saturated with the life of the stage. And the certainties are appealing too for they are so extravagant. Know this: the singer says, in this exotic world I came from it's either high success or . . . or . . . death. Wow! And what did I have drummed into my head? The things that all children have, to say please and thank you, to try to hide my appetites and, perhaps more unusually,

64

to keep secrets and never, ever to divulge information or opinions that had been expressed to me by another. (Even now my instinct is to conceal what I've done or thought or felt or heard for fear of I don't even know what. Is it because the amounts might look wrong or not tally in some shaming way?)

Working hard

And then into this highly disciplined framework of training and yearning the exotica of theatrical hierarchy is introduced. The song doesn't challenge this, it accepts it fully: to be on the bill, to be the headline, to open the bill, these are all quite different propositions. The point about this kind of hierarchy is that it's oddly reassuring.

If the call comes you drop everything. It's not about letting people down; it's about self-respect.

I love the little short story in the middle of the verse about the team of hoofers. It makes me think of Ruth in the alien corn in Keats's 'Ode to a Nightingale'. It's atmospheric and tender – the calling of the hoofers to New York – a sort of eternal truth in this ancient of professions, but more than this it is such a wonderful gift for any stage-struck listener. For if the hoofers are ditching the star spot in Dallas just to *open* at the Palace, then who'll fill the gap at the Majestic created by the errant dancers? Me! I wouldn't expect to headline – oh no – but if all the other acts moved up a spot could I not open the bill down in Dallas, just this once?

The modesty of the last line of this verse is utterly enchanting. Why, it's almost ostentatious! In this highly hierarchical world only the true superstar can refer to herself as 'on' the bill when she is, in fact, at the top of it. To all intents and purposes she *is* the bill. When the melody reaches its apex, then plateaus and falls in a little echo of the star's bow, the sense of the journey travelled and the achievements notched up are exhausting. The singer's entire life has been a preparation for this moment. Finally, she's arrived, she's absolutely a star and it feels wonderful. Hooray! Was the work ethic ever made to sound more appealing?

The
Rescuers

I was born into a family that takes making people feel better very seriously. My great-grandfather invented psychoanalysis.

My mother's heart goes out to strangers in trouble faster than anyone's I've ever seen. I am on a register of trained volunteers who are called on straight away if there is any sort of public tragedy in London. We used to form part of the government's disaster action plan but we have been renamed – in the fashion of a modest band of upbeat cartoon superheroes – the resilience team!

*

A highly sensitive child will very often develop an attendant facility: the art of consolation. You can be your own best friend, the adult world proclaims, and these children soon master the skills they would like their peers to possess. When I was younger and less developed than I am now, consoling people was my favourite pastime. When I met someone I really liked my first thought was, wouldn't it be wonderful if you suffered some sort of minor crisis/mild illness and I could be the one to help you through?

By the age of eight I was good at all manner of consoling. I got results. My technique was one of acute listening paired with high-octane cheerleading. You had to create an environment that was completely uncensorious, where anything was allowed as long as it was true. Then you had to dazzle the consolee with an undiluted beam of your highest personal regard. And this two-pronged attack cheered people up, it really did. I could turn round your mood in half an hour.

My range, as I grew older, broadened dramatically. I became known as a little oracle. The phone rang day and night: boyfriends with a gift for disappearing, delinquent parents, French homework, lemon meringue pie? I would calmly dispense my advice. I was forever crossing town in the small hours with a quarter-bottle of whisky and a bunch of droopy tulips to go to the aid of a friend. It was tiring at times, but I couldn't be happy if you weren't happy, so in the long run it did make sense.

In November 1968 Judy Garland injured her head on the corner of a marble table, falling out of bed in a Boston motel. A doctor was called and the wound was taped together. It wasn't serious but Judy needed somewhere to rest for a day or two. John Meyer, her principal romantic companion for autumn 1968, was too exhausted to manage her alone. He telephoned the owner of the Beef and Ale House where the pair had dined the night before. The proprietor, a man named Vinnie Toscano, and some of his family had joined the Garland party. It was all very festive. As they left the establishment Vinnie had said, 'If I can do anything for you, either of you, ever, I want you to give me a ring.'

So John picked up the telephone and appealed to their new friend. Could Judy come and stay for a couple of days to recuperate? Vinnie said it was really not convenient. It was Thanksgiving and he had his own plans. (Do people ever mean it when they say you must let me know what I can do? Think very carefully before you issue these words.) Vinnie did however arrange for one of the waitresses at the Beef and Ale to take Judy in. 'In her forties, with dark hair beginning to streak grey, a flat Irish face and a nothing-can-faze-me look, Mahgret was just what the doctor ordered.' He was not wrong.

Margaret's* second-floor walk-up in Ashmont, a suburb of Boston was surprisingly pleasant. She prepared a meal of chicken and potatoes, and asked if she might play the recording of Carnegie Hall. Hooray! A fan! Everyone relaxed. All present began a poker game and soon the vodka came out. It was all rather convivial. Judy changed in to one of Margaret's jerseys and started to entertain the little gathering. When she was appearing in Houston, she recounted, the Supremes were appearing on the same block and one afternoon they telephoned Judy's room and asked if they might come up and meet her. 'Impossible,' Judy's companion said. 'Miss Garland is taking a nap.' Diana Ross asked, 'Well, can we come up and just *watch her sleep?*'

I myself would have loved to watch Judy sleep, from the respectful distance of an upright corner chair. I'd have liked to appreciate her without asking for anything in return, not entertainment of any sort, nor confidences or explanations. Her head might be turned from me, her hair flattened in repose, her shoulders hunched, her

---

*I can't bring myself to spell her Mahgret, as Meyer does.

face glistening with night cream under the blue bedclothes. I would keep watch and ensure she wasn't disturbed by a shout in the corridor or heavy footfalls from the rooms above.

After a while, at that modest Boston Thanksgiving party, Meyer went off to fetch some Ritalin for Judy, leaving her to rest in Margaret's capable hands. Afterwards, his sweet hope was that he might be allowed to sleep alone for a night with no interruptions, no further late-night chemist capers or impromptu recitals or counselling sessions or arguing or madcap rat pack hell-raising. Most famous for his witty, dissolute anthem, 'I'd Like to Hate Myself in the Morning', Meyer wanted to *like* himself in the morning, is my guess. A night with no long bouts of reassurance about his loved one's status in the public hearts or in his own seemed within his grasp. Vincente Minnelli described Judy's need for reassurance as 'pathological'; when she made a cake, even, she required a minimum of ten compliments. Who doesn't? (Me? I like a spontaneous round of applause such as I received last night when I produced a five-tier ice cream gateau in shades of pink from soft strawberry blush to cassis, decorated with sprigs of frosted redcurrants and piped meringue rosettes.) The vision of an uninterrupted night of sleep shimmered before John Meyer like a beautiful mirage. He was so tired he actually thought he might die. Judy viewed Meyer's sleep – it seemed to him – as a bitter rival, as treacherous and alluring as any Lana Turner type. Betrayal was what it meant. But Meyer could not resist sleep's call. He decided to head back to town for the night. Besides, Judy was entrusted to the highly reliable Margaret. She was close to sleep now herself. The prospects looked good.

Like a father of a newborn, he tiptoed away.

Margaret held the fort admirably. She was a good sort. If lifelong friends we couldn't be, nor family, nor colleagues, I would have liked to have been this Margaret woman, tending to the injured bluebird, lending sweaters – she could have had my best charcoal-coloured

70

jersey with the floppy mink trim – cooking dinners, supplying Judy with a cosy domestic arena in which to shine. It's almost like a scene from the Bible, the wounded traveller and the Good Samaritan.

I feel ashamed that a person of Judy's stature and reputation should have been left with a stranger in her time of need. It's a scandal that no superstar, or non-superstar for that matter, should have to endure. And yet Margaret's skill and grace were quietly spectacular. She knew all the right moves: ordinary family cheer, food, drink, calm admiration, unquestioning hospitality, a listening ear and the suggestion of a party. In that modest Boston apartment, Judy was oddly comfortable. For a few hours Margaret supplied her with the conditions in which it was possible to flourish. It was a small masterpiece of care. *And she didn't once ask her to sing.*

Sometimes in the insomniac hours I wonder if 27 November 1968 (when I was minus two months old) was actually the best night of Margaret's life? Was there much competition? I hope there was. Competent, unflappable and kind, I wish there had been more such people in Judy's world. Sometimes I muse on what Margaret might have said when her boss telephoned with his unusual request. She had no husband and no children, and didn't people just know it! Did it cause her offence that she was expected to drop everything, and at Thanksgiving too? I think she leapt at the chance, affecting an acutely casual tone with her employer in order not to seem too keen and raise alarm. (It's easier for people to give what you like than what you crave.) 'Sure, no problem . . . bring her over . . . I'll put the heating on. I'll sleep on the couch and she can have my room.'

When Margaret awoke the next morning Garland would be gone; she had insisted on being driven back to Boston and delivered to a drowsy Meyer in the small hours. Did Margaret feel she had been through her own personal trip to Oz? She would have kept close to her, I assume, the vodka glass that Garland's warm hands had cradled and the hoop of lipstick on a crumpled Kleenex; perhaps for a week or so Judy's crisp rejected baked potato skin might have sat on the mantel like a prized seashell. (When I met Liza Minnelli and she left me alone for a moment with a half-full ash tray – 'It's my last remaining vice,' she said – I almost pocketed her god-ends, I mean her dog-ends, *and* the quarter club sandwich – chicken, bacon, tomato – that had been abandoned on the hotel side chair.)

I expect the following Judy-less days and weeks seemed unbearably flat to Margaret. Like the victim of an attractive one-night love bandit, did she find herself chained to the phone? I would have been. 'You'll never guess who dropped by the other day!' she might regale each new waitress at the Beef and Ale with the little story, behind the counter, down the years. 'And such a lovely woman, so funny and warm and down-to-earth.'

'You already, like, *told* us,' would each new intake of waitresses sigh?

One night thirteen years ago I had some louche and reckless cult rock stars in *my* home. It all happened very quickly. One minute we were falling out of a club called Smashing and the next we were in the kitchen of my little mews flat with its blue gingham Formica table, its curtains printed with fruit and vegetables and its come-down-in-the-world sheets and towels labelled *second housemaid* and *square butler's room* for it had once been the staff accommodation of a nearby grand house and had never quite shaken off the association. Semi-automatically I made bacon sandwiches (isn't that what rock stars eat at three a.m.?) and put on a Stevie Wonder record because it seemed a safe bet. It was hot and I had a case of wine and vodka left over from my recent book launch – I assume that was why I had been chosen to host the gathering. There were six or seven of us and I was the youngest by far. My guests dazzled in their exquisite cloth-ing, with the requisite rips and stains of a fierce night out. I felt so proud! The pop stars, one toothless, one legless, were rather fastid-ious: they wanted ice in their drinks, which I didn't have. They were vegetarians! It wasn't a serious failure on my part, but I ditched the crispy bacon pretty sharpish. In two hours almost all the drink was gone and I felt my popularity wane, but life is sometimes like that, I self-consoled.

Someone suggested we go out on to my flat roof and look at the dawn, so we gathered up our drinks and one by one climbed the ancient ladder that went up to the large expanse of pale grey lead. We sprawled out and gazed at the backs of the nearby grand buildings, six-storied, Crown-cream-painted Nash houses, bulging conservato-ries and looped spiral staircase extensions, their cobbled gardens primed for summer entertaining with Italianate furniture and elab-orate wrought iron rose bowers. One of the singers called out for a guitar. I held my breath and went to fetch it. At the ladder going down I met the last of our party. I moved to one side to let her pass, but suddenly her leg slipped and she grappled for her moorings, falling sideways slightly and stumbling as her foot hit some rotten wood that framed a skylight in the garage below. In a semi-second the glass shattered and she shot down through the smashed window, and was clinging with clawed fingers to the edge of the skylight with a twenty-three-foot drop beneath her, on to concrete and my brother in-law's amassed sculpting tools. She was calm, hanging there; she even smiled faintly, cartoonish in the half-light, her delicate hands thick with blood. I screamed for help. My friend was six foot one. She was fashionably narrow, but even still. One of the rock stars, reed thin and no weightlifter, appeared. His lank black hair flopped against his neck as he gripped her wrists and bent and flexed his forearms – he hadn't a whisper of a chance and I could not bear to watch. But from somewhere there came to him the strength to hold my friend fast, then he took a deep, concerted breath and hauled the entire hanging, dripping, trembling seventy-three-inch body of hers up to safety.

I was so shocked at what I had seen I ran into the kitchen, half-hysterical, sobbing and clutching myself. I closed the door. I'm not a good person to have around when people fall. It's too painful, even when the ending is good. I don't know how to bear it. A platinum blonde woman I'd not met before – dressed in silver with scarlet lips – she knew what to do and she walked in and tried to cheer me. Open your mouth, was her command. Sit down. Dazed, I obeyed while she poured vodka in from the bottle. It did not feel good but she was being kind, I suppose. Someone told her I'd had a friend – the best person I knew – who had died recently through falling. Was she trying to anaesthetise my pain? She knows more of life than you, do what she says, was what I thought. But when she started unwrapping a folded square of paper I just shook my head and said, 'No. Please, no.'

What I wanted, what I had sought and found, was something I wasn't built for. It was Oz all over again – my dress that night was of blue gingham. I quite like adversity, its prompts and challenges, the opportunities it presents and its chastening heroic spur. At least I thought I did, until that night.

*

When I think of Judy Garland in pain, or Judy struggling, or Judy stung by disappointment or betrayal, or Judy petulant or deliberately misunderstanding, or Judy uncertain of the size of her star, or staggering under the weight of her talent, or reeling from her 'medication' too much or too little, or being maltreated or turned against and rejected, or denying herself food, or neglected or simply in despair and facing the world with the sharp accusation, 'You demand a great deal of satisfaction for the little you give', I'm always trying to think what I could have done to help. How do you console someone who's in the sympathy business herself? An expert who knows all the tricks of the trade?

I sometimes think of Judy in the week her television series recorded its final show in 1964, and wish for a way to reach out to her. The last few days were almost operatic: the vanquished heroine embarking on a harrowing series of endurance tests, the absolute fidelity of the studio audience fans, the shadowy power play from above, the bitter rivalry of the deeply ungallant Mel Tormé (Mel Torment, as we good fans like to think of him), the demolition of the original sky-high hopes and the ludicrously cheery-banal villain of the piece that was *Bonanza*, the most popular television series in America, against which the *Judy Garland Show* was cast.

The deal negotiated for the *Judy Garland Show* was, according to *Variety*, 'perhaps the strongest contract ever elicited by a TV performer'. All the signs were good. Judy's glamorous and witty performance on the previous season's *Jack Paar Show* had won her many new fans and delighted the millions she already had. Every inch the star in a demure black silk dress, she bewitches her host with her confident and powerful allure, her quick wit and her irrepressible personality. She was not playing a part of any sort; she was finally and magnificently herself, the best of herself, the best of America, brimming with mystery and inner resources. *This* was what and who she would be on her television show. 'She's magic, so abracadabra – here's Judy Garland' was her introduction, and it was true. Judy was strong enough too, and humorous and debonair enough once the contract was signed to make light of her previous difficulties in the most public of arenas. At a CBS function packed with senior executives from the station, on 11 April 1963, Judy Garland sang a specially tailored version of 'Call Me Irresponsible', which went approximately like this:

> Call me irresponsible,
> Call me unreliable,
> Throw in undependable, too.
> Do my foolish alibis bore you?
> Are you worried
> I might not show up for you?
> Call me unpredictable,
> Say that I'm impractical,
> Rainbows I'm inclined to pursue . . .
> But it's undeniably true –
> I'm irrevocably signed to you!

The audience exploded. She had met their fears head on. It was the perfect mixture of mischief and courtesy. It doesn't always work in life, if you regale your doubters with a catalogue of reasons to be cautious about you, but it did in this instance. Notice she doesn't make any promises not to live down to people's worst fears; she just says, 'It's a done deal!' It's very stylish. I've always loathed the dictum 'never apologise, never explain', it's guaranteed, it seems to me, to result in mistrust and alienation, but I do understand the point of it here. The first time I saw Liza Minnelli in concert at the Albert Hall she said, 'You've probably read a lot of terrible things about me in the papers. Well I'm afraid most of it's true.' How can you argue with that?

*

There's no doubt that the *Judy Garland Show* had the potential to transform, utterly, the day-to-day life of its star. What it represented cannot be underestimated. It might have underwritten almost every aspect of Judy Garland's personal and professional life with its promise of enduring financial security, removing a whole portfolio of anxieties from the star's slight shoulders. It could have changed the often hand-to-mouth nature of the later part of Judy's career and paved the way for an unprecedented level of control, which would promote family sanity while assuring its star a place in the nation's hearts and homes for ever. It would also have meant she could have stayed in the same place for months on end, something her concert career never allowed her. Her life could be *comfortable*. And with all this, once the promised money had rolled up there would be what accountants term a healthy sum, delivering a future that was endurable and, more than that, one that could be *lived*. There would be work schedules that were not debilitating – and thus requiring more and more stimulants – but could be undertaken by a Judy Garland with the power to cut her cloth to suit herself, to work infrequently or not at all, to have the sort of life that she had long craved.

Yet the project from the first was mighty ambitious, a tall order in every respect. It would require from its tenacious star almost the equivalent of a Carnegie Hall spectacular or the 'Star is Born' movie-within-a-movie production number every week. Judy Garland, everyone involved agreed, was giving the shows her all. When did she ever give anything else? All the network had to do was 'maintain (and, at the same time, dispel) the myth of "The Legend" that was Judy Garland, keep her tremendous appeal intact (but somehow distil it for weekly television), make her an event on a weekly basis that would, at the same time, not overexpose her tremendous larger than life personality that had to conform to all of America coast to coast – while still remaining unique.' A tall order indeed.

There are so many high points in this body of work. Looking at a picture of Judy on the last note of 'Come Rain or Come Shine', which she sang on shows 3 and 21, gives you an idea of quite how much of her all Judy gave her television show. Her arms, her feet, even her fingers and shoes seem to be singing *in excelsis*. Her right thumb is going all out.

The best lines in this song are 'Happy together, Unhappy together, And won't it be fine!' This to me is one of the greatest sentiments of any love song ever written. It takes the rather stolid and punitive segment of the Christian marriage service, 'for better or for worse', and translates it into the stuff of crazy high romance. The idea that the bad times could somehow be as good, possibly even better than happy times, is quite revolutionary and extremely appealing. In a novel I wrote a few years ago, the highly optimistic marriage guidance counsellor heroine thinks, 'Bad people were not worse than good people, of that she was sure . . . Or was it just that goodness and badness mingled together were a far better proposition than goodness alone, because goodness alone equalled a sort of bleached insanity and bad in isolation was so rare as to be non-existent, give or take the obvious exceptions.' Howard Hirsch, the man who played the bongos for Judy for this number at Carnegie Hall in 1961, told the singer Rufus Wainwright, 'I loved Judy. I would have died for her.' He used to take his bongos to the place where she is buried and sing 'Come Rain or Come Shine', with its heavy promise of lifelong devotion, 'I'm gonna love you, like nobody's loved you, Come rain or come shine.' I'm glad about that.

Judy was informed on 11 March that her series would be terminated after show 26. It was a terrible blow that arrived at an impossible time: a nasty custody battle for her children had begun, in which her estranged husband Sid Luft accused her of attempting suicide on at least twenty occasions. Financial ruin and lawsuits from previous employees also loomed. The *Judy Garland Show*'s ratings weren't sky high, but they were always respectable, especially when you consider that thirteen of the fifteen most popular shows of the time were straight comedy rather than musical variety shows.

Bill Colleran, the executive producer, commented at the final recording: 'Judy was broken-hearted . . . I had the distinct feeling that deep down, she was thinking this was the end of her life. She knew it was her last chance, her last act. A few days later, when the final recorded section had to be completed, Judy was too distraught to sing another note. Production consultant Bob Wynn said, 'She stood there alone. It was all over for her. Judy didn't ask me to, but I walked out with her, put her in her car, and sent her home. She insisted on taking tons of stuff with her. Sheets, pillowcases, all kinds of crap from her trailer. It was very sad.'

This image of Judy utterly vanquished, trailing linen, stayed with me for a long time. I thought of her 'we're a couple of swells' down-at-heel persona, spying an opportunity and seizing it. I didn't find the image as desperate as her observer did. I was glad that in the absence of human consolation she found something else to cling to. A pile of crisply folded pillowcases in a cupboard in my house represent, to me, order and plenty in their tenderest incarnation. I was happy to think of Judy with the bedding. When at low ebb I sometimes browse the bed and bath sections of department stores and marvel at the thickness of the towels, the strict, dry lustre of a very high thread-count sheet. It can be very consoling. Sometimes, when I wonder about performing ordinary domestic tasks for Judy, I think about taking care of the ironing; being in her house in a sunny side room, pressing sheets and pillowcases while madam slept upstairs or breakfasted in bed, oblivious to my light industry and its accompanying scent of starch and scorch below.

I wish I'd been in the car with her that night, although the pressure to come up with some outlandish gallows humour might have been almost more than I could bear. What do you say to a person who feels she has lost everything? Car talk has never been my forte. I tend to speak so much that people wind down the windows to let a bit of me out. John Berryman quoted his friend R. P. Blackmur's assertion that poetry was to be distinguished from verse by language

> so twisted & posed in a form
> that it not only expresses the matter in hand
> but adds to the stock of available reality.

At this point in her life, as options closed in, Judy would have needed an additional stock of available reality. I have one idea: I imagine embarking on some kind of wild and childish slapstick spree with her, but slapstick with meaning, which the best sorts always possess. I imagine driving and driving until we reach dense woods like the miles and miles of beautiful plane-tree forests I passed on my four-hour drive from Minneapolis airport to the town of Grand Rapids, where Garland was born. I have never seen so many trees in my life. As children we went once to a wood in France where something was wrong with the trees, and when my youngest brother leaned against one it just fell over. We couldn't believe our luck and, half-deranged with glee, we just ran around crazily felling trees with our bare hands. We were superheroes to ourselves. It was very reviving. Could I somehow manage to recreate that experience for Judy?

I can't bear to think of Judy Garland (or anyone really) feeling unloved. Lack of love, she makes clear, *can* kill. In just two lines from 'Me and My Shadow', a wry song in others' hands, Judy paints a scene so vivid in its starkness that the images haunt and disarm long after the song's close:

> And when it's twelve o'clock
> We climb the stair.
> We never knock
> 'Cause nobody's there.

I see her ascending the stair of some decrepit boarding house or unspeakable flat, slowly and wearily, utterly alone, in elaborate stage clothes, trying as she climbs each step to keep her spirits intact, to self-insist that she remain jaunty no matter what. The days are blank, the nights irretrievably bleak. The burden of herself! She absolutely won't accept that her morale is shot, but things aren't looking good. Willpower and self-discipline help with this of course, she knows you know, but there's a sense that the closer she gets to her dim room the nearer she will be to the inevitable slump she's been staving off all day, all month, perhaps all year. There is such a quiet humility to Judy's version of this song, and so much good-natured acceptance, but the words grate, startlingly bald and frank against the easy melody, and, to me, the performance conveys acutely the day-to-day strain of trying to be modest and reasonable about human expectations when all the while your existence is underwritten by a continual muffled howl: How can I bear it that there isn't any love in my life? And then come the ignominious attendant cries of doubt: What if I fail myself? How do I *know* I'll never give up?

Sympathy can be a limp instrument, cosy, conservative and banal. Sometimes it can even impede progress by stemming feelings rather than allowing them free rein. Yet in Judy's hands sympathy is powerful, anarchic and revolutionary. It stuns and mobilises. It's a sort of violence.

During the worst period of my life, autumn 1989 to summer 1990, I watched an eighty-five minute PBS television special called *Judy Garland: The Concert Years* every day, receiving from it something that just wasn't available to me elsewhere. What to do when you are twenty, bereaved and grieving, living alone, an owner-operated pain factory dwelling right at the very edge of what you can bear? You can't foist yourself on friends or family, however kind, for repeatedly provoking and enduring their alarm is more than any of you can take. You're a risky prospect. You may not have the courage or wherewithal to let a professional take up the vast unholy slack of you; besides, you do not wish to pathologise your grief or have the dead person's electric absence counselled right out of your life for good. Others have managed it, since time began, and so should you. And then you scarcely even want the pain to diminish because without it you have absolutely nothing to your name. So I sat with Judy and she sat with me. Most days our meetings, in my draughty sitting room with the low hum of the condemned gas fire sending out damp heat and fumes, were absolutely terrible, almost blacker than death or Hell, but it was an arena in which it felt possible for me to stay a person.

No one else, it seemed, knew how I felt and could bear it, let alone face me with a heart frank and sweet. This is what the world sometimes is, Judy sang to me; sick, rotten and sharper then swords, and it absolutely shouldn't be allowed, but nowhere is there more life than the sphere you currently inhabit. There is a sort of ancient private human dignity in what is happening to you, however squalid and desperate you feel. There was such a huge weight of camaraderie between us and then, oddly, and with a lack of regard for good taste which was quite breathtaking, from nowhere notes of elation would creep in. Where had *they* come from? And the humour! This is so completely terrible it's almost funny, she would remind me, now and then. Is it? I asked. Is it? I couldn't see it but the idea certainly appealed.

I don't know how she did what she did, and her technique for healing was without doubt excessively severe and I still don't quite understand our extreme daily psychic pain ritual, but I know it was bigger than I was, larger than life certainly, not magic or anything fantastic in that way, but nonetheless astonishing. She was irresistible. I kept going back to her face and her voice on the television screen and they were sometimes worse than awful, our repeated and lengthy excruciating sessions together, but something in me could not quite stay away. We sat it out together. The tiny figure in clown's garb, sitting on the apron of the stage at the Palace in the half dark, where it wasn't clear if she was young or old, black or white, male or female, did not know of my specific loss; she had been dead for twenty years but that didn't count for a minute. She had something I needed and she gave of it freely, repeatedly, and it kept me functioning in a very modest way, until the experts came in.

I don't quite know what the opposite of never forgiving someone is, but that's how I feel towards Judy about that time. It's more than extreme gratitude and it's less external too, for it was a form of collaboration between us. I could feel as bad as I needed for days, for weeks, for months on end and she would meet me there, and the person we made me into was fractionally less afraid and less lonely. Although nothing she did diminished the pain exactly, she brought to me a sense of its value and a sense of my own, and knowing that meant there was just about enough to survive.

The singer Rufus Wainwright told me that after 9/11 he found himself listening to Judy Garland's Carnegie Hall album repeatedly. It's true that the soaring high spirits and the jokes on that record are exactly what are required when life's losses loom large. The ease with which Judy sings, the subtlety, the control and the avalanche of clear, undiluted feeling led her audience on 23 April 1961 into a sort of ecstatic collapse. People had wanted her to be happy for so long that when they saw that she was they just couldn't take it. She didn't know what she was capable of until that night, her friend Kay Thompson remarked. When I waited outside Carnegie Hall to hear Rufus's version of that epic concert in June 2006, a woman who was passing the theatre (fifties, spectacles, floral shirtwaister) murmured to her friend, 'It's a bit like he's restaging the crucifixion.'

Well, *The Concert Years* is of even stronger flavour. It's an ambush of unadulterated super-human emotion and the places it takes you are as shocking as anywhere you'll ever see, but what an excessively lovely rendering of those awful places it is. Yet there are lighter moments, lots of them, extraordinarily skilled and celebratory interludes like Garland's 'Get Happy' number. This song is suffused with so much theatrical artistry. The play of light, the sharp shadows, the limbs at once smooth and angular reinforce the lyric powerfully; and then the underlying sense you get of a vamp who's somehow the most innocent person in the room is so charming and captivating that nothing about it seems to do with anything as leaden as human selves.

'I would not dare/Console you if I could', wrote Philip Larkin in 'Deceptions', picturing a young woman whose life had been undone by a brutal attacker. Good consolation does require daring. It's a risky business. Sometimes muscles and millions are required, not just intelligent and delicate feminine instincts and a supply of soft knitwear.

One night, when the chips were down, Judy Garland telephoned Tony Bennett from her suite at the St Regis hotel, asking for help because a man was beating her up. Tony Bennett was just about to go on stage – opening night, in half an hour – and couldn't get there but his ex-wife said, 'Call Frank.' So Bennett phoned Sinatra, who said he'd do what he could and would call back in fifteen minutes.

After twelve minutes Judy phoned Tony backstage: 'I have five hundred policemen outside the hotel and six Jewish lawyers in my suite. I asked for help – but this is ridiculous!'

Three minutes later Sinatra phoned Bennett. 'Is that all right, kid?'

Often afraid in the night in my flat on my own, twenty-one and paralysed with anxiety and a certain knowledge that there was someone in the next room about to attack at three o'clock in the morning, I asked my father if he could get me a gun.

'I wouldn't dream of using it, of course, I'd just keep it under the bed so I can sleep at night.' I heard my voice slip into its acutely casual register that fools not a soul. 'Oh you know the way that when you make an appointment for a few days' time with a very good doctor, if he's worth his salt, your symptoms will vanish and you can cancel at the last minute? Well it would be like that. Make me feel safe. Wouldn't probably dream of ever—'

'I can easily get you a gun,' my father said. 'That's fine.'

Hooray! The arrival of the cavalry is always a nice moment.

We chatted on a little about the world and his wife until it was time to say goodbye. There was suddenly a note of awkwardness and he cleared his throat. 'Is it definitely a good idea, though, the gun?'

After I trained as a bereavement counsellor in my mid-twenties my attitude towards consolation shifted subtly. I learned that people in distress need support that is diversionary and support that is cathartic. Most people are good at the diversionary sort, suggesting interesting and pleasant distractions, but few people can bear their loved ones to state their despair at its bleakest and most unbearable without trying to tidy it or improve it or usher in a distant note of cheer or hope or resolve. Distressed people need to be allowed to reject your optimism now and then without taking responsibility for your hurt or alarm.

> YOU: I sometimes feel I just can't bear to go on.
> I: But you have *so* much to live for! You're so talented and beautiful and everybody loves you!
> YOU: I sometimes feel I just can't bear to go on.
> I: Almost as if nothing means anything; nothing's worth anything any more?

Which will make a person feel more understood? Judy knew you need both.

I like exacting people. I like the feeling that you can't get away with anything and nor do you want to. I like the sort of people you don't dare interrupt, the sort who, when they're stuck for a particular word and look to you to provide it, you never oblige for fear of suggesting the wrongest possible thing. Judy could see straight through people. When talking to her you would have to summon your best

87

words and your finest feelings. How easy it is to go through days where you don't say a single sentence that you haven't said before. Judy would require original thought; otherwise she would be on to you. I'm usually careful in what I say. My father once stopped speaking to someone because he used the word 'mishmash'.

Yet when I think about consoling Judy Garland my worry is this: how do you use *words* to try to affect the morale of a person whose manner of singing enabled her to get so much more out of her songs than the songs themselves seemed capable of expressing? How could my meaning have meaning when her meaning went so far beyond even the idea of words?

Judy Garland sometimes responded best to consolation that was humorous and pitch black. After she nicked her throat with a shard of glass in an extremely half-hearted suicide attempt in 1950, shortly after the termination of her MGM contract, she received a telegram from her friend Fred Finklehoffe:

DEAR JUDY, SO GLAD YOU CUT YOUR THROAT. ALL THE OTHER GIRL SINGERS NEEDED THIS KIND OF BREAK.

'Isn't that sweet!' Judy said to her then husband Vincente Minnelli. It concerns me that a twenty-eight-year-old Judy found this so consoling, because it is very much not my style. Confident and sophisticated, I can see, but that sort of comment is more daring than anything I'd say.

When my boyfriend was killed in a climbing accident, a falling accident, two months before his twenty-first birthday, in June 1989 – twenty years to the day that Judy died – a fellow mourner standing next to me at the funeral leaned in and whispered, 'You're very lucky! You can get away with absolutely anything for the next five years.' I was so shocked I fell over straight away. The woman helped me up, kindly assuming I had the jelly legs of one so fresh to mourning. Perhaps she sensed she had spoken too harshly for moments later she gave me a pound for the collection plate that never materialised. Her sharp words were attempting, I can now see, to extend to me a note of permission for the foreseeable future. 'Don't feel you have to look or act or feel a certain way, just do what you need to do' was perhaps what she meant – although I do wish it was what she had said. I imagine Judy might have responded well to such a comment.

Before 1950, Judy's fans admired her for her strong feelings, her delightful moral effervescence, her bearing both radiant and trembly, her picturesque yearning, but all the feelings had to be pleasing. Imagine the pressure. It is required that you are dewy, sincere and optimistic, brimming with a cadenza of bright feelings, but only ones that do you credit. You must convey extremes of emotion, but

89

they must be extremes that are ornamental and upbeat. Was it a relief to Judy that within an hour of her injury a newspaperman got wind of her so-called suicide attempt and shattered for ever her image as a cheerful and wholesome all-American girl?

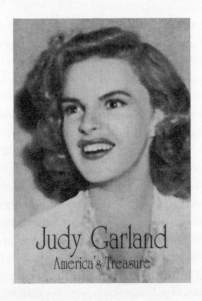

Judy Garland
America's Treasure

Might she have had someone make the call? If you feel your inside is so misrepresented by your outside does it make you feel even crazier? Finally, perhaps, there was permission to be sad and angry. Everyone needs that. Was this what my straight-talking mourning neighbour was thinking?

Sometimes I dream of showering Judy with luxuries. It wasn't that she was particularly stimulated by fancy things – it's interesting that not one of her five husbands had what you might call *money* – but the extent of the luxuries available to Hollywood stars of her era was so extreme that it would have been nice to have distracted and *amused* her with the dazzling trinkets and outrageous bibelots that ought to have been the natural trappings of her world. I sometimes think of a little scene described by Hedda Hopper in her first volume of memoirs and wish that the heroine of the piece had been Miss Garland. For who, it must be said, is Paulette Goddard?

I went to interview Paulette Goddard after one of her European tours. 'I can't give you dinner,' she warned, 'but we'll have a little snack.'

The walls of her apartment were covered with famous paintings by Diego Rivera, Waldo Pierce, Renoir, there was no more room to hang them on, so she had stood them on the floor against chairs. The latest one, a personal discovery, was done by the local taxi driver.

Paulette reclined in a black satin princess dress, held up by her personality. Her ears were weighted with dollar-sized gold earrings crusted with diamonds. On her feet were strapped golden sandals.

The snack consisted of fresh shrimp, caviar, buttered pumpernickel, sandwiches, iced champagne in silver buckets, vodka, and a spicy sauce in a scooped-out red cabbage . . .

'There was a time I dreamed of being a great actress. Now I'd rather have a short role with long eyelashes than a long role with no eyelashes.'

She left the room and came back with a diamond tiara and gold bag, solid gold.

'For a girl who doesn't want possessions,' I said, 'you certainly travel heavy.'

'But Hedda, that bag is only to carry my lipstick in. The tiara? Not much, really, but beautiful workmanship, don't you think?'

I am aware, of course, that discretion is necessary when offering consolation. Amounts are very important too, for the economy of sympathy is mighty complicated. To over-console is to insult and to inflame. No one wants the howls of conjoined despair, the inclined head, the excruciating facial contortions and the deep intakes of breath. No one wants to hear, 'I am soooooooooo sorry.' Are you? Aren't you also a tiny bit pleased?

When people draw their breath in little paroxysms of fellow feeling at your trouble it sometimes feels as though they are trying to cause humiliation. Matters of status are involved, and relish and power struggles that just aren't pretty. When you console someone eagerly it is wise to question why. A distressed person needs to talk about something painful happening and be met with calm. Handy suggestions and professionals' phone numbers may be useful later on, but in the face of the storm they can seem dismissive and belittling. A friend of mine who separated briefly from her husband some years ago was alarmed by the throbbing consolation that arrived concerning her new arrangements, from people she hardly knew. She'd spy them at a distance, weighing their words, approaching oh-so-carefully to ambush her with their expertly honed sympathetic outpourings. By suffering, it seemed to her, she was doing them some kind of terrific service. 'Sometimes,' she said, as yet another approached, moist eyes blazing, 'it feels as though these people are trying to kill me.' Nobody wants such 'treatment'. Judy herself caught at this human phenomenon in a television interview with Barbara Walters in 1967: 'maybe it will distress a lot of people, but I've had an awfully nice life, I really have'.

Judy once remarked that she was forever receiving get-well-soon cards from the public when she felt absolutely fine and she found the experience rather dispiriting. 'I hurt people where they think they want to be hurt, that's all,' she said to Dirk Bogarde in a rare moment of cynicism. In interviews, Liza Minnelli sometimes refers to a time she saw her mother laughing and asked her, 'Why do people not see how funny you are? Why do they always say you're so sad?'

'Because they need to,' was her mother's sober reply.

If you love someone, I'm always telling myself, the very least you can do is respond to the facts of her life in a way that doesn't grate. I try not to send her great piles of get-well-soon cards, I try to send jokes and Valentines.

In my writing room I have two photographs of Judy with an infant Liza Minnelli. In one, framed and on my wall, she is costumed for her role as Manuela in *The Pirate*, a vision of calm and affectionate smooth film star mother-glamour. She seems so tenderly and affectionately linked to the child that the little curve of the baby's eyebrow and the shadow in the crease of her mother's chin have become one line.

In the other photo, the one I keep in a drawer in a bed of pink tissue paper, there is an image of the same pair taken a few months earlier. Judy is wearing a simple striped dress in which she looks strained and empty and somehow *wrong*. She has the appearance of a person who has split from herself. The stark stripes bring her lack of focus into focus. There is a sense of effort, as though she is trying to be what she is – a young successful film star, wife and mother at home, off duty and at ease – but when I look closely, into the face of this twenty-four-year-old, I feel there just isn't anybody there. The baby looks anxious in her finery, like an artist's impression of a junior member of a troubled aristocratic family, which, I suppose, she was.

But I won't carry on in this vein. I can see it's not right. I wouldn't like someone to examine a photo of me and my baby when I'm having a bad day and cast aspersions about my state of mind. All new parents know it is the best of times and the worst of times.

When these photographs were taken Judy Garland had already made the acquaintance of several psychoanalysts. Amongst the first was Ernst Simmel, a distinguished colleague of Sigmund Freud. If Freud had settled in America (which he loathed – he called it 'a gigantic mistake') rather than England (which he liked – 'a blessed, a happy land'), or if he had lived for another few years and ventured to Hollywood, he might have had Judy as one of his patients. Sigmund Freud never saw *The Wizard of Oz*, but if he had done so in the last year of his life and heard Garland sing 'Over the Rainbow' I wonder what he would have thought. Do psychoanalysts share their fellow human beings' desire for some place where there isn't any trouble? If they do, they are very altruistic.

The early refugee psychoanalysts in America had many obstacles; not least was the fact that the people in America had quite different problems to the people in Germany and Austria, and this just didn't strike their analysts as quite right. In the old country people were obsessed with their fathers, but in America, where the family was structured differently, people were obsessed with their mothers.

Simmel was interested in men and women with drug and alcohol problems, a section of patients that psychoanalysis had not traditionally been known to treat. In an essay written by Simmel in 1947 and published in the *Yearbook of Psychoanalysis*, the author distinguishes, interestingly, between two types of sufferers: those who use alcohol or drugs 'as a means of escape from reality' and those who use them as 'a means of mastering reality'. Judy Garland's use of drugs throughout her adult life was conceived of as a prop to her better functioning under the extreme pressures of a job to which, apart from her huge talent for it, she was quite unsuited.

What does it mean to have an excessive talent that necessitates a style of life to which you are constitutionally unsuited? Trouble, is what it means.

Perhaps the most charming account of Judy Garland's psycho-analytic career concerns the sessions she attended as an outpatient following her stay at the Peter Bent Brigham Hospital in May 1949. During her stint at the hospital Judy had learned the rudiments of self-care, and by adhering to a regime of three good meals a day and lights out at nine, had mastered the art of eating and sleeping properly. Her analyst's name was Dr Augustus Rose, an eminent neurologist who, at six foot four, was seventeen inches taller than his illustrious patient.

On the first day of her outpatient treatment she was driven to Dr Rose's office from the Ritz Hotel in Boston. A few passers-by recognised her and waved. Her troubles and health concerns had received a good deal of coverage in the press and the American people, on the whole, had a great deal of good will and kind wishes for her. The following day there were more people present as she arrived at the building and as she left, and on the third day there was quite a little crowd. The word got round Boston about these regular sightings and soon it became almost festive, with people lined up waiting for her car to arrive and shouting endearments and kind wishes, and making declarations of love. She was terrifically buoyed up by this support and encouragement, and would float into Dr Rose's office, or so the story goes.

The analyst and analysand had humorous exchanges over this along the lines of, 'Judy, calm down. Just because you had a few people clapping outside—'

'Oh, you're a mean man.'

Part of the treatment was Dr Rose's desire to return her to the reality and solidity of her true Frances Gumm identity, the person born in Grand Rapids in 1922, rather than the manufactured adored

Hollywood creation that was Judy Garland. Judy Garland, world-famous entertainer, was meant, for the duration of her sessions, to be left outside the consulting-room door.

Judy Garland with notes
of Frances Gumm

Judy Garland

But she was simply too clever for Dr Rose. Garland knew she had her audience outside. They adored her; they would now wait for hours to see her arrive and leave; they could be plainly heard from the consulting room; and the doctor was telling her it wasn't real! 'Look,' he said. 'We can't do this, Judy. If you're going to come to see me we cannot do this. You're trying to make me into one of your fans. I can't help you in that way.' How dare he tell Judy that this love wasn't real love, that her desire for applause and mass approval was a delusion? How dare he suggest that the public's intense feelings for their star could be dismissed as a branch of her own neurosis? It seems to me an extremely unimaginative response.

There were three windows in Dr Rose's office, and one day in the middle of all this she stood up, threw them open and began to sing. Her voice filled the room and outside there were roars of applause, paroxysms of approval and she looked down at the gathered crowd and waved and sung them an encore as if to say to her doctor, and with defiance, 'So that's not real? You're telling me it's not real?'

This story doesn't exactly throb with the ring of truth. In fact, this account of Garland's analysis plays like a cut scene from *A Star is Born*. It could have come from only one of two sources: the doctor – and God forbid that psychiatrists talk to biographers – or Judy, whose information regarding herself could be awfully unreliable. This account does have the hallmark of one of Judy Garland's created anecdotes, but I hope with all my heart that it is true. The work that a patient undertakes when embarking on a course of psychoanalysis can be so gruelling that a crowd of adoring fans heralding your every arrival and departure might lend you sufficient ballast to engage confidently with the process.

THREE THINGS THAT HAVE CONSOLED ME GREATLY AT LOW MOMENTS

1. A letter from my mother while I was at university and very, very sad.

Darling Suse,

I hope so much that you are feeing better. I think you are being very brave about everything. All this immense golden

98

sunshine seems very extraordinary – when I went to the market early it was cold, even wearing a coat. One old lady fly-pitching on the pavement: 'Yesterday the Caribbean, today Siberia!' and she was repeating it to every passer by, accompanied by lots of laughter.

The tree outside looks like a firework display of golden shooting stars aimed at my window and the air is rotten with the smell of lawn mower, except for our front garden where some roses are out. They are called PEACE; I might put some little labels like the sign TAKE COURAGE at Finsbury Park.

I'm going to see Enid tomorrow. Last week I stayed there till midnight, we were recounting the days of our youth, I could remember a lot of things about her that she had forgotten. I must see if she can do the same for me.

Tomorrow there is a circus in Highbury Fields, no animals but lots of funny acts. I'm hoping to take Frances* after school. I should think it would be very exciting for us both, though not so exciting without the smells of lions and elephants.

Some time in the summer after your exams, perhaps we could go on a little holiday together, for one or two days, stay at a posh hotel in Brighton for the night or something. Wouldn't it be lovely, we could go to the Variety Theatre in the evening and stroll along the pier. And take photographs. What do you think?

I hope and pray you feel better, I have a strong feeling that everything is going to go really well, and you will be really pleased with all your hard work and exams.

I hope you like the little enclosure [a rose key ring].

All the love in the world. Mum.

*My lovely niece.

2. Something my husband did after I attended a family party and dis-covered there had been a smaller, better one the night before, to which I hadn't been invited. I don't know why this upset me as much as it did, but I just couldn't bear it: the sense of being on the outside of things, the perceived lack of status this suggested, the sense of a slight and then the treatment I had to endure from those who had been included as they tried tactfully not to mention it. I don't know why I minded as much as I did – my morale was low, I suppose – but at the time it felt like the most final of straws.

Tears started pouring down me. My husband scooped me up and put me in the car, where I just sobbed and sobbed. We passed a small supermarket.

'We need a few bits,' I said through tears, ever the shopper. 'Can we stop?'

We went into the store, arms locked together.

'Lets go crazy,' my husband said. 'Get everything you like, stuff you would never ordinarily buy.' He swung a super-sized trolley into my hands and said, 'Go insane.' And with his forearms he made a little gate, which he then threw open. 'Ready, steady, go!'

It was such a funny idea, to pretend you've won a trolley dash and go berserk. At the end of my first novel the heroine is alerted to the fact she's won a trolley dash by a letter from her local supermarket, after her slogan for the store's new baked-potato outlet wins first prize. (At Spuddies . . . We cater for every taste in potata.) On my own spree I only chose some green Chinese noodles and some crunchy-nut cornflakes, two things I love but never normally eat, but it was very consoling and we went home and put these things squarely in the cupboard for safe keeping and went to bed and I did feel better.

3. A note my father sent me

He could see I was very low for he painted me most mornings and I just couldn't stop the tears from rolling down my face. 'You are a person of the highest calibre. Love Dad.'

My father-in-law told me that when Paula Fichtl, Sigmund Freud's housekeeper, was feeling down in the dumps and homesick he would complain to her that he'd lost something important, like his book or his glasses, knowing she would find them in an instant and that this little success would improve her mood.

'Did she realise what he was doing?' I enquired.

'Very likely. She wasn't stupid and she had a good sense of humour, but it cheered her up none the less, that he took the trouble.'

In the last weeks of her life, when Judy Garland was on tour in Copenhagen, her new husband Mickey Deans had urgent business in Stockholm, chasing after cheques, and Judy was invited to stay at the country house of a well-known radio personality, Hans Vangkilde. Vangkilde had been a friend of Margaret Hamilton, the Wicked Witch of the West, during an American stint in his youth, and it was owing to this tenuous connection that Judy agreed to an interview with him. Interviewer and interviewee found an instant rapport although Vangkilde was shocked at how frail his heroine was, her skeletal appearance reminding him of the horrors he had seen as a reporter at the end of the war. Judy was comfortable with Hans's wife Grethe, their children and their dog, and sat in a chair by the fire singing 'Over The Rainbow' softly to herself with the children playing quietly at her feet. But at night the familiar terrors came back and she begged, like Dorothy, to be allowed to go home. She asked Grethe to sit with her all night and Grethe stayed with her, holding her hand until she fell asleep. Later on Judy awoke, unsure of where she was, and Grethe found her sitting by the fire in one of the Vangkilde girls' nightdresses, her arms tightly clutching the family's dog.

'You must try to sleep,' Grethe told her, and wrapped a robe around her bare shoulders.

'You know who I am?' Judy asked.

'Yes, of course. You are a great star – so great that in a couple of moments you can give ordinary people something they will never forget.'

'Please say that again,' Judy begged, as a child beseeches a mother to repeat a familiar story over and over again.

I can't think of anything better that Grethe could have said at this point. I marvel that she was able to put this feeling in to words so plain. When you are dying, it seems to me, you should be gazing into eyes that are full of love for you. When I feel sad that Judy died on her own, in the bathroom of a rented London flat thousands of miles from her children, I think of these words of Grethe's, seven or eight weeks earlier and of the comfort they must have brought, and they comfort me also.

Judy Garland in Copenhagen in 1969, signing autographs

Of course, rescuing people has fallen out of fashion. It has been out-lawed and pathologised. Even the emergency services are drilled in the health and safety procedures that forbid some forms of attend-ing to the drowning, for instance. Have-a-go heroes are derided for their irresponsibility as often as they are praised for their courage. The desire to rescue has also become subject to deep suspicion. The same clinics that treat alcohol and drug abuse have programmes designed for compulsive helpers.

Not all helping is harmful. In the right place, at the right time, helping is lovely. Where helping becomes harmful it steps over the dividing line between caring (which is healthy) and caretaking (which is unhealthy). Helpful is where we care for others in our life – but we do not step over into taking on their responsibilities for them, which is what happens when we compulsively help.

When I compulsively help, it is in order to run A. N. Other's life for him or her and to take the focus off running my own life. When I feel good because I am focusing on someone else and I am unaware of anything else except what I am trying to do for the other person in my life, whether family member or friend, whether addict or not, then that is compulsive helping. Someone who is leading a balanced life will not wish to have those respon-sibilities taken over, unless of course there are extenuating circumstances such as acute illness and so on.

I would regard as unhealthy someone who allows someone else to compulsively help. Of course we can help others, in a caring, non-intrusive way – but compulsive helping is not the way to go about it. It gets in the way of a good, healthy relationship between the two people, and hence is destructive.

Either way, as far as you are concerned, keep out of it and look after yourself if you can't keep on the caring side of the compul-sive helping boundary.

In rescuing others, many are motivated by what they see as a stab at heroism. The men who loved Judy Garland were not immune to this. She was, undoubtedly for some of them, a project, a fine cause and a chance to flex their chivalric muscles in the noblest way, an opportunity to bring meaning into their own lives. John Meyer, her companion in the autumn of 1968, wrote:

> I never had a war. Never had a cause to believe in; not Kennedy, not civil rights, not Vietnam. All those concerns of the sixties that my friends had been so exercised over, these things didn't mean shit to me, just didn't move me, and I never pretended they did . . .
>
> Which is why I embraced Judy so fervently . . . Judy took my talent, my wit, my heart . . . and then validated them for me, made them important, by pressing them into service for herself.
>
> And I could go into bat for, yes that was something to fight for, that was, that was something to believe in all right. And in fighting, in believing, so fiercely, I found myself stretched way beyond my limits, uncovering resources, uncovering strength and intelligence and compassion; yes, working for Judy I found all this . . . and in greater abundance than I'd ever dreamed was there. I was fantastic, I was as powerful and effective as I'd ever been in my whole life.

I don't look to Judy to provide my heroic opportunities. I have felt like a heroine all my life, in any case. I don't ask that Judy understands me in a way that no one else does or provides me with occasions to be my best self. It's very important to me that I ask nothing from her. I feel modest about anything I could have achieved for Judy. I don't need her to validate my pain or joy, although I do receive from her permission, on occasion, to feel as strongly as I desire. I don't think of Judy when I ought to be thinking

105

of myself. She plugs no gap in me, although she has provided immense comfort and cheer that I will never forget as long as I live.

Judy makes me feel extraordinary things. She allows me to view the world in a way that I like, but scarcely dare. I love our fellow feeling. She's not a problem I wish to solve and nor am I. I'd like to have helped, naturally; to have provided good solid care and peace and calm and kindness and jokes (and money) in a way that would have aided her happiness. Her suffering doesn't stimulate me. I do like looking after people, but I much prefer it when they're well. Yet I know it's complicated. For one thing she is no longer with us and I do understand what that means. How do you reach back into the past to provide care? I would have done or given anything that could have assisted her, but I hope too that there's always an easy and dauntless element to our relation. I'm not a tower of strength. I'm good in a crisis and my friends rely on me but I didn't, like Judy's third husband Sid Luft, survive twenty minutes on a plane that was blazing with flames. I haven't even done a course in first aid. And I'm not making up for lost time or looking to Judy to provide some sort of glue for a fractured state. I don't need her. Perhaps I did once, but now I just love.

I'm not naive. I know that if you want people who take drugs to like or love you, part of it involves keeping them well supplied. Yet I also know that every time in her life when the pressures were reduced, when the demands were taken away and there were hammocks and friends and fun and no financial worries and the correct psychological network of support, Judy's lifetime of drug-taking dwindled and, at some points, completely fell away.

There's a photograph of Judy dancing at a party with Lucille Ball in the fifties, with arms outstretched, on some kind of genuinely gleeful Hollywood spree. It's not all about helping and suffering, and recovery and dependence and catharsis. There are moments of carefree abandon between friends. That's how I'd most like it to be.

106

The
Things
that Judy
Taught
Me

When I was a child my greatest fear was that I would conceive an unshakable passion for someone who did not much care for me and this would severely impair my life. As far as I could see, this was what a love affair was.

A friend brought up by evil nuns was taught that the punishment for a love affair was eternal damnation. No one in their right mind would risk it, she thought. My secular view was rather similar. If I did conceive of a love affair, I felt instinctively that it would be safer if all the feelings remained on my side. That would stop things getting out of hand, wouldn't it. Wouldn't it? For it was when you involved the other person that the trouble began. Love should be utterly discreet and self-contained. It was disrespectful to something as sacred as love even to speak of it. There was something illegitimate, to my mind, about expressing the pain of love. It was cowardly and unfeminine. What did you expect? Had you not realised that love would require your greatest strengths? Its management, the stoking and nursing of it, might be the biggest job of work of your life.

To dwell on its difficulties or tribulations was a sort of betrayal that defined you as a person of low worth. No, it was not to be spoken of except in the endless painful shuttles of enquiry that went between your heart and mind. That loving was its own reward I had no doubt, for it was cheap and grasping to expect anything in return. It was to be borne bravely and privately, with inward care but no outward signs.

Many of Judy Garland's songs pitch the central character headlong into a form of romance where the question of the other party's reciprocity is almost irrelevant. I often marvel at a song called 'It's All For You': the fierce intensity of the lyric on the page, before you even allow for the extra meaning Judy's delivery brings to any set of words, positions love as more harrowing and more magisterial than any other human business.

> It's all for you.
> I live just for your sake.
> With every move I make,
> Breath I take,
> Rule I break.
> Each day I live,
> Each thing I do,
> It's all for you.
> All for you
> All for you
>
> Let not a day go by
> When I don't reach the skies,
> Try to fly,
> Touch the sky.
> Some day I will
> And when I do,

It's all for you.
All for you

There's no one else my heart adores
And no one else's heart for me but yours.
When life is through,
When all my days are done,
By every star above
It's you I love
The only one.
And let them say
This much is true,
It was all for you.
All for you.

I am torn by these words. They represent utterly unarguable emotion in its purest form, but I know that they are trouble. Perhaps a baby in its earliest stages might wish to be loved in this way, if a baby can wish with words; and possibly Jesus Christ would welcome such love and loves this way Himself, but I've always been fairly sure that no male human person could endure being loved in this way by a female human person.

'Once you've found him/Build your world around him' Judy sang in 'Make Someone Happy'. Well, yes, I thought as a child, but do make sure he doesn't see you constructing your little love-cage.

Could I tell then that a love such as this might be considered a form of assault? Did I know that you cannot foist yourself on others in this fashion? Is 'It's All For You' the sort of song a person might sing before pulling out a gun and shooting everybody down? I don't know. But I've always known that love this strong is anarchic and dangerous and possibly deathly and must be hidden, for everyone's sake. And I've always loved it.

110

As a child I knew I was the kind of person who in life would be prone to over-love. A book set in a ballet school, that I adored, had a little boy whose friends called his mother his 'Smother'. I knew I'd be that sort – the type to kill a plant by over-watering. I knew my feelings needed to be diluted many times before I gave expression to them. The excesses of love were a person's undoing. Something about my natural style of attachment, I knew, was on the wrong scale. My devotion to Judy Garland helped me manage all this. Sometimes I think that when I was a child Judy Garland's songs deliberately instructed me in the ways of hero worship so I could appreciate her all the better.

I've always been a hero-worship person. I thrive on all the enthroning and ennobling. It's genuinely nutritious for me to reckon up daily, weekly, all the startling extraordinarinesses of those I admire. I turn to my heroes as others turn to alcohol and cigarettes.

Hero-worship can be seen as a modest and ill-adjusted form of love, but it can be so productive. You may consider it essentially deranged, and deduce that therefore nothing good can come from it, but you are wrong. In 1841, in his lecture 'The Hero as Divinity', Thomas Carlyle expressed what, for me, are some of the chief benefits of this kind of love. I have changed the words 'great men' to 'Judy' or 'Judy Garland' throughout and altered the pronouns accordingly. The word 'humanity' replaces the word 'manhood':

One comfort is, that Judy Garland, taken up in any way, is profitable company. We cannot look, however imperfectly upon Judy, without gaining something by her. She is the living light fountain which it is good and pleasant to be near. The light which enlightens, which has enlightened the darkness of the world; and this not as a kindled lamp only, but rather as a natural luminary shining

111

by the gift of Heaven; a flowing light fountain, as I say, of native original insight, of humanity and heroic nobleness; in whose radiance all souls feel that it is well with them. On any terms whatsoever, you will not grudge to wonder in such neighbourhood for a while.

What Carlyle neglected to add was that hero-worship broadens one's love horizons wildly, for if love doesn't require the merest hint of participation from the other party then the number of potential candidates is infinite.

When I started at my secondary school the teachers were so odd. They were ancient, almost all on the brink of retirement, and this had made them reckless and madcap. After a lifetime of extreme self-control, their edges were fraying slightly and now and then curious outbursts came: there would be shrieking, bouts of spite and bile, extraordinary revelations about lost loves and other kinds of compelling personal hysteria. I think they felt their power over the girls ebbing slightly and this seemed to them the beginning of a chain of humiliations relating to age. All the clothes they wore were coming to the end of their life also: long gathered skirts that clung on lumpily from just under the bosom and eked their way down to the waist as their mistresses gesticulated wildly at the blackboard. Now and then there were embarrassing incidents resulting from perished elastic. These women – brilliant, many of them – saw teaching as a vocation. They were dignified and high-minded pioneers, and few of them had families. Husbands or children would inhibit and restrict those whose life was dedicated to improving the minds of young women. They would have got in the way of the life of the school and the life of the mind. Instead, these women ranged themselves among elegant and distinguished pets, King Charles spaniels, haughty and faithful, or artistic-looking pedigree cats. One or two lived with their increasingly elderly mothers, waxed-faced, reed-thin women with startling eyes and equally fierce brains. Many of these teachers became regularly furious, their faces as violet, with choler, as varicose veins by Friday afternoon. Did they feel cheated by the choices they had made, the cards that life had dealt them? A great many of the staff seemed to be confronting some sort of pressing personal predicament. The atmosphere in the school was, at times, electric. It was very exhilarating.

Perhaps in order to feel the soothing presence of their own moorings, the teachers had acutely ingrained ideas about what was intolerable and what was correct. They were passionate about this. The school was groaning with rules and other instruments of control. Flaws and lapses were wildly stimulating to the staff. I'm sure they were discussed into the small hours over soup and bread in local mansion flats.

Tidiness inspections were carried out daily and points feverishly awarded to each form. Once a term deportment badges were distributed. Simple though these systems sound, they were complicated and mysterious. You couldn't score the highest mark for tidiness just by presenting a front that was neat and clean. Subtle things were being judged, inner immaculacies, aspects of human nature that you barely knew about and could even less control. There were all sorts of crimes stemming from vulgarity, I suspected, and it was possible to be considered of the wrong sort of constitution and therefore utterly ineligible for tidiness awards however physically spotless you appeared. Deportment was self-carriage in the widest possible sense: goodness, moral energy, kindness, courage, modesty and cheer were all constituent parts. Triumphs in the shape of difficulties overcome were respected and rewarded: rapid unprecedented academic success, a shy person excelling in the school play, a girl with a bad leg shining on the games pitch.

113

I respected my teachers and tried to please them. They were growing frail and did not know, I guessed, quite how severe they seemed. I found the matrix of recherché regulations oddly comforting too. It was the end of an era. We were all clinging on to it together.

One autumn term a new English teacher arrived. Miss M was thirty and astonishingly, heroically normal. She made jokes and laughed. She was nearer our age than that of our grandmothers, and it was almost impossible to believe. A modern person – the only teacher in the school to wear trousers – she was pet-free and even drove a car, a sunny little yellow Fiat, that appeared on the steep bank outside the school every morning like a smile. Sometimes I'd time my arrival at the school gates to match hers so that we could exchange a cheery good morning. She herself was always smiling; not inanely, but with intelligence and interestingly. She was a large woman and my heart went out to her because I was large too. She had had polio as a child, I remember hearing, so her size wasn't her fault, as mine was, so our predicaments were utterly different, but even still. Once I showed her a photo of Judy in a black lace dress with a white rose in her hair, that I had bought in a theatrical record shop in Soho. It was on my bedroom wall for seven years.

'I wish I looked like that,' I ventured.

'Don't we all!' I was shocked that she'd want to be anyone other than her rather splendid self.

My mother had struck up a relationship with a Welsh antiquarian bookseller who drank quite a bit. He considered himself some sort of wildly romantic character, but it was not what I saw. In addition to this, a much-loved relative was in the grip of a heroin addiction and would sometimes drop in for the evening to use the phone or raid the fridge or . . . or . . . I didn't really know what it was that he did, but I saw little nests of syringes in the rubbish.

I was acutely aware that if my home life was subjected to the same sort of scrutiny that the most modest misdemeanour met with at school, I would be thoroughly sunk. There would be disgrace on an international scale. My two worlds could not have been more at odds. I tried to reconcile my lives, principally by eating a lot of cake (lemon cake, malt loaf with salted butter, still-warm yellow sponge sandwiched with jam that my mother made), but this of course was only the most temporary of solutions.

Miss M's smile soon became what I lived for. The smile in the morning by the Fiat, the smile in the lunch queue – neither of us, I had noticed, ate the school food; big people can't afford to eat in public – the smile as she walked in to our class and we all sprang to our feet. It was a long game that I played. I would never speak to her of my worries but fancied that on some level she knew. If anything very bad happened, I was sure she would take the right action: she wouldn't be heavy handed; she wouldn't cause humiliation as so many people who try to help do. In placing my happiness in her hands I knew to censor myself, not to follow her round too much and only utter every fifth or sixth remark that crossed my mind. The situation was fragile and delicate. It had, I could tell, the potential to become excruciating. The beacon of friendliness that she represented would diminish and die if I asked too much of it. But it was the age-old conundrum – how much is too much?

At home we had discovered a brand of delicious, low-calorie American-style ginger and chocolate chip cookies that comforted and thrilled, named – we could scarcely believe our luck – Slimmer's. They were three inches in diameter and came fourteen to a pack. I ate quantities of them, ravenous after school as I took no breakfast or lunch. The lure of cooked sugar, its scent and its promise, then the moist chewy texture beneath the crisp first bites, the potentially harsh note of ginger reprimanding, mellowing then vying with consummate sophistication for supremacy over the plentiful drops of chocolate that studded the biscuit's face. It was an exquisite battle. I wondered about buying some for Miss M, but one of my rules was that I mustn't present her with gifts. It was the least I could not do.

I did begin to tell her about them once, though, as we walked along the raised bank that led to the school gates one wintry morning. 'They've got some marvellous new lines at Safeway's,' I broke out boldly, but then I couldn't quite continue the conversation. It was too domestic, too personal. It was what grown-up women might have said to each other. I felt out of my depth. About a year later I discovered, perhaps I had always known, that the brand name of the biscuits was actually Simmer's. They weren't a dieting product at all.

I met Miss M again recently. I contacted her through her educational consultancy business and she suggested we might cross over at a bar called Black and Blue in four weeks' time. Should we meet at eleven for coffee or at five for a glass of wine? she asked. We were both grown-ups now, but the rules were still in place. Part of me wished to say, 'Or at midnight for a crack pipe? It's awfully more-ish,' but it would have been extremely rude. 'We can raise a glass to Lincoln,' I said rather randomly, because my diary stated it was his birthday that day.

'Excellent,' was how she judged my idea.

When you seek out people from the past and confront them with their behaviour, the standard model, it seems to me, is one of recrimination and reproach. How *could* you! How dare you! Or you may be moved to apologise for your own rough conduct: 'I'm so much sorrier than I can possibly say.' How much trickier to express gratitude and demand it be received. How awkward to accuse another of inspiration and life-saving kindnesses. I had prepared myself for it. I could afford to be embarrassed. Embarrassment doesn't frighten me as it once did. Now and then, it had even occurred to me, it is a feeling to be prized. I had planned that our meeting might be excruciating for I have felt excrucation many, many times and there are far worse feelings. *I really loved you with all my heart,* I would say. *Your kindness during a difficult time for me made the difference, between – and no exaggeration this – sinking and swimming.*

These were Judy-ish feelings I felt even at the time. In his book *The Theatre of Embarrassment* Francis Wyndham writes that embarrassment is an intrinsic part of many theatrical experiences. We mistake it for other, more valuable strong feelings. Squirming with discomfort is easily confused with a satisfying night out at the theatre or concert hall these days. Fear of Judy's failure, he argues, failure to dazzle, failure to flourish or finish, failure to show up even, was very much caught up in her audiences' excessive responses. Its alternative, relief at her success, Mr Wyndham suggests, sometimes even came as a disappointment.

In the taxi to Black and Blue I wondered how Miss M would respond to my declaration. Would it strike her as an assault? I bought a wrap of lilac-coloured hyacinths at a greengrocer's, to break the ice. She had been a headmistress for eleven years, at a girls' public school, since we last met. Could she take mention of my girlish ardour in her stride? I absolutely didn't want anything back.

Seated at a round table in the empty confines of Black and Blue, Miss M looked exactly the same only the colour had gone out of her hair. We shook hands warmly. 'Did you know how much I loved you? Did you think I was going to be all right?' I didn't quite blurt out. We decided in a spirit of crazy splurge to order a half-bottle of red wine.

I made a list to her, to kick things off, of the most particular things I remembered about her. About Her and Me.

1. You once used the expression 'by and large' thirty-seven times in one lesson.
2. In the alternative school magazine I put together, you shocked me by answering the question 'What is the meaning of life?' with 'A long preparation for death.'
3. You once told me your favourite wine was St Emilion and when you left the school I gave you some. (Also, one large chocolate cake, sandwiched and iced, a Victorian silk handkerchief and a letter.)
4. You once gave me your own personal unopened tube of Bonjela when I had a mouth ulcer.
5. You once gave me 97 per cent for an English literature exam and apologised for having deducted three marks due to my poor spelling.
6. In a 'Who's the Baby?' competition on the stairs that led down to the dining hall you were pictured as an infant on a very glamorous frilled and starched linen pillowcase, which suggested to me both riches and fastidiousness in your family background.

'My nanny was very particular,' she said, about the pillowcase. 'She was Scottish, and when I was a baby she fed me lemon juice. When my mother complained that I was always crying, and could she please stop the juice, she said it was so I'd get used to the fact that this life was full of bitter things.'

'My God – that's terrible!' We chatted for a while. I don't think she said anything to me she hadn't said to others before. She was very polite; she asked after my mother. Every now and then I hoped she might say she had followed my career, or hadn't I turned out lovely, but no such luck. Two questions she asked startled me slightly.

'Are you on your own with your children?'

'No,' I said, 'I have a lovely husband and we've been married for ten years.'

'Do you do anything else apart from your novels and journalism and the children?' (My youngest child was five months old at the time.)

'I work a little as a bereavement counsellor,' I said.

'How did I seem to you, when we were at school?' I finally asked.

'You were proud and modest, modestly proud, no, not modestly proud because the adverb would qualify the adjective wouldn't it? You knew you were bright, but you didn't go on about it,' she said approvingly.

Hooray! Compliments!

'Did I seem particularly sensitive?'

'Not excessively.'

'Is it hard to handle someone who's very, very fond of you if you're her teacher?'

'No, I just felt that sometimes you and I could see the irony of a situation, because you were more mature than your contemporaries, that others couldn't see, and although I would have liked to acknowledge this feeling more I didn't want to single you out in this way because it might have been very annoying for you.

'You had,' and she paused, 'a *very* well-developed sense of irony.'

She talked to me at length about the people who had inspired her, encouraged her to take her career more seriously. She had wanted to be a surgeon, she said. 'Like Keats!' I enthused.

John Keats

She ignored this, but told me that her school said it would be impossible due to her disability. One of her hands had no strength because of childhood polio.

'I never knew,' I said.

'I worked hard to make sure people didn't know.'

'Call myself obsessed! What an amateur,' I sighed.

She raised a brow and proceeded to talk animatedly and at length about two other girls, one of whose mother was a television personality, and another whose face, she remarked almost poetically, 'looked very cross when in repose'.

She said she always trained teachers to be very careful of what they said. I told her about the worst moment of my school career. Mr Hamilton, my English teacher, was asking the class what the word bulbous meant.

'In the form of a barrel?' someone suggested.

'Or indeed,' and he shook out a houndstooth-check bell bottom-clad leg in a sort of flourish resembling a human fleur-de-lis, and smiled warmly, 'or indeed, Susie Boyt shaped!' There was no venom to what he said, it was just intended as a jolly remark, but the room darkened instantly. Tears leapt into my eyes and I started to shake. I told Miss M how I put the lid of my desk up and pretended to root about for some hidden thing so that no one could see me cry. I hadn't thought about that incident for fifteen years.

'Just look at you now, though!' Miss M did not say.

'When I'm training teachers I tell them you can't overestimate the effects you have on your pupils. Very likely people will remember the things you say and do all their lives. You must be extremely cautious.'

We parted cheerfully: 'Lets definitely do this again. Perhaps in, I don't know, a year's time.'

'Great!' I said and we shook hands warmly.

Two days later a card arrived, thanking me for the flowers. It was Valentine's Day.

Devotion, devotion of a general nature, devotion even in the abstract, is a feeling I know well. It's one I enjoy. 'It's all for you,' Judy Garland sings, and as I listen I think, Yes, of course! That is as it should be! I like all forms of extravagance. Sometimes it seems to me that the most authentic kind of everyday human interaction is saving someone's life. Yet occasionally, when I listen to this song, it strikes me rather differently. This song doesn't always make me think of the people I love best. It doesn't even make me think of the people who love me more than they love anyone else, and there are a few of them. No, 'It's All For You' can make me think of all the people I never came first with and of the times in my life when none of it was for me at all. It makes me reel at the thought of the people I have loved for whom I have barely counted. When I hear this song it can make this tiny group of three or two swell in number to almost the size of an army. There is, bizarrely, some sort of bitter pleasure involved in this feeling, a sort of epiphany. It feels like a crazy sprint away from health towards something that could destroy, but the views en route are awfully good.

When I listen to 'It's All For You' in this vein I find myself styling the events of my life so that they appear in their starkest, most painful aspect. I set-dress my sandpapered hopes and fears until they are all that count. I cling on to negatives as though they are life rafts and I even take pleasure in the fact that I have the worst eyesight in my entire extended family. Through these bad eyes I see only bad things and it's such a relief.

After a while it's all reproaches and repercussions and I know for certain that the sheer undiluted beam of emotion from Judy to another in 'It's All For You' was most assuredly unwanted. I feel angry and implicated in this. Is Judy close to saying, I gave you everything and look what you did to me? She doesn't mention a single thing about the other person. It is, it suddenly seems to me, a terrible song about being on the receiving end of un-love.* About what un-love feels like, for it can be as strong and blinding in its effects as its opposite. More so.

Yet sometimes the worst times with Judy are actually the best. I'm sure it's good for you every now and then to turn your back on happiness and health. Happiness and health are well and good, but sometimes you need a holiday. You can't always always always take the sensible path, and if you generally do, is it so very wrong to follow a slip road now and then into a world where the feelings are so strong they can kill? Oh the tyranny of sanity! You can turn the tone of yourself down, and the colour and the sound, so you are fit for the purpose of everyday life without too much chafing, without

*un-love: the absence of love where love should be.

too many tears, but is it bad now and then to experience yourself at full strength, to give wings to the matrix of longing that lies at the centre of your childish heart?

Is it really bad?

Sometimes as a teenager I fancied myself a nineteen-fifties American poet-professor's wife; he'd be a tall man, shaky and brilliant. Self-effacing and stoic in narrow tweeds, intense, with a frank look that could grow on a person, I'd write my novels in the scratched moments that occurred in between crisis management. I thought with longing of women like Jean Stafford and Elizabeth Hardwick, in their highly polished brown lace-up shoes, lurching happily from disaster to disaster.

Jean Stafford

My role would be to provide good cheer and sound sense, an island of calm and soft charm. It would be an utterly feminine managerial style, permissive, accepting. My capacity for discretion would

124

impress, but I'd take very good care of myself. The Princeton of the fifties was 'a cosmopolitan community with a density of brilliant minds'. It sounds very inviting.

I imagined myself travelling with suitcases heavy with books, not clothing, to holidays in the Midwest with a steady 'influx of poets'. These men were not easy husbands. Jean Stafford once claimed that Robert Lowell, the world's champion reviser, began a poem with the title 'To Jean: On her confirmation . . .' which ended up being called 'To a Whore at the Brooklyn Navy Yard'. And that wasn't the half of it . . . 'She was very beautiful you know, before the accident,' was the kind of thing people would say.

The danger, of course, is that the dark and stormy slip roads are steeper and longer and more hazardous than you imagined. (I'm no driver.) The trouble is, the signs on this road say health and happiness are facile and hollow and indicate a life half lived. It's sorrow and struggle that are truly worthwhile, all the picturesque views proclaim – well they would, wouldn't they? It's such a seductive paradigm, for the part of you that is still a troubled child. And the increments creep up on you so skilfully! The pile of losses mounts and it's such a slippery slope because one minute you turn your back on umbrellas and gloves and the next it is roofs and clothing and food that seem as irrelevant and risible as scatter cushions. Come with me somewhere so dark, the music claims, that the pain you feel is truly exhilarating. In this sort of mood a simple question like, would you rather put the kettle on or undergo a bout of ECT? can genuinely tax your mind.

When you're in this mood so dark that not a chink of hope can pierce it, life from every angle feels astonishingly vivid. Even a frayed lapel on a stranger's coat seems unbearably affecting and everything's passion and mourning.

There is almost no togetherness in this 'It's All For You' song, no vision of a shared future, hardly even a prospect of a meeting. The

125

love has a deathly quality to it. Well, true love does, you find your-self agreeing with banality. If it's a lover Judy addresses in this song, it is clear the relationship is already doomed, but if, as many fans believe, it is her audience she's serenading, things are more compli-cated. There are responsibilities to be shouldered. Adulation and exploitation, in the case of Judy Garland, are so inextricably linked. She worked herself to death, everyone agrees. Do all we who love her have that on our hands? Did we kill her as surely as Dorothy killed the Wicked Witch of the East when her house fell on top of her, an accident but none the less a sort of manslaughter? Did I, in some way, kill her – even me, a little baby of five months that couldn't hurt a fly?

When you nurse an obsession, when you feed it and rear it, you are always on the alert for others who live in the same way. You may not share my love for Judy Garland but if you have a similar connection with another, in some small or large part you may feel as I do. I salute and applaud that part, I am interested in it and drawn to it and reach out to it. I may even find myself obsessed with your obses-sion; not with the object of it – for how can that match my own? – but with the forms it takes, the way you service and administer to it, how you respond to its flow. Does it ebb away with a dearth of stim-uli or is it quotidian with you, and regular, almost tidal, in its habits? Even though the object of your affection inevitably lacks the grandeur, the spectacular mixture of gravity, warmth and glamour of my own (*mine* own, I nearly wrote), I may turn your obsession over and over in my head at night, view my own love through your love and the rites and dilemmas and crises of my relation to my heroine with these things as they fly between your hero and you. It is possi-ble that the object of *your* obsession is unequal to your heroic feelings, as mine will never be, and that you are a tiny bit (and I whisper this) *misguided* in your choice, but your feelings are good and true, I see that. Your obsession may be the mightiest thing about you, despite or even because the individual you are drawn to isn't quite worthy of your love.

To the young girl who said, 'If nuclear war was declared my first thought would be, I hope Boy George is OK,' I sincerely say, 'I hope so too.'

Harbouring obsessions is a pursuit whose status is low. Obsessions are the territory of children or the infirm, or so the view of my circle goes. Fanaticism equals embarrassment because of the vulnerability and ardour it betrays. These human facets are quite out of fashion and have been so for more than half a century. If opium is the king of the drug world, unadulterated, fabled, mysterious and of natural derivation, then obsession as a mind-altering construct dwells several rungs below, beneath Valium, cider and even glue. It inhabits an equal axis, perhaps, with that dented slot machine with a 72 per cent return mechanism, poorly installed, at an angle, on linoleum, cracked and warped, in the corner café, with dim piped music and half its flashing lights and buttons shot. Well, I don't care. Obsessions are a modest way of making life bearable when it plainly isn't, detractors say. How *quaint*. To be a fan acknowledges a lack of equality, for if my hero towers on a pedestal, exalted, then where lurk I?

Wrong! Hero worship, when properly entered into, has a great deal of poetry to it. It inspires and motivates, renews and revives. It encourages introspection, investigation of desire, personal moral inventory and all manner of fruitful examinations. The cargo of goodwill that spells of extreme admiration create, can provide personal ballast against discouragement and grief. To be in the habit of fixing another with your highest personal regard over time increases your capacity to love. Hero worship can aid relaxation. With your hero you can be amused, complacent, compassionate, idle, quiet and solitary. It can also augur self improvements, for through the text of a life that is shared you can investigate past behaviours (your own

127

and your idol's) and prepare and facilitate behavioural strategies to come. You can interpret and redefine to your heart's content, experience your own rough workings while discovering what the fair copy of yourself will entail. There is the tenderest sort of human interaction at the heart of such connections, in its crises and its swoops and triumphs of fellow feeling and separation. I don't think such relationships are second-hand life, second-hand love, or a modest form of existence. Hero worship can be an emotional Olympics, a way of testing one's lowest and highest drives. My Judy-love strengthens and inspires what is already good in me and what is bad. It helps me become more completely and entirely myself. And if the poetry of hero worship imparts some measure of heroism on the practitioner, then that is all to the good.

All obsessives become great measurers. How long since I have thought about him or her? How long since I haven't? These are calculations similar to those that mourners make, looking out for a day without crying, a day where you don't notice you haven't cried, a day where you haven't thought about the lost person, a day where you don't register this lack of thought. A great many obsessions *are* painful – but this sort isn't in the least. In your devotion you may imbue life with more promise and more texture than it actually has, but in doing so you transform it so that it is richer, it is fuller and suddenly it actually is more *in almost every way.*

As I am trying to get to sleep I often think about the telegram girl in Henry James's novella *In The Cage.* Her thorough preoccupation with her favourite customer, Captain Everard, is an obsession of the highest order. Her obsessive nature is immaculate, artistic and astounding, quite the best thing about her. It is treated by its creator with a great deal of dignity and respect, despite the fact that the Captain himself is vastly inferior to the girl who worships him. James's heroine is fascinated with her relation to the Captain. She examines it continually.

Part of the nature of obsession is not just the primary fascination with the person, but all the deeply pressing satellite concerns that hover around the relationship. You think about the person and then you think about what the thinking means. You even wonder what all the wondering about the wondering will lead to. Everything? Nothing?

As I examine the telegram girl's obsession in my insomniac mind, I often picture the physically diffident Henry James wondering, a little, what it might be like to be the object of a stranger's romantic fascination. I watch James experience himself as though viewed with the same levels of scrutiny that he habitually brought into his relations with other people. It's an interesting vision.

Henry James

But mostly when I read this novella, or think of the girl taking down the telegrams of the man she so admires, I wonder what it would have been like to work in a shop or menders or cobblers of which Judy Garland made regular use.

I found the location, the perfect premises for just such an outlet, on a trip to the house in which Judy Garland died. The house itself was empty and uninhabited, in a small modest mews behind a row of grand houses, a five-minute walk from the mews house behind grand houses that I lived in from 1989 to 1997. The curtains were drawn and, peering through the letterbox, I made out an enormous fridge, propped open with some cardboard, in a dim back kitchen. The décor was olives and moody browns.

Adjacent to this little house is a dry cleaner's, a boutique dry cleaner's named after a fictional butler of international renown. Watching me peep through the letterbox of Judy's old mews house, the manager pops out and regards me carefully. Elegant and immaculate, he inclines his head with sympathy and asks if he can be of help. 'Just come to see Judy Garland's house,' I offer, pointing.

'Yes, dear Judy,' he murmurs. His face lights and warms. 'Dear, dear Judy.' We stand silent for a moment, then he gives a little bow. He has been the manager of this grandest of dry cleaners (men's suits start at £28, a lady's simple day dress is £24) since 1989 and knows everything about the area. I walk in to his premises to continue our talk and lean against the polished counter. Established in 1969, a brochure about the business proclaims. In 1969 Judy lived fifteen yards from the place I am standing.

I imagine Judy coming in to my little shop, the air thick with dilemma and adjustments, the assorted self-checks and self-measuring that passionate interest requires. I take hold of some of her clothes, laying the precious garments across my arms: perhaps the ill-advised feathery blue chiffon confection she wore to her fifth wedding to Mickey Deans on 15 March, her Blackglama mink, the pale linen coat she wore at Heathrow airport before her flight to New York on 21 May.

I listen carefully to her instructions and agree with everything, quickly and easily. I thank her for her custom but I do it reasonably, even though my entire face is a smile, my whole body is; yet there is also sadness that needs hiding, for we are just weeks away from the end of her life and although she was never in her life fragile, she is frail. I try to convey, just with my eyes, in the mildest, most casual way possible, that there is nothing she could ask me to which I would say no. I ground this silent appeal in good cheer. Of course, the cleaning is on the house. 'It's the least we can do for a neighbour!' I exclaim. I might add – and I'm not sure of the wisdom of this – 'If there's anything I can ever do, no job is too big or small . . .' but I don't wish to sound like a plumber's van. I offer my services as a cheery and strong good sort might, 'Always a pleasure, never a chore.' I would casually mention that I'd happily deliver her things to her home, but I'd not bombard her with offers. Everything to do with an obsession's success hinges on the amounts involved. What I mustn't say is, 'Judy, I have loved you all my life.'

The girl from *In the Cage* doesn't ask much of Captain Everard's liking, 'she only asked of it to reach the point of his not going away because of her own'.

It would take practically nothing to drive Judy into a rival establishment where the assistant was less emotional. Those soppy eyes! In order to stand out you need also to seem not to do so, yet there must be occasional gleams from you that indicate firmly that you have more promise about you than your setting suggests, a legion more strings to your bow and mysteries and depths.

The proper management and care of an obsession when you are going to come into contact with your chosen one fairly regularly are:

CONTAIN – contain your excitement within excitement when
    your hero appears, allowing a very controlled amount of
    your feelings to show very rarely, and in the most
    subliminal of ways. There needs to be muteness to your
    effusions, I'm afraid. Only suggest at the strongest. Avoid
    James's 'anything vulgarly articulate'.

REVEAL – a very occasional fractionally revealing remark can win you some sort of notice if limited to every fourth or fifth casual encounter. In James Joyce's short story *The Dead* the maid Lily answers Gabriel's gentle enquiry with, 'the men that is now is all palaver and what they can get out of you', deeply shocking her interlocutor. Well, your tiny revealing thing must not be anything even a quarter as strongly flavoured as that.

SYMPATHISE – restrained fellow feeling can be winning; a natural entering into the mood or the spirit of the person without seeming to do so can be affecting.

ASSIST – be primed for anything that is asked of you at any time. Know rudimentary first aid and remedies and stain removal strategies, be DIY-wise and shorthand-happy. In the course of years crises will occur and if you seem reliable and available you may be called upon to help.

GIVE – presents may be dangerous, but can be very successful also: dilute by prefacing with the fact that you won the bracelets/tablecloth/floppy hat with a flower in a raffle and have no use for it yourself. The odd cake lightly given – you were making one anyway and found yourself with too much batter for one tin – may not hurt.

SERVE – make everything as clear and easy as possible for the other person with a standard of service designed to stun. Economise on words. Answer questions with the simplest possible phrase. This always feels like high courtesy. For even asking the time or straightforward directions often leads to all sorts of complicated explanations, prevarications, margins for error and a litany of unwanted opinion and comment. *Don't say anything like*, 'Ooh, I'm not sure, hang on, let's think, I seem to remember – but don't quote me – that it's about half a mile down that street, turn left and then third right, I *think*.'

Judy would have required regular praise or acknowledgement of her position as the world's greatest entertainer from time to time, and this would have to be done in the most dextrous and humorous ways, in passing and with the sort of spry emphasis that only an aside, in a stage whisper and inverted commas, can achieve. Oh the precariousness of an obsession with someone real! The unbearably delicate balancing act! How much better to love someone who's quite out of your reach. How much closer you'll feel.

My career as a shopgirl began in Madeleine's, a high-class lingerie boutique in St John's Wood, which was all silk satin lemon-coloured shorties and ivory Belgian lace bra-and-panty sets. It's a coffee shop now. I progressed from that excruciating environment to the more neutral setting of catering equipment, dispensing chefs' checks and copper sautée dishes, olive pitters and oven guards, ending up in a small bookshop in a busy tourist-filled piazza where the majority of the enquiries concerned the local attractions, of which I hoped I myself might soon be one.

It's hard not to harbour romantic notions about yourself standing, behind a shop's counter, with the plate glass window for a frame and only the throbbing till to dilute you with its green liquid-crystal display. The driest transactions are made bearable by such fancies. You think about ways of distinguishing yourself, endlessly, of seeming engaging and remarkable. Your mind wonders about some spectacular occurrence that might CHANGE EVERYTHING.

Fancying yourself rather an alluring young creature as you ring the purchases through the till, you can tell you are admired. You imagine it to such an extent that you falter at all the fences and your professionalism withers and dies so that everything is confusing and even the most basic of facts, such as who gets the book and who keeps the money, seem hazy and open to interpretation.

*

133

Obsessions are often born out of avoidance. I've known for a very long time that these sorts of electric flashes of fellow feeling take people over when there's something else looming that you are trying hard not to see. My own love of Judy Garland intensified at a particularly acute period when I didn't understand a single fact about my life: what could I do to make myself less sensitive and cut to the quick by anything sharp enough to qualify as a remark? Why could I not stop eating for a single second? Why was my father always painting? But my obsession outgrew its spur, redeemed and transcended it. Although its causes are long left behind, it hasn't diminished in the least. There's lifelong loyalty there. Besides, as with all fairly obvious facets of psychology, they never quite seem to apply to those one knows best.

Gazing at the curtained windows of the house where Judy Garland died, I'm not sad that I can't enter. I don't like this house. Lorna Luft said to Rex Reed in 1972, 'The only sad thing is that she ended up so far away from all of us, with a husband she hardly knew.' Judy Garland took her last breath in the bathroom, with the door locked, sitting on the loo. A friend tells me this fact is commemorated on the 'They Died on the Toilet' website, but I'm not minded to look.

An elderly English caretaker, charming and courteous as though from another era, comes out to tend to me as I stand slumped against the wall in Cadogan Lane. 'I wrote to the owners asking if I could look round but there doesn't seem to be anyone there.'

As you may know Judy Garland spent the last few months of her life at this address. I am currently writing a book about her and wondered if you would be kind enough to let me have a quick look round at a time that is convenient for you. I would be happy to do you any reasonable favour in return: huge bunch of flowers, home made cake etc. etc. Best wishes . . .

How Judy might appear if she had read this book

How it all began

This was on my bedroom wall for seven years

She is one of the loveliest human beings who ever lived

It's so charming when Judy re-enacts her long day at rehearsal for her delicate spouse in A Star is Born

Reading telegrams backstage at the Dominion, London 1957

This is the picture of Judy I carry in my purse

Me looking at Judy's address book, seven months pregnant in New York

I never got a reply.

The caretaker informs me that the house is owned by Italians now, who may sell up soon. 'You know I saw Judy Garland on the television yesterday,' he tells me, 'I'm not an . . . aficionado like you, but she was . . . captivating.'

I had seen *A Star is Born* on the television the day before also, while assembling mini trifles for the baby's first birthday party. A little sponge cake, a layer of lightly cooked berries, a spoonful of canary-coloured custard and a slick of white cream all meted out in time to 'The Man that Got Away'. Crystallised rose petals go on top and a sprinkling of a pink decorating powder called edible lustre. When I was a tiny child the first six times I ate trifle I was sick, but still I persevered with it for some reason. These munchkin portions are perhaps a concession to that fact. Trifle and being sick, good and bad, ring through my mind as Judy sings Harold Arlen's melody, 'Since this world began/There's nothing sadder than/A one-man woman looking for the man that got away.'

The faux-rehearsal quality of the performance is beguiling. The way Judy stretches out her arms! 'They're fools,' the Cocoanut Grove restaurant manager says (or something very similar), 'they sing their hearts out all night here and then sing there for free.' This is no rehearsal. The humming at the song's start may suggest a sort of elegant vocal tuning up, a concession to the notion that this is a woman who happens to be singing spontaneously and casually, to no audience, just *because*, but this performance of 'The Man That Got Away' is, in fact, spectacularly polished and full of victorious theatricality. As Esther Blodgett sings, you don't imagine her suffering romantic hardships as you do in some of Judy's later concert or television versions; nor do you think of Frank Gumm, Judy Garland's beloved father, or indeed your own. What faces you squarely as you listen is the fact that the singer knows, the song practically knows, the film certainly knows, that the triumphant and transforming power that a performance of this calibre contains mitigates majestically against the vanishing of any so-called *man*.

Sometimes I think that all the things I would have liked Judy to have – peace, health, hammocks, a decent wardrobe, a calm yet dashing doctor husband with a large private income and no other patients and, of course, *me* – I'd also like to procure for her eldest daughter, Miss Liza Minnelli.

Because a star is a star is a star and should be treated as such, I asked a florist friend to pick me up one hundred long stemmed Dolce Vita roses from the flower market on the day I was set to meet Liza. I wanted to walk in to the interview, my body obscured by a small pink tree. I thought it would seem pleasantly surreal, as if a rose bush had legs. I had resolved to wear some cherry-red patent shoes that would lend a distinct nod to the famous ruby slippers. The roses arrived in sheaves of crisp white tissue and crackling cellophane smelling of Turkish delight. They were four feet tall, only eleven inches shorter than Garland herself. I was going to make an impression.

I put the bank of flowers in a bucket by the door and topped them up with water. The hall looked festive in the extreme and also strangely sylvan in the Tchaikovsky style. I wandered about, bouncing the baby happily, feeling a little corps de ballet-ish myself. At ten I went out for a walk with my notebook and the baby. My list of questions looked like the scrawlings of a mad scientist: there were diagrams, arrows, speech bubbles, treble underlinings, asterisks, equals signs, a train of capital letters in bold written vertically down the page and some crosshatching. I was sick with nerves about seeing Liza. There were six hours to go. I went to a café and ordered a cappuccino. When I told the waiter about my next port of call he wouldn't take a penny for it. I sat there as the baby slept, electric with anticipation: I was longing to meet Liza, I'd been longing for it half my life, but why then did it seem like such agony? The stakes were so high. What if I was unable to summon my best self during our interview? What if my best self did not have any sort of appeal? I was already planning our second meeting, our seventh, our twelfth. A friend of mine, while in labour, announced to the midwives (they were very impressed), 'I just can't wait to have my next one!' Now I knew what she meant.

I had it so well planned; what she would say and what I would say. I saw the arc of our meeting through Liza's large-lashed eyes: her trepidation would segue into trust, followed by acceptance, interest, appreciation and affection, culminating in a lifelong friendship. She could absolutely do with a friend like me. It wasn't too much to ask, was it? Was it?

The day wore on unbearably. My nerves, which had seemed madcap and a little hysterical earlier, now hovered towards fullblown anxiety attack. At eleven I took the baby for her one-month check. Although I was feeding her almost continuously she had not grown any bigger and in fact had shrunk by two ounces since the previous week. The midwife was quite severe with me. I telephoned a friend to confide this sad news. 'Don't worry,' she said absently, 'it's always good to lose weight, isn't it?' I didn't have the strength to respond.

By five to twelve I had cranked myself up to such a feverish pitch I didn't know whether I'd still be able to function by the afternoon. My head was plagued with regrets. I wished I had a few more days to research Miss Minnelli. I wished the baby was already two, or six, or in her second term at university. After childbirth you have to close your emotions down for a few months because the slightest, lightest thing feels deeply poignant, even a litter bin in the street, a piece of white toast, cold and elastic. As it was I couldn't bear to listen to music or sing songs. My old anxiety-slayer, whistling, was also out, as all tunes were barred for being harrowing. A passer-by had caught me singing the alphabet to the baby and accused me, harshly, of trying to kick-start her academic career, but it was the only song I knew that didn't make me cry.

Just then the telephone went. It was Liza's genial PR. 'I'm so sorry,' he said, 'but we're going to have to change the interview to the end of this week. Is that going to be possible?'

Reprieve! 'Fine,' I said. 'Not to worry, that suits me much better. Thanks so much! Yeah-er-great!' I would have four more days to ready myself. The baby would be that much older, maybe even bigger, I would be better rested, I resolved. I've always loved any sort of a cancellation. In fact, if I long with all my might for one it generally comes, although the circumstances can be horrific. In the past my concentrated dread has caused extreme illness, breakdowns of vehicles and psyches, sudden feuds and, once, an earthquake . . . But even still.

Hooray! I thought, my entire body slumping with relief. Then I remembered something. The poor flowers!

By Friday the Dolce Vitas were three-quarters dead but my fears had grown even more lively and strong. It was a complex pull of

138

loyalties I was embroiled in now. I had woken up in the middle of the night from a bad dream and sat bolt upright. It struck me forcibly, the bald, blank truth, and I gasped at the realisation. *There was not a single thing that Liza Minnelli could ask me to do to which I would say no.* I would give her anything and drop everything. I would follow her anywhere, like the passage about Ruth in the Bible that her mother so admired. This made me, I realised, quite vulnerable. I felt myself swinging from my hinges wildly. The baby awoke with her customary one a.m. gurgling, hoping for some high jinks. She made a noise that sounded strangely like 'How are ya?'

Remember your responsibilities, I self-instructed firmly.

I saw myself in some bizarre form of employ. I'd be guardian of the eyelashes and the eyelash curlers, careful assembler of club sandwiches, chief sharpener of the kohl pencil and keeper of the liquid liner, canny contract small-print scourer, palazzo pant presser, friend-from-foe shape sorter, a benign force-field between Miss Minnelli and the reality she so famously likes to rise above. What was the line that Judy loved from *Death of a Salesman*? 'Care must be taken; attention must be paid.' Well, I'd do just that. It would be my pleasure! I'd be ears, eyes or even legs to the star, endlessly responsive to the demands of the moment.

On the morning of the interview it becomes apparent that there's something wrong with my milk. There are waves of burning pain in my chest and on the advice of my doctor I go to the hospital and express a few white drops to be sent to the lab for analysis.

'You feel such a failure when everything doesn't go right,' the nurse said to me, transfixed by the tears streaming down my face. I stiffen.

'You been up all night too?' she asked.

'No. No, of course not. Not at all! I'm completely fine.'

'All right, dear,' she says. 'All right.'

Two hours later I was waiting to meet Liza Minnelli, who was running late, in a boutique hotel in Fitzrovia. I am sitting on an overstuffed sofa in a private sitting room. Opposite me is a baronial-looking chair in whose seat is a bottom-sized indentation. Liza's, I thought. My splendid intentions for the interview had become cruelly modest, through necessity. No longer concerned with conveying acutely my simply marvellous personality, in all its recherché and altruistic glory, my reduced hopes were these: do not cry and do not be sick. I felt raw and wild with tiredness and fear that I would somehow blow my main chance. I drank six cups of tea hoping, in that English way, it would restore my moral energy. I swallowed some painkillers. I could barely string a sentence together. What was it my eldest brother always says when he sits down in the hairdresser's chair?

Do you mind if we don't talk?

Well, that would hardly do.

After one and a half more hours I am perching next to Liza who is patting my knee in the friendliest way. Dressed in a black fleece and black palazzo pants, she is made up in a manner that far exceeds the nines. Her features are unmistakable. A Work of Art. She has a curious build, the two halves of her body mismatched as though taken from different people, the top large and strong and expansive, the bottom half narrow and spindly. Instantly it is clear that despite all her difficulties catalogued, in detail, by the world's press down the years, the shaky, highly strung person in the room today is me. Who am I in this situation that feels so much like a reunion? Her long lost niece? Her hysterical auntie?

Liza knows exactly who she is and she likes herself too. She is childlike, but she is childlike with authority and experience. She is a strange and beguiling mixture of who she was, who she is and who she might have been. But Liza doesn't do regrets, mistakes, blame, hindsight or if onlys. Where's the glamour in them? They're not, she believes, appropriate territory for a star. Lovely as she is, it feels as though there is a sheet of Plexiglas between us. There's no hope of any serious intimacy. Who can blame her?

She wants, I tell myself, far less from me than I wish to give. It's a very familiar feeling. All she asks is that I am over with quickly and unnoticeably. She wants things to be pleasant and polite, of course. But it is an encounter that is unmemorable that will please her most. And I do so want to please her.

In seconds I resolve that I mustn't mention anything at all difficult. Liza does not like to talk about her mother. What is there left to say? She is legally obliged not to talk about her soon-to-be ex-husband David Gest, who always seemed to me not so much a man as half walrus, half fish hook. She does not appreciate being quizzed on her problems with alcohol or drugs, I suspect, and surely she would baulk at anything crass such as requests for tips on smiling through tears.

This suits me well as I am a terrible interviewer. It was drummed in to me as a child never to ask people personal questions. I was brought up to keep secrets about almost everything and to expect the rest of the world to follow suit. Even now I never ask people what work they do or where they live. Suppose, like most folk, they are in between things and feel sore about it? Suppose their house went up in flames the night before? My friend Albert once teased me that a typical conversational opener of mine might be, 'Do you tend to use a name at all, or not especially?' But what is wrong with that?

Besides, we are meeting because a newspaper asked me to talk to Liza about a DVD reissue of *Liza with a 'Z'*, the multi-award-winning television concert spectacular put together for Liza in 1972 by John Kander, Fred Ebb and Bob Fosse, the team responsible for *Cabaret*. It is a documentary of a stunning performance. Minnelli, by turns, is goofy, sexy, poignant, brash, thrilled, wistful, sophisticated and sardonic in this concert of fifteen songs. Bob Fosse's choreography is severe and wild, the atmosphere intense. Would I have the nerve to say that I inwardly compared the 1972 special to

141

her mother's Carnegie Hall triumph eleven years before? Instead, something wholly different emerged from my lips.

'When I watched the film,' I venture, 'what I kept thinking was, if I were your mother I'd be insane with pride!'

'Oh that's so sweet, that's so sweet.'

We chat a little about how she gets in character for each song, making notes about every aspect of the person singing, from her chequered relationship history to her fridge magnets.

'One of the things I admire about you,' – I am speaking very slowly – 'is that you never complain about anything. I think courage is kind of the moral arm of glamour,' I tell her. It's a belief I've long held.

She looks at me as if to ask, How is that a question? But still she finds an answer.

'Oh I complain, but I give myself a time limit. You give yourself a certain amount of time to complain and then you get on with it. And I do that, too, with temper and stuff; I give myself twenty minutes and then it's time to get back to schedule.'

Because I am nervous I tell her that I try never to complain or get angry and I can go on for a long time like that but then I crack and everybody suffers.

'You got to go into a room and complain for twenty minutes.'

'Every day, can I?'

'If you need to, if you need to, but do it alone and do everything you have to do to get it out the way so you can move forward. Honour your feelings. They're your *feelings*! They may not be facts, facts and feelings are different. You know that better than I do. "You should be grateful!" "Well, I'm not!" We've all felt that.'

Liza as therapist! Liza as life coach! Sister, auntie, employer – yes. This I had not foreseen. Much of what else was said goes under the heading of neither here nor there. I was allowed to shine in tiny unrefracted drops, once or twice, but no more. I mentioned that I wrote books.

'What sort?'

'Black comedies about family relationships.'

'How fun!'

'They're rather dark, I'm afraid.'

'Well – whatever.'

I bite my lip.

I can't think of anything to ask that will not displease her. Nothing feels neutral. I have talked at length about my deep appreciation of her work, with the sort of intricate detail designed to stun, but there are only so many compliments you can heap on someone. After a while it could start to feel like an assault. The minute the interview is over I realise what I should have asked. I should have asked her if she would let me sing the first few bars of *Cabaret* with

143

her. I'm pretty sure she would have said yes. I just wanted to be in her presence. There's not always a need for words.

'Lovely shoes,' she murmurs, cocking her head expectantly, as if to remind me I need to say more things.

Just to fill the gap I ask her what her favourite food is. Does she have any religious beliefs? And to both these questions she gives rather disappointing answers. She likes anything made by Sara Lee and the reason she says this, I know immediately, is so that she can tell me she sometimes sings a song about how much she loves the rather un-inspiring frozen cake brand. I am very familiar with the song. It's not one of the greats, although it always makes me smile wryly when she sings, 'I love my mother but you can't compare 'er/Not to Sara.'

'Religions, someone once said,' she continues, 'let me get the quote right, is for people who are afraid of hell; spirituality is for people who have been to hell and back already.'

I laugh although I've never gone in for that kind of talk.

Do you love her? I ask myself, but before I can answer, out of the blue I hear my voice tell her that I am slightly in awe of my father, that other people's excessive interest in him makes me very uncomfortable.

'But don't you understand where they're coming from?'

For an awful second I feel I am about to say the wrongest possible thing, like, 'Do you . . . do you like a foggy day? *I* do?' or, 'I know, we'll stay all night and I'll sing 'em *all*!'

Instead, 'I do understand,' is what I say, 'but, you know, it's just really, you know, it's sometimes so hard to . . .'

Liza looks me hard in the eye. 'I know exactly how you feel, honey. *Exactly* how you feel.'

And this, in our thirty-eight minutes together, is the nearest we get to discussing her mother.

The
Disillusionment
Stage

At a party last night I was introduced to the son of the man who played the cowardly lion in *The Wizard of Oz*.

After dropping a few remarks we cut to the chase.

'You know, Judy Garland was a nightmare,' he tells me.

I take a step back and contemplate some form of attack.

'We are all nightmares some of the time.' This is the most popular line employed by 'good fans' when facing Garlandian challenges. We're all 'Who *doesn't*? Who *hasn't*?' when others speak of her excesses or the difficulties or chaos of her own making, or when accusations of bad behaviour descend. You show me a family that *isn't*?

'Yes, but—' and he gives an elegant, dismissive little flourish of his hand and what I seem to hear him say is that whatever sort of nightmare I may foolishly imagine myself to be, in the quaint little sphere from which I hail – well – it's absolutely *nothing* compared to the unbearable, terrible, indelible levels of behaviour meted out by Miss G.

I'm not quite sure why this seems so insulting, but it does. I feel I have been labelled a lightweight. Half of me wants to recount to him, in no small detail, all the worse things I have ever done. I begin to list them mentally and before long there's quite an array. Have you any idea that when I was six I stuck a ball of juicy bubblegum into my best friend's silky white-blonde hair and after two hours of her mother's painful unpicking and unsticking she had to have it all cut off, and – hooray – I was suddenly the prettier one! When I was eleven and my mother struck up a romance with a man I didn't like, every evening whenever anything really dreadful came on the television I used to call to her to come and watch it. 'Mum, it's that programme you really, really love,' I'd coo generously in the hopes that these scandalous lapses of TV taste would eventually drive the man away.

But you're trying to make Judy look good, not blacken your own name, I self-advise. All sorts of wild comments jostle in my brain. I face the man squarely, 'You're a coward, just like your father was before you!' I don't quite say. I don't have the nerve.

Is there anyone in the entire history of the entertainment business – or any other profession, for that matter – who, despite psychiatric difficulties from teenage onwards and a problem with drugs that spanned almost thirty years, managed to hold down a world-class show-stopping career for her entire life? I mean, have you even seen the reviews from when she was a child? I don't say this either.

My friend Francesca was raised in a Malibu household where she wasn't allowed to mention the words Judy or Garland. They were powerful nouns, inflammatory and forbidden. Her father Mayo Simon wrote Judy's last film, *I Could Go On Singing*, and his Judy experience was such that he didn't ever want to hear her name again. All children learn how to curse from their parents. I love the idea of a mini Francesca stubbing her toe or unwrapping an unwanted gift and hissing '*Garland*' under her breath.

*

'I've been thinking about this for a long time.' Mayo Simon begins to speak into my tape recorder.* 'Judy Garland had a hunger for love that could not be measured. The only way I can explain my experience with her was that she was kind of like a three-year-old who said, "OK you love me, do you? If I write all over the wall with crayons will you still love me? You do, huh? If I piss on the floor will you still love me? Oh, you do. Well, what if I set fire to the room will you still love me?" She would do all kinds of crazed things and I can only think it was all, "Even if I do this will you still love me?"

'My psychoanalytical friend, he was her analyst for a while, he once said to me when one psychoanalyst wanted to do a dirty trick on another psychoanalyst he handed him Judy Garland as a patient. "I can't help you any more, but this guy down the street he's really wonderful!" Well, she was crazy, that was my scientific evaluation.

'Example: the producers of the movie rent her a house and after two hours she decides she doesn't want it and they say, OK, they'll find her a flat in Central London that she likes better, and they do, and the next day the real estate lady calls and there's a bill for I don't know £4700 – a pound was a lot of money then – and the producer says, "For what?"

'"Well, it's for the damage while she was in the house."

'"She was in the house for two hours, what did she do?"

'Real estate lady says, "Well the fire on the ground floor actually didn't hurt the floor too much, but the rug is ruined and it's an expensive rug so we have to replace that and the broken windows and they were made of this special old leaded glass and that's quite expensive to have re-made and the door off the hinges we can easily repair, but the—"

'And the producers say, "Fire? Broken windows? Door off the hinges? How did this happen?"

*I did not ask Mayo Simon questions. This is simply an account of his Judy Garland life.

147

'Nobody ever found out, nobody knows how it happens. This was Judy, the kind of crazed wake that went behind her.

'Judy gets picked up and brought to the studio every day but one day, no Judy, and they're spending thousands of dollars on people standing around. Where is Judy? She would get upset and try and leave the country, so they stole her passport so she couldn't get out of England. "But I'm Judy Garland."

'"We know that miss but you still have to show your passport . . ."

'So she couldn't have run away. At five o'clock as the doors are closing the driver comes up with Judy. Where had she been? Well, the driver's little girl was in the hospital recovering from something or other, not feeling well, so she had the driver take her to the hospital and she sat there all day singing songs to the little girl. Is this Judy's generous spirit or is it crazy Judy saying will you love me if I don't even show up? Well, you can pick and choose but it's sure bizarre.'

'I bet the child made an instant full recovery,' I say, picturing myself in a sky-blue hospital gown, golden hair splayed on the starched pillow, and Judy hovering over me like a dark angel singing health back into my heart.

'Yes,' Mayo Simon beams, 'that is probably so.'

'Another time, Sid Luft came to town – he used to be married to her, kind of a gangster type. She calls him up, "Sid come on over," so he leaves to see her. Then Judy calls the police and says Sid Luft tried to attack her, some story about shoes which I never did get straight; did he want the shoes back that he had given her? I don't know what, but suddenly the police were called. This is the middle of the night, of course, so the producers are called. They say, "What happened?" They get through to Sid Luft and he says, "I don't know what happened," but suddenly there's this whole huge commotion with lights going on all over the place, with Judy creating tremendous commotion over what? No one could ever quite find out.

'The producers took her out to dinner one night; they had a pleasant time, then at three in the morning she calls one of them. "Larry I want you to tell Stuart that I'm just not going to come down any more and do the picture until you've decided you're going to treat me like a goddam fucking lady." Larry calls Stuart and Stuart calls me. Who said what? Nobody knows. The dinner was very pleasant, what is she talking about? What do we do now? We have four hours, we've cut the script down so she can make it in the time she has left, but now what's she saying? Who apologises? For what we don't know, but we'll apologise anyway.

'"Shall I call her?" says Larry.

'"Shall I call her?" says Stuart.

'When shall we call her? Will we wake her up? Should we go there? All right we'll go there, with flowers! We'll take flowers to Judy. We'll go there at eight o'clock, meanwhile lights are on all over town and now Judy can sleep.

'This wasn't like crazy; by this stage it was typical.

'She tried to kill herself several times, so we hire a guard to check

149

on her all through the night. Well, Judy calls Frank Sinatra in Australia, "I just can't take it any more, Frank, I just want to say goodbye." So Frank calls Hollywood and Hollywood calls David Picker, head of United Artists in New York, and he calls the producers in London and the producers call the guard who's asleep, naturally, and he breaks into the room and she's taken some pills and they take her to the psychiatric hospital and they pump her out and then she comes back and finally when lights are on all over the world, she can sleep.

'Another time the psychiatrist calls – this is so bizarre even now it's hard to believe – and he tells the producers, "You mean, evil, corrupt people are destroying this girl," – this is the psychiatrist – "she can't come back to work, you're just going to destroy her," so now the psychiatrist is Judy's agent.

'So they say we have a picture we're trying to make, we want to accommodate ourselves to her somehow; could she come back at all . . .?

'"Well she might be able to come back for a few days."

'"Well how many days is a few?"

'They negotiate that Judy will come back for ten days. 'Course, then they call the writer and I have now to fix the script to take Judy out of scenes, to cut scenes to see if we can still have a picture if she only comes back for ten days instead of the sixteen or the twenty that she's supposed to and they negotiate that and then the psychiatrist says, "Oh, and she wants you to pay her phone bill." They say, all right we'll pay her phone bill, and the phone bill is so astronomical it's thousands of pounds. How do you run up a phone bill for thousands of pounds in 1962?

'Well, apparently she was talking to her psychoanalyst in New York endlessly and somehow his bills got tied up with the phone bills – thousands of pounds – so they pay the phone bill, so she comes back for the ten days, and this is adding up to she'll never

150

make another movie because in order for a star to make a movie the star has to be insured by somebody and this kind of activity means that no insurance company will ever insure her again because she has a history of trouble-making. So she's now guaranteeing that she will never make another movie. She has no money, she never has any money, and she mixes with people who siphon off her money endlessly. David Begalman and Freddie Fields her agents, her former husbands – the IRS took her house away from her finally. She had no concept of money, money was kind of meaningless to her, so she finally comes back and she tries to get the director fired now. He grew up at Shepperton, he is a child of the studio – he refused to sleep with Judy was the story that I heard – so the crew at Shepperton say they will all walk off the set unless Ronnie stays; it's a battle of wills and finally she gives in, they make the picture, but this is like daily occurrences with Judy, this constant crazed turmoil. I remember Larry, the co-producer, saying one morning, and he's a very sober serious guy and it wasn't meant as sarcasm, "Well at least she hasn't tried to kill herself today." This was dealing with Judy.

'By the time the picture is finished the producers have split up, best friends, they never make a movie together again. I have split with them, best friends; I never speak to them again. My mother, who came to visit – we don't talk for the next three years; one of the producers gets divorced and the guy who does Judy's hair tries to kill himself. Dirk Bogarde, one of her best friends who kept her functioning, secretly rewrote the stuff that I was rewriting; I was secretly rewriting my script because she'd fired me but the producers kept me on to secretly rewrite my own secret rewritings but they didn't tell me that Dirk Bogarde was secretly rewriting some of my scenes. And everyone is mad at everyone else. In Hollywood films there is a certain amount of attrition, problems creep up, but this is pretty unusual and by the end of the film Dirk Bogarde announces that he

151

cannot devote his entire life to Judy Garland he has his work to do and they break their friendship of thirty years.*

'I was *so* angry, I couldn't work for six months after that film and I had to support a family, I had to write but I just couldn't face the typewriter. I literally did not talk to my mother for three years. It was madhouse when my mother came and I wasn't easygoing and tolerant, I'd had these terrible days at the studio where I'd find out that someone else is secretly reworking my scenes and I'm not even supposed to be doing the script, I was only doing it as a favour, I was supposed to be working on another script and I'm getting madder at the producers who didn't tell me they gave Judy the right to fire me and I'm getting mad at Judy for fucking around with me like this and I'm mad with the director. Why didn't he tell me she had the power to fire me? And I'm mad at Dirk Bogarde: what right does he have to rewrite me – and I don't like what I'm writing either and I have to keep the script together in my head all the time so I'm grinding away and I'm writing quickly like I've got to finish today for tonight or tomorrow morning and I'm not doing good work and I'm mad at myself so I didn't have any tolerance left for my mother's craziness when she came to visit. My mother said, "They're spying on me."

'"Oh mother!"

'"Yes they're spying on me in Holland, your friends there are all Nazis."

'"They are not Nazis."

'Then my mother would say, "You go out, I'll babysit. No, no! I insist you go out, have a good time," then she called my father and said, "Know what they made me do? They made me stay in with the children while they're out having fun . . ." I just couldn't take it. I mean I wanted to strike out with a knife.

*Actually, they met in 1956.

'It always starts with a big love fest with Judy; she requires that love fest. Every Judy Garland project starts with the producer saying, "Judy, those other guys didn't understand you, they really didn't love you enough. We understand you, we love you, we're going to take care of you." Then there's crises and consternation and everyone ends up not speaking to everybody.

'David Begelman, her agent, used to carry round an editorial from the *Minneapolis Tribune* – "Our Judy is Back: How Wonderful for America" – which he used to read to her. I noticed it was getting yellow around the edges. She needed that love more than appreciation, we love you we love you we love you we love you, and yet the most grotesque things would happen to people around her so she lost all her friends except for these gay guys who would pick her up when she was unemployed and broke and nurture her, take care of her, bring her back to life and then, you know what would happen? She'd walk away from them; she'd go and find some guys who'd beat her up or something. I don't know if those two things go together, this tremendous need for love and this need to cause consternation wherever you go. Is that two sides of something? I don't know. It's just what I saw.

'When I saw her in New Jersey in front of forty-five hundred people it was not a performance, it was way beyond that. I mean, she was a terrific singer with a wonderful sense of timing and a really terrific dancer and she had that quality that brought us up on our feet. I don't know if you've ever seen religious revivals, when the audiences get so excited they stand and they raise their hands in the air like this – I think it's something about heaven – that was a "Judy Garland" audience. They stand with their hands upraised as though some god was going to descend to them. You had thousands of people struggling to get close to her, to throw bouquets at her, and by the end of a concert she was dripping wet, totally exhausted, and she was small and the stage was enormous and the last thing she

153

sings is "Over the Rainbow" a cappella, sitting on the stage, her little legs dangling over the edge, under a spotlight. And the audience wasn't like, "Oh what a great performance," the audience was, "Judy, we love you! Don't die!" And her whole performance was sort of like, "If you don't love me I'll die!" And the audience was saying, "Don't die, we love you!" She required a lot of love and the audience were just crazed to give it to her . . . It wasn't like emotional blackmail, it was like a drowning man giving you his arm.

'I think you know the real life of stars is quite different from their public life. In public they project something that's like them but really much better than they are, but the private life is a different thing. I think the real Judy Garland was the one you saw on the stage, the private Judy Garland was all chaos and craziness and pettiness, but when she stepped out on the stage there you saw the real Judy.

'I remember at New Jersey sitting in her dressing room before the show, listening to the audience out there waiting for her to go on, slow hand clapping, which is disapproval in America, and her not noticing and no one else mentioning it. I tried to figure what it was like. You go and see a really sick person and there's a bunch of you in a hospital room and you haven't discussed it beforehand and you know you can't talk about *that* and we should really be terribly considerate about *this* because boy, is she sick – that is how they treated her. No one mentioned there was an audience out there who was getting impatient. It was like, "Let's sing another song" in the dressing room, no one mentions there's a show tonight, an audience waiting. It was that kind of very delicate. Then, finally, she says, "Hey, let's have a show!" And everyone goes into double speed to get the thing organised but everyone's aim is be nice to Judy, everyone professional backstage is like, "Be nice to Judy because she's sick and really delicate." You always knew what you shouldn't talk about. And of course she had this blond boy carrying the little suitcase full of

154

pills – unnamed, I don't know what they were. She swallowed at regular intervals, I don't know if they were pep pills. She had a lot of pills.'

'But surely she wasn't well enough to be working?' I can't help saying.

'On the last day of the shoot Judy sings the songs. She did not record the songs until the last possible moment. Why? Because as soon as she had recorded the songs they could throw her out, yet without the songs there's no movie. She does the songs on the last day. I'm not invited because I'm not there officially, but people tell me what happens.

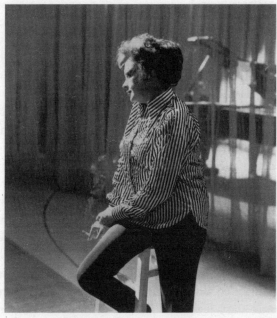

Judy Garland recording the songs for
I Could Go On Singing *in London*

'This is the only time that she recorded the songs live. Usually all of her songs are recorded afterwards but in this film they're all live. "Second violin is a little off," she said, "tell the bassoon to be tuned a little better, not sure I like the flute . . ." She is so super-professional when it comes to recording the songs. All that craziness is all gone and she is super-super-professional, hears everything, sees everything musically, knows everything that is going on. It's like a different person walks in to record the songs. That's Judy the professional that lives inside of her just as much as Judy the crazy person, so that's another side to her. When she had to be professional, boy was she ever. Everything was on the first take and everything was perfect with Judy Garland, she doesn't forget a word, a note – she's all there, she was a super professional.

'But she had this need for love like no one I've ever seen, unable to cover it up, but she constantly chose the wrong associates. Who's the worst guy I can go with? Who's the worst manager I can be with? Let's make a list of all the worst people I can conceivably trust with my money. How anyone could marry Sid Luft!

'David Begelman, her agent, making an awful lot of money, turned out he was putting in bogus expense account statements for Cliff Robertson, an actor, and then collecting the money himself and pocketing it. Ten thousand dollars against a salary of half a million; he was what we call a *ganuf*, he couldn't stop stealing. He couldn't stop – it was natural to him. These were the people she chose. Both Fields and Begelman used her to start that agency, but then when she got too crazy and they had enough other talent they dropped her.

'During the film, when we called New York and said, someone's got to come and do something to help or we can't get the picture finished she's so crazy, Fields was going to come but he said he needed fifty thousand dollars to cover his expenses because he wouldn't be able to service his other clients. Well this was really unheard of,

Hollywood did not operate that way. The producers said, we won't do it, so they came anyway. Begelman came – he who was sleeping with her at the time. Begelman loved to sing and would stand in for Judy in the light and sound checks; he loved that, doing his Frank Sinatra impression. He was actually a very charming guy, tough Brooklyn Jewish, self-made but ebullient and charming. He was very nice to me, but then all this other stuff came out that he was so corrupt, but in the pettiest way, and he stole a few thousand here and a few thousand there what was the point of it all? It made no sense. These were her companions.

'But on the set, in front of the camera, she was always excellent. The out-takes were always excellent, even when there's a little bit of her coming in to a room she's coming in to a room but there's a liveliness and a presence about her that's terrific. She never schlepped through a scene: she always knew her stuff. The real Judy was the one who was performing, I never saw her do a bad thing when she was performing. She never made a mis-step when I saw her in New Jersey. Where did all that wonderful patter come from? And her segues from talking to music were terrific, wonderful, unexpected, rhythmic – where did all that come from? She didn't rehearse it. She was super-professional on stage and super-professional making the film.

'There was like this crazy Judy, which we learned to fear, then there was this real professional, she was a great actress, and then when it came to singing there was this Goddess Judy – she really was the best popular singing talent that we've had in this country, nobody like her. She had such . . . gallantry.'

I click off the tape recorder and conjure up Judy's face, watching Dorothy's soft expressive features grew more defined and elegant, see the dark curls of Oz redden and extend into Esther Smith's sleek auburn locks, then Esther Blodgett's modest elfin crop. I see the late-fifties doughy, almost oriental-looking visage narrow into

157

mannequin CBS TV show Judy in long, narrow column dresses or white matchstick slacks. I see Jack Paar, 'off-duty' film star glamour Judy in a black cocktail dress, accessorised with arch and smouldering repartee.

I had listened, braced, to Mayo Simon speak, and much of it was hard to hear. I walked downtown for twenty blocks taking deep breaths, thinking, thinking. That someone who hated you so much he banned all mention of your name in his house for several years can speak about you now with this degree of warmth and admiration and respect after everything, well, I *have* heard worse.

When people who knew Judy came to the end of the road with her their experiences were often very similar. A strange sort of exasperation mixed with claustrophobia spread over everything. A nervous and physical exhaustion, financial and/or professional disarray, the bitterness of defeat, lawsuits, chaos and the dread of being caught up in Garland's own bad ending usually characterised the splits. The all-out quality that enabled her to captivate 108,000 people in one night in Boston, and have each one feel she was singing just to him or her alone, when directed at one individual was a pretty powerful proposition. And her disciples did not abandon her lightly. 'People put themselves through the most outlandish contortions, they left jobs, broke friendships, deserted families for this woman.' The ruin she could wreak on a person was no joke.

In the early days of songwriter John Meyer's romance with Judy Garland, an ex-beau of hers, Tim Bass, dropped off a manila envelope of printed matter at Meyer's mother's apartment. This included:

A letter from Judy's Boston attorney advising her that a
    Californian storage company was about to auction her
    furniture unless charges were paid.
A copy of a letter from Tim to Mr Wong of the IRS, stating
    that he, Tim, had pawned two of Judy's rings at her
    request, and that she was sole recipient of the money.
A bookkeeper's ledger of expenses incurred by Tim on Judy's
    behalf, carefully detailed. Over a two-year period
    (1967–1968), these expenses amounted to $58,815.62
A statement signed by Judy acknowledging her debt to Tim of
    some $19,000.
A copy of a legal document instituting suit by Tim against Judy
    for the recovery of monies Tim claimed he was owed. The
    document was a summons.

A note: 'You know this is the last thing I'd want to do, but if
   you try to get me out of the club, or some other way keep
   me in the awful condition we have both gotten "Tim Bass"
   into, then I have no choice.'

Did an examination of this material deter John Meyer in his
fledgling romantic entanglement with Judy Garland? Did he take
alarm at a man who felt so squashed and broken that he actually *put
his own name in inverted commas* as if he were some sort of provisional former person? What do you think?

If you look at how people broke with Judy, examining the last
straw that made her loyal comrades' backs collapse, it is their aware-
ness of her refusal to help herself that often lies at the heart of
things.

Vincente Minnelli described the 'shocking confession' that came
from his wife in 1950 that made him realise that they couldn't go on
any more. 'Someone at the studio had counted up the number of
psychiatrists she'd been sent to. They totalled sixteen, Judy was told.
"So what?" she retorted. "I never told any of them the truth. There's
more than one way to get even with you people."'

'She hadn't even tried . . . at least not as much as she should have.
It was damn near impossible for me to forgive Judy for this. I opted
for sanity.'

This scene makes me extremely uncomfortable. I know that it's
impossible, really, ever to form accurate judgements about other
people's affairs, because very often the one fact you haven't been
told is the thing that makes sense of everything. Yet why did someone decide, right then when Judy was at a very low ebb, to remind
her how many psychiatrists she'd seen? It was hardly a neutral communication. Was there any context for this pronouncement? Did
the representative also mention the tens of millions of dollars she
had made for the studio? The part that the studio had played in

her early difficulties, when intensely pressurised fourteen-hour days for a girl in her mid-teens were the norm? Analysands have always claimed to lie to their therapists. It's bravado and defensive pride. Judy's outcry was surely the vanquished boast of someone who felt she was being unfairly attacked. Besides, how do you tell someone the truth when you yourself don't know what it is? Isn't that part of the problem? Taking a moral approach to mental health is very complicated. Is it fair or even sensible to expect focused, rational behaviour from those who are being treated for their instability?

John Meyer's break with Judy – for all the heroism he located in himself in her service – was linked to her own lack of I don't quite know what.

Oh Judy . . . It was difficult to speak with my nose full of tears and my mouth contorted with anguish. You just do it to yourself, every time . . . and there's no way to fight it . . . it's inside you, and I can't help you . . . it's inside you.

You just make it impossible . . . for anyone to help you . . . because you won't let them . . . something inside you defeats you . . . and destroys you.

Of course I love you . . . That's why I'm crying . . . because I love you and I can't help you . . . nobody can . . . it's inside you and you're the only one who can do something about it . . . but you can't . . . you can't.

Dirk Bogarde, a man Judy decided might be her romantic saviour, was unequivocally unsuited to the job in *many* different ways. He wrote:

The demands had been too many and too strong for me to support; she had gone her own way, as she always said that she would,

161

and I had determined to go mine. As she spiralled slowly down-wards into her particular black well of despair and fear, I had ignored the outstretched hands imploring for help. How can one help a blazing meteor in its fall? It was no consolation; I walked up to the villa filled with shame, but also fuelled with a fury at the waste, the sheer bloody waste of a husked-out, rejected, once glorious life destroyed by cinema.

There are several things wrong with this. Self-aggrandising phrase-making and the fashioning of elegant little metaphors out of someone else's misery is not quite right. There is also a modicum of venom in 'husked-out'. Similarly, 'destroyed by cinema' is a ludicrous euphemism, meaningless and banal. 'It' is how Bogarde confessed Judy was referred to by the end of the *I Could Go On Singing* shoot, in a television interview he once gave.

John Carlyle, her charming but dissolute bit-part-actor on-off companion during her last year or two put it very simply: 'I was afraid that she was no longer a survivor, and I had to be.'

I'm very interested in the exact point in life at which the love stops. I always count how long a smile lingers on a fellow's lips before it vanishes into the quotidian frown, and I've foreseen in the quickening of this process the sense of an ending many times. What makes people stop loving people? More often than not, it seems to me, it is something to do with mistaken identity. If I were to find out that Judy Garland was not the person I thought she was, would that change things between us? Is there anything about Judy Garland I could discover that would make me not love her any more?

I'm not someone who believes bad things easily. When I did jury service some years ago we were confronted with a young man whose gas meter cupboard was found to be stuffed with cheques that really ought not to have been there. Our case concerned just one of these cheques, which was being accused of being a 'false instrument'. I sent a question to the elegant judge in my best handwriting. 'Does the term false instrument have to mean forged or could it mean generally dishonest or untoward or dodgy?'

It has to mean forged. The kindly judge looked up as though she was impressed by the question. This man lived in desperate circumstances. He was obviously not profiting from the scams and there was the small matter of his three children. How could I say that he knew for certain some cheques he was harbouring were forged and not just stolen or illegal? How could I say, beyond all possible doubt, that he knew *anything* for certain?

It's actually beyond *reasonable* doubt, one of the jurors reminded me after the not guilty verdict.

Oh! Of course. Never mind!

I formulate some questions to test my Judy-love. Would my love stop:

IF I FELT JUDY'S DIFFICULTIES HAD BEEN ASSUMED AND EXAGGERATED IN ORDER TO GAIN THE SYMPATHY OF THE PUBLIC?
This discovery would strike me as extremely good news.

IF I FOUND OUT THAT THE TRUE EMOTION SHE TRANSMITTED WAS IN FACT FALSE?
In 1951, Judy Garland had a difficult conversation with her early love Artie Shaw after he came to see her record-breaking Palace show for the second time. She could sense he was disappointed to see her repeat certain 'spontaneous effects', the kicking off of her shoes, the jokes she made against her dress. 'I knew that would get you,' she said afterwards. I have no difficulty with this. She was a theatrical performer.

Liza Minnelli has said, 'My whole life, my mother was truly

163

hilarious. And people would go, "Oh, really?" They just want it to be such a tragedy and it wasn't. She understood that her vulnerability in performance was something that we all recognise in ourselves. She knew how to portray somebody in flux, somebody in pain, very well. She understood it deeply enough to be able to portray it. She created the legend. She did it, and she knew exactly what she was doing. [After a performance of "Over The Rainbow" people would be] standing up and falling down and screaming and crying. I'd rush up to the middle of the stage [in the blackout] thinking, Oh my God, she's a wreck, and she'd look at me and say, "You want Chinese food tonight?"'

I can accept these comments easily and most certainly want them to be true.

IF SHE KILLED SOMEONE?
She didn't kill anyone but there are two recorded incidents when, in the grip of mad despair, she pulled kitchen knives on people, once on her son Joey and once on one of her young assistants. Neither sustained any physical injury. What can you say? Intolerable circumstances made a monster out of her on occasion, but that's very often what they do. None of us would like or even perhaps deserve to be remembered for the worst thing we have ever done.

IF I FOUND OUT FOR SURE THAT SHE WOULD HAVE
DESPISED ME FOR MY FELLOW FEELING, REFUTED IT,
RESENTED AND RIDICULED IT?
'I have a voice that hurts people where they think they want to be hurt,' Judy Garland said. Ouch. But on the whole Judy Garland was as in awe of the amazing powers of healing and cheering contained in her voice as her fans.

IF I KNEW FOR SURE THAT ALL HER EMOTIONAL EFFECTS
WERE PLANNED IN THE GREATEST OF MINUTIAE AND SHE
MANIPULATED DELIBERATELY THE EMOTIONS OF HER
AUDIENCES TO SERVE HER OWN ENDS?

Judy asked John Meyer, when they were preparing to do the Dick
Cavett show, 'My God he's nervous . . . why do I make everyone
so . . . nn . . . uncomfortable?'

'Because, Judes,' he said, 'no one knows whether you're going to
sing "Over the Rainbow" or open your veins.'

Judy giggled. 'Sometimes I do both . . . at the same time.'

Who doesn't?

IF I DISCOVERED HER TERRIBLE FINANCIAL
PREDICAMENTS WERE CAUSED IN PART BY HER
PROFLIGACY AND EXTRAVAGANCE?

'Judy would often keep a limousine waiting outside for, like, days . . .
and those things add up,' a former employee said. Muddle and instability make people careless with money. I wish Judy had been more
extravagant and had had more luxury in her life. The fact remains
that in her last decade she saw very little of her earnings, as others
siphoned off her fees and left her with the tax bills.

On the last afternoon of the thirty-second Judy Garland festival in
Grand Rapids, Minnesota, an eleven-year-old girl called Lorraine
approached me. A serious child, with an odd intensity to her, I had
already heard her Judy story. Ill at home for several weeks the year
before, she had passed her mornings watching the *Rugrats* movie and
her afternoons in front of *The Wizard of Oz*. By the time she was
better she was Judy-hooked.

'Can I ask you something?' Lorraine came and sat with me.
Together we had already sat through many JG sessions, including:
Judy Through the Years; Judy Garland: The Dressing of a Legend;

They Remember Judy; Judy Garland Alive in our Hearts; Ruby Slipper Caper Mystery Dinner; Munchkin Luncheon, with real munchkins in attendance nearly seventy years on.

I turn to Lorraine, who is weighing her words. 'I think it's weird that no one is mentioning that she was on drugs and alcohol her whole life and yet still managed to be so mellow and nice.'

It was true. For over forty-eight hours of talks and conversations there had been not one single reference to what good fans quaintly term the '*medication issue*'.

'The reason no one is mentioning that stuff – and I agree with you that it is a bit weird – is that there are a lot of other people who *only* talk about that stuff and that makes the people here very angry. I guess the people here want to put the other side of the story. They feel that dwelling on that stuff is a way of reducing the amazing achievements of her career. It's a way of doing her down somehow, of belittling her. There wasn't the kind of help available to people with her problems back then. People just didn't know that much about it. So I guess the people here feel those things need to be addressed with respect and, well, love. Does that make sense?'

'No.'

'Did you ever read any Jane Austen, because at the end of *Mansfield Park*, when people are doing stuff that they shouldn't, she writes, "Let other pens dwell on guilt and misery", because I guess it's just not what she wants to do. It's not what she thinks is the interesting or important thing.'

Lorraine is not convinced. 'It's just not right,' she says. 'It's not right that nobody mentions it.'

Lorraine has read a great deal about Miss Garland. I expect the next question to be something like, 'What do they mean when they talk in some of the books about "Frank Gumm's sad frailty"? That was her dad, right?' I prepare an answer for her. 'It is,' I would say, 'the largely accepted view of many "Judy People" that her father indulged discreetly and occasionally in sexual relationships with men. At that time, in the nineteen-twenties, a lot of people would have thought this was very wrong. People think differently today. Which is good.' I would not mention to Lorraine that when one of my Judy-friends recently remarked to his Christian fundamentalist brother that the weather was unbearably warm, his brother's reply was, 'It'll be a lot hotter than this where you're going, unless you change your ways.'

I sometimes wonder how affected Judy was by the discord between her parents when she was a child. A porous personality, which she undoubtedly possessed, absorbs any sort of floating anxiety. The texture of displeasure and disagreement can most certainly affect the quality of air in a room and taint the colour of everything. But I don't think about this very much; the guesswork and suppositions that cause some writers to emphasise and almost glory in this aspect of her childhood do not tempt me. I prefer to think of her singing.

Yet Lorraine's frank features haunt me sometimes. By not talking about Judy's darker struggles am I abandoning her in some way? Am I walking backwards out of the room, smiling and waving as she told Dirk Bogarde people always do when they have had enough? Judy Garland was undoubtedly a consumer of people. My five-year-old pokes her head into the room where I am writing. It's late. 'Mama, can you come down?'

'In a minute sweetheart, in a minute.'

'If Julie Garden was still alive would she be your best friend?' she sighs.

When a person is talented in the extreme, dwelling on her difficulties is a way of denigrating her achievements. I know this for certain. Yet banishing all mention of her difficulties isn't quite right either.

I don't like to think of Judy in despair, not publicly. *Judy in Love!*, *The Young Judy Garland*, or even *Judy Alone* the names of her album covers proclaim. But *Ill Judy*? I don't wish to desert her in her cruellest hours. It's just I feel that by describing them at all I am prolonging them, extending their power.

There is an Ill Judy record. It's called *Judy Garland Speaks*. You get it from the 'Celebrities at their Worst' website, which describes it as 'ultra-rare home voice tapes which were recorded as notes for her never-written autobiography'. The back cover proclaims, 'I'm the one who's had to live with me . . . all my forty-four goddam, marvellous, failing, successful and hopelessly tragic and starlit years . . . I've sung, I've entertained, I've pleased your children, I've pleased your wives, I've pleased YOU – you SONS OF BITCHES.' I bought this record years ago, but I won't listen to it.

I'm not a cock-eyed optimist. A friend and I were in a café yesterday and one of the things on the menu was *affogato*.

'What is it?' I asked.

'It's a small cup of espresso poured over a scoop of vanilla ice cream.' We ordered one.

'But what does *affogato* mean?' my friend pressed.

The waitress darted back into the kitchen and returned with the dish. 'I asked the chef, he's Brazilian. He says it means drowned. But I guess you could kind of interpret it and say it means floating.'

We looked differently at the courageous little dessert after that, presented by its pathologically hopeful waitress. Not drowning but floating.

You cannot prize someone for the strength of her feelings and desert her because her feelings become so strong that they are no longer to your taste. Love doesn't abandon its object in illness. At the end of her life, it was patently clear Judy was drowning. Lorna Luft's own memoir states, 'She had to keep on working to deal with the debt. Working meant expending more energy than she had left, and that in turn meant more amphetamines to carry her through. As the cycle continued, her anger and despair mounted.'

When it comes to the difficulties that Judy Garland had, I feel obliged to turn away with compassion rather than with distaste. But can you turn away from someone with compassion? Does it actually mean anything?

When my first novel came out everyone seemed certain there ought to be a picture of a cake on the jacket.

I was rather a keen cake-baker, yet this idea caused me huge embarrassment. It felt too personal. If I had a cake on the cover of my jacket, might it be confusing for people? Might people – it could happen – actually think it was *me*?

I asked my father for advice, for we had suddenly grown very close. A strong cake, a robust cake, he seemed to think, would be fine. The kind of cake, he added, that Virginia Woolf would have loathed. We had spent a very pleasant morning working together, chatting in part about Iris Murdoch in our breaks and eating pear and almond tart. I wrote down on the back of a bus ticket one of the things he said: 'Some of her books are so muddled it's like a drawer with socks and shoes and even feet in it.'

'I'll do the cake for you, for the cover, if you like,' he offered. It was decided that I would make a cake as a sort of life model and my father would draw or paint a picture of it.

The following day I rose early and set to work. I put my heart in to that cake. I made the springiest fatless sponge I could muster, beating six egg whites with a hand-held balloon whisk until my wrist had cramp. It was an old Robert Carrier recipe my mother used for all our birthdays. The cake rose to four and a half inches, and when it was cool I split it in two and sandwiched the halves together with some raspberry jam and some fresh raspberries and loosely whipped cream. I spread another layer of cream on the top and piped some curlicues and rosettes with cream I had dyed pale pink. 'Life is just a bowl of cherries,' I sang as I arranged some heart-shaped strawberries in the centre and strewed a handful of redcurrant sprigs over the whole thing so it wouldn't look too contrived, so it might have something of the forest.

I took the cake round to my father's with some ceremony, holding it firmly on the top deck of the bus braced against my knees, much to the amusement of my fellow passengers, marching it proudly to his front door, bearing it up the five flights of stairs to where it was to sit for its portrait. It was a boiling hot day and the cream glistened and warmed in the sun but I willed it to stay in one piece and it did. I set the cake on the kitchen table and left it to its fate. A few days passed. Something had gone wrong, I just knew. In life, the longer you have to wait for news the worse it generally is. After a week I summoned the courage to ask my father what was happening. 'Can you put me in the picture about the picture?' I said.

It hadn't worked, it transpired. I never knew if the cake had dissolved in the heat, or had been ignored in favour of a more pressing human situation, or whether the picture had been begun and scrapped, something that has happened to me four times and never feels very nice.

So the next day, as we agreed, I made another cake and took it round again, only this time it didn't seem like a jaunty adventure. The second cake, though respectable, was not half the person the first one had been. My morale was low. I asked my friend Jon to come with me for support. There are only so many lovely cakes you can make in life. We travelled in a taxi and he waited in the street while I took the cake inside. Although it was still hot I wore a great heavy coat.

It was an anxious moment when I put the cake into my father's hands, and as I had feared I burst into tears. 'What's the matter?' he asked, or something along those lines.

'Everything's a terrible muddle,' I said, 'and I'm sorry to say it but when I was making the cake again I couldn't stop thinking about how sad I was that I didn't see you all that much when I was a little girl. I thought of the first cake and everything and I just felt—'

'Oh no!' he cried, putting an arm on my shoulder and kissing me. 'You must absolutely banish that thought from your mind. Please.'

It did seem like a sensible idea. 'OK,' I said. I made some tea, which we drank black.

'How did it go?' Jon said kindly when I came out of the front door.

'All right. Could have been a lot worse.' Although it was Sunday I had my job in a bookshop to go to and I said goodbye to my friend and made my way there.

Three days later a beautiful picture of a cake, better far than either of the two I had made, came my way. It's hanging on the wall in front of me now.

I will never abandon Judy but I find it as agonising to hear about her difficulties as I do with all those I love. People who are making bad choices need their loved ones more than ever, but how best to show love is not always clear. Addiction is not like other illnesses, for as you tend to the patient it is often the sickness that grows lively and strong.

One night I put the *Judy Speaks* CD in the machine and lie down on the floor. It's a hot summer evening but I feel myself shiver. The talk begins and Judy is there in the room with me. It's not intimate, the communion between us, she's addressing me as if speaking to some sort of public gathering, but it's her all right. I close my eyes. Instantly her voice, even in its introductory technology uncertainties, swells into the high ceilings. It's a rich voice with so many different emphases and modulations, perhaps three or four different kind of italics and occasional bursts of an intonation as arched as a

171

pair of pencilled brows. It's a form of performance, an interview of sorts. She's asking and answering herself, straight into the machine. She is setting the record straight. She's chatty and witty and charming and angry and hurt. Who isn't? A few minutes in she rewinds the tape to see if it's been doing its job correctly.

A seminar on Wordsworth I once attended revealed that in an early draft of, I think, 'The Ruined Cottage' the poet had written the number 20 or 18 when that many lines had been set down. He must have been pleased with it to have done that, the tutor, one of Wordsworth's descendents and a guardian of his flame, declared. He has sat back and counted and that indicates a certain sense of achievement. Well, Judy's rewinding had a similar effect. This *is* going to work, is what she seems to say.

The pain in Judy Garland's voice, after a few minutes, is more than I can take. The charm has diminished and it's all sadness and depression. It's come so quickly. I want to reach her speaking into that machine in London in 1964, but I don't know how. You can root for someone with all your might, like a deranged cheerleader, trailing ribbons into the past. You can think whatever happened to Judy – and I'm still, after more than thirty years of wondering, not exactly sure what it was – must never be allowed to happen again. In the face of her pain I feel militant and tender. It is traumatic. My eyes fill.

In John Berryman's* first really successful poem, 'Homage to Mistress Bradstreet', he goes back in time to love and befriend an early female American poet whose life-sufferings and pure heart touch him greatly. Is this what I am trying to do?

Not everything Judy Garland says – and I don't like to write it – sounds absolutely sincere, and some of it isn't even true, but it's certainly *meant*: the feelings behind it are true. She is having a very, very bad day, I tell myself. She's alone and she minds it. Who doesn't? In

*My favourite poet.

172

a lengthy lament, witty and bitter, she curses her children's fathers, saying how useless they are and always have been. I recoil at this soap-opera rant. I imagine it through her daughters' ears. I think of Vincente Minnelli giving Liza miniature versions of what the screen's leading ladies are sporting, from Hollywood's best couturiers, each Christmas. In Minnelli's autobiography he allocates Liza a few pages to paint a picture of her father in her own words. This seems to me extraordinarily respectful and stylish. I cannot think of any other autobiography that does this. In the Liza-written scenes their life together is pictured vividly: his yellow shirts; their breakfasts in bed delivered by the housekeeper, with him endlessly reading scripts; Liza's arrival at the studio to watch the filming, hoping that it's a musical, it's Fred Astaire today – hooray! Their sing-songs in the car on the way home as they pass through the studio gates are charming and even possibly therapeutic. It's not everything, but it's not nothing either. I don't like to hear Vincente cursed, nor Sid Luft called a monster. The jury is very much still out on the latter who played a key role in Judy's heart and career from 1952 to 1965. This ambivalence was central to his obituary in the *Atlantic*, which appeared under the headline, 'The Least Worst Man [in Judy Garland's Life]'. It's a modest distinction, or is it? If she had stayed with Sid she might still be alive, some good fans believe, crediting him not just with his physical support of the legend, and a brand of very careful handling, but also a vital contribution to her marvellous second act, the concert years. Others disagree:

Sid Luft was a man of considerable human charm but one of the great fourth-rate human beings of all time. When you are given command of your wife's money and you gamble it and spend it profligately on yourself and you don't pay the taxes for three or four years and that huge burden is hanging over you of four hundred thousand dollars . . .

173

It means a great deal that in all the time I've known them neither of my parents has ever said anything negative to me about the other one.

Judy's cursings of her husbands I accept, but they aren't pretty. She's blustery and incensed. Little of what she is saying has the ring of fresh thought. She is parading grievances and wounds. Who does-n't? The press she rails against very powerfully. They're not in such great shape themselves, she says of the gossip columnists. She's spoken to their make-up people and knows the long processes involved in making them look like women. This tape recording is a kind of performance but it's not a good one. Now she's *really* angry. It's as though she's reacting to a specific set of betrayals but she's not entirely sure what they are. Every so often the tape clicks on and off as she stops and starts her recording over a period of days. These moments are almost the most intimate of all. The stumbling fingers, the fresh beginnings.

And then the dramatic and the articulate evaporate; the gesturing and the actressy pronouncements and a very heavy and quiet sadness fills the room. The quality of the sadness is so searing that when she uses words like 'crooked' and 'treatment', in reference to former friends it is clear that the effects of these things have struck her almost as a murder attempt. For all her vulnerability, Judy never seems fragile in the least because she has such a strong survival instinct, but here she sounds *frail*. The words are extremely slurred and I have to crouch next to the machine to be able to hear at all, whatever the volume. I don't know what to do. It's awful not to be able to comfort her.

The telephone rings – reprieve – and I rise to answer it, pausing Judy in despair. It is a friend asking me if I am aware of the musi-cals and gender conference that is taking place in three months' time at London University. Pal Joeys and Calamity Janes is its provisional title. Would I like to come? The keynote speaker is a man whose essay on Judy Garland website postings and attendant controversy 2000–2005 is quite legendary in some circles. I may have heard better news but I can't think when. I jot down some dates.

I once listened, in a similarly heightened manner, to a tape of someone else I've greatly admired, the poet John Berryman, giving a reading at the New York Public Library with his friend and rival Robert Lowell.

I had expected to swoon at his severe and charming delivery, his laser-guided witticisms and his gauchenesses, and to be enthralled by the sudden intimacy of a man caught, like the person in the Michael Andrews painting, at the exact point of falling over.

'A Man who Suddenly Fell Over' by Michael Andrews

I locate in Berryman's poetry the startling image of someone repeatedly turning himself inside out and back again, but with the natural ease and lack of fuss that one might correct a newly laundered jersey pulled over the head in haste.

I was shocked at Berryman. His drunken swagger, his boom and that self-hating, self-aggrandising see-saw; the muscular arrogance of his growl. Where were all his delicate instincts? He was spoiling for a fight. He didn't even seem attractive, much less great. It wasn't even funny. There was banality there. You could almost smell the whisky in the clotted jolts and starts of his voice. Being an alcoholic seemed to me then and suddenly the tritest way to solve the problem of yourself. Think of something original, why can't you! I almost wanted to roar. A poet's wife? What were you thinking? I scolded. Then, after a while, I didn't feel sympathy or betrayal or kinship or embarrassment. I felt in my shoulders the beginnings of a small shrug.

John Berryman

I read this morning of the death of Elizabeth Hardwick, 91, writer and co-founder of the *New York Review of Books* and Robert Lowell's second wife. Under the photograph of a woman, with eyes soft and piercing, it says, 'The public humiliation of abandonment was multiplied by a violation of trust. Suffering with his own guilt Lowell published poems in which he transcribed parts of telephone conversations and letters that revealed Hardwick's anguish and desire to have her husband back.'

Lord protect us from poets.

I don't un-pause *Judy Speaks*. It's late at night. I can't end on such a note and think of sleep. I listen instead to Judy's beguiling stage patter from Carnegie Hall on 23 April 1961 as an antidote. I'm not proud of myself for making this switch, but it feels necessary.

> I've got to tell you about another, another thing that happened to me when I went abroad. I went to – er – to London first.
>
> 'Welcome back!'
>
> Ah . . . ah . . . it's lovely to be back, thank you. It's lovely. And they're, ah, they're terribly sweet, they're wonderful, they're very sweet to me, but if you know anything about the English press, they're rather odd. They really are. They just say terrible things about people, you know, and they say miserable things and then somebody sues 'em and then they pay 'em off and then they say 'em again and then they sue 'em again and it's a never-ending thing.
>
> Well, anyway, I landed in London and I was taken to a press conference in a hot – err – airless little room and . . . er . . . er all these photographers and reporters and so forth were asking very impertinent – very rude questions, you know, and, and I was being so nice and there was, there was one young girl though and she was kind of cute she was, er, next to me all the way through this party and she kept saying, 'You look marvellous! I've never

seen you look as well, you look so relaxed and you look – what have you been doing?'

And, and I said, 'Well I er, ah, er I feel fine,' and she kept following me all around the room and saying, 'I can't get over how . . . what have you . . . ah come on now . . . what . . . you've never looked so well!' and so on and by, you know, I was there for an hour and a half and by the time I left I felt pretty good with this, with this, girl and, er, just as I was leaving she said, 'Would you mind dropping me at my hotel because I'm afraid I can't get a taxi?' and I said, 'Come on!' I wanted to hear more about all this so we got into the taxi and all the way to her hotel she kept saying, 'I really, I really just can't can't get over – I've never seen you look like this and I've seen you for a long time but I've never seen . . . what I . . . but . . . and I . . .'

And I dropped her so I picked up the paper the next morning to her column and her – she had a whole page and the headline said, 'Judy Garland arrives in London and she's not chubby, she's not plump: she's fat!'

A terrible girl, a, er, miserable thing to do after all that time taking her to her hotel and then she said she, er, went on in her article and said, 'but she's jolly, she's jollier than I've ever seen and if you say anything funny to her she throws her head back and her chins jiggle happily!' Oh, and then she said, 'she has a lovely smile' and I'm quite . . . 'and her teeth are crooked but I think they're her own . . .'

That's all.

I go to bed. All the Judys are there with me! Intelligent Judy; dewy Judy; 'I can sing, you know' Judy; glamour-girl Judy; 'I'm no glamour girl' Judy; ranting Judy; Dorothy; the Judy beloved by bad fans: vampish and curled or sprawling in a lesbian nightclub in New York autumn/winter 1968. I recite the thank-you letter Judy wrote to Vincente Minnelli before they were married:

Vincente Dear,

[The simple inversion of the conventional opening seems utterly charming to me]

Your beautiful birthday gift has changed my outlook on life. It used to be a difficult task for me to walk into a room full of people with any self-assurance. But not any more. Now I merely hold my handbag at the proper angle, descend upon the group and dazzle each individual.

Thank you for one of the loveliest gifts I've ever received.

Love, Judy

Judy Garland framed beautifully by her director husband-to-be, Vincente Minnelli

As I fall asleep my thoughts drift back to the Carnegie Hall concert patter. Why would a London journalist be staying in a hotel?

Next morning I slide the *Judy Speaks* CD into the machine in my daughter's tiny pink bedroom. I climb into her bed, which is festooned with pink tulle and stickers of Snow White and Sleeping Beauty. I don't much feel like hearing it.

In bereavement work, in the face of another's extreme pain, some practitioners imagine a figure of eight both linking and separating the counsellor and the client, ensuring that the spirit of fellow feeling does not descend into an identification so strong that both parties are undone. I enclose myself in a figure of eight. The job of a true friend, I self-remind, is not to take away another's distress but to listen acutely to it, to witness it, to stay at the side of the person who is grieving. (I know I will never ever play this recording again.) Not to leave.

As I listen I feel and feel along with Judy the devastation of betrayal. Physical, emotional and financial betrayal from the people you once, and perhaps still do, love. I think of a passage written by Judy's first grown-up love, bandleader Artie Shaw, the man who went out with Lana Turner one evening and came back . . . married:

> I have never since been able to entirely dispel that original loneliness and lose myself in the crowds for whom I performed. If anything, the larger the crowds and the warmer the waves of admiration and love that I have felt pouring up from them, the more intense the loneliness and sense of isolation I have felt standing up there between the two separate worlds of my band on the one hand, and the audience on the other; with myself drifting, apart, between these two worlds, like a desperate island, or some sort of lost planet, alone in dark, cold outer space, wandering, like Shelley's moon, 'companionless among the stars that have a different birth'.

Hmmm.

I don't claim to know Judy Garland, of this I am sure. I feel very close to her, I love her, but I don't understand. Perhaps I never will. I accept there are layers and layers of things. Very often the one thing that makes sense of everything is the thing that you don't know. And then I can't entirely trust myself either; my favourite interpretation of her life states that Judy's childhood was so wonderful, her greatness so prized and she herself so entirely respected, cherished and lionised by her family who gave her everything, that it was ensured, unwittingly, that she would be forever disenchanted with the adult world that followed.

Face to face with John Fricke, the world's foremost expert on Judy Garland, I put it to him tentatively. 'I know we're not meant to dwell on her difficulties but I still don't understand why she found her life as hard as she did. I hope you don't mind my saying.'

'It's all right,' he reassures. I thank him.

'Feeling unwanted, terrible pressure always, being pushed beyond her strength, really miserable home life, and then by her mid-twenties her nervous system was completely shot through. And then of course all her luck was bad . . .'

'I can run faster than my body can handle,' I heard a lithe young woman boast to her companion in a Lebanese restaurant. What did she mean? I imagine her legs and trunk several yards ahead of her head and shoulders, cartoonish with triumph. Did Judy begin life able to run faster than her body could handle, then suddenly, imperceptibly things changed until the truth of the matter was that she needed to run faster than her body could and there were no healthy reinforcements for her? In 1940 and 1941 she starred in six films, made forty radio appearances and cut eighteen singles for Decca. How could anyone manage that? In her memoir, Lorna Luft states that by the time her mother was seventeen she was an expert at hiding the 'medication' that had been prescribed for her by studio doctors. She always seemed to be able to get hold of more pills, Luft writes, sewing them into the seams and hems of her costumes, stowing them behind furniture in her dressing room for future use as she had hidden candy when she was a child.

Does it seem a courtesy to Judy, on my part, to claim not to understand the root of her difficulties? I know a great deal more about her than I do about either of my parents, yet I shy away from defining her, from defining anybody. The time to make up your mind about people is never.

I move in the sort of circles in which hero-worshipping people with addiction problems raises eyebrows. It is mildly scandalous, frowned on and a cliché. Listening to the *Judy Speaks* recording I force myself to think about Judy's drugs life. It interests me less than any other aspect of her. It's not that I avoid it exactly, I just don't know what to do with it. You absolutely loathe being round people who are on drugs, is a fact I occasionally repeat to myself, especially people who take speed. The twitchiness, the accelerated facial movements, the angularity of all the gestures, the completely unpredictable behaviour all underwritten with a sort of staccato, paranoid aggression. You can't stand it, remember. It's hardly something I could forget. Does it make nonsense of this whole thing? Of me, of me and her?

I sketch out a little moral hierarchy of drug taking in my mind. There are all sorts of kinks and complications of legitimacy. I see a paradigm forming in pyramid shape.

Those who take drugs for pleasure, to enter Baudelaire's 'artificial paradise', for no reason, just because.
Those who take drugs to relax, or out of curiosity or to 'systematically derange' all their senses – a change is as good as a rest.

182

Those who take drugs to escape life's pressures.

Those who take drugs to escape psychological pain that they cannot bear.

Those who take stimulating drugs pragmatically in order to fulfil their responsibilities, to facilitate strenuous work as Judy did, as W. H. Auden did, and who goes on endlessly about that?

Those who take drugs to cure extreme physical pain.

I'm not sick enough to see a heroism in Judy's drug-taking, although the fact that she took Benzedrine in order to achieve more is rarely disputed. Benzedrine is, after all, the most utilitarian of drugs. At first you get more things done. A relative was prescribed it at Christmas, to make things jolly for the children when she was at low ebb. My mother said that when she was a child it was given to people with colds to help them meet their commitments.

I pause the recording once more and telephone a family friend who is something of an expert on both music and drugs. As a seasoned manager of recording artists, these sorts of dynamics have been a constant of his career. 'People who take Benzedrine are hyper-sensitive, hyper-reactive, paranoid and impossible to please and they become very exacting of themselves and other people and they don't understand why. The damage to the nervous system and the balance of the brain and the wear and tear on the body is really terrible,' he says sadly.

'Right.' None of this is exactly news.

But he is still talking: 'One side effect is that it makes people unbelievably excessively emotional.'

I am completely shocked by this. All the people I've known who've been very involved in drugs have been made almost entirely devoid of emotion. It's usually been a motivating factor of their addiction. I feel myself unravelling wildly. I've always nursed an

183

anxiety about loving people for the wrong reasons. What was it that first drew me to JG?

It was her extreme, excessive strong feelings. Was it just the drugs that I loved? Was it the drugs singing? It's an idea that ruins everything. I had listened to *Judy Speaks* with the fear that it might make me like her less. It hadn't occurred to me it would make *me* less likeable.

I spent half my childhood in a house that sheltered an addict of one sort or another. I learned how to love and care for people with these problems. I became thrilled by the drama they provide. I knew about the best rehab centres: the strict ones where no books were allowed and, oddly, no miniskirts or shorts; the genteel ones where upper-class girls made apple charlotte, which was served and eaten on benches in the grounds. The ones that were so tough – five hours of group therapy every day with co-patients who let you get away with not one trick – that prison was more attractive.

Getting an addict into rehab is complicated, requiring luck and good timing. It's like starting divorce proceedings, making Christmas dinner and moving house all rolled into one. You have to get all the different pieces in place at the same time in order for the thing to come off. You might start by securing the finances, then seek the agreement of the addicted person, which ebbs and flows depending on all sorts of things: supply, demand and despair. Sometimes a grunt is all you get in the way of acquiescence and you've no idea if he means it but you act as if it's true. Then you have to make sure a place is available; as these things come up and go very quickly you may have two or three treatment centres in mind. Sometimes you do these three things in the reverse order. You speak to the admissions person about your case, trying to be clear and unemotional. Thinking positively, you have to arrange the sort of net of transport through which an addict cannot fall. Then, when things look promising, the pre-treatment binge must be negotiated.

184

During this time all manner of things can go wrong: the finance may fall through at a perceived lack of commitment, the acquiescence may be retracted or the place at your favoured centre may no longer exist. Sometimes the addict suddenly disappears for a few days, during which you fear the worst. You phone every number you can find. The people you speak to! You get him back. He's alive, sheepish and angry by turn, but what does that matter? You begin the process again. Hooray! A place comes up at your second choice and you leap at the chance. Some say it's brilliant! Others now say it's terrible, really worse than . . . And you falter. Should you hold out for your first choice? No, no, no, keep going or you'll lose the momentum. You're so exhausted you hardly know what you're doing. Are you the one with the problem – a fixing problem – after all? There's no time to answer. Suddenly he's in! The relief comes and all you want to do is sleep.

Only sometimes, on the grounds of the treatment centre a patch of magic mushroom grows and the inmate/patient/bastard over-indulges and is expelled with a friend and they turn up on your doorstep in disgrace at teatime and your mother takes everyone out to the local taverna for kebabs! (You have a chicken shashlik, you actually have two because the charred greasy meat is very calming.) The Christmas decorations, in the restaurant for some reason, are all still up, red lanterns, robins, gold and silver garlands in May. Or sometimes his girlfriend, she with the jangling nerves and the leopard-print cardigan, sends *your* addict a 'care' package and he's out on his ear before the weekend. And you take a deep breath and you fish the syringes out of the kitchen bin when he comes home and you wonder why you're the only one who seems to have seen them, but you do your homework, you make and eat an enormous cake, you turn up for your exams the next day. And if you're lucky and he agrees, the whole process begins again.

185

But sometimes it works. You can breathe again. You're going to get him back. You've got him! The old self, abandoned in teen-age, starts to re-emerge. You get to know each other. You knew he was pretty great deep down – you could always see it – but now he's far better than you ever hoped! FINGERS CROSSED!

These are powerful lessons, but I decided, quite deliberately, to waste this education. I have not looked to replicate its thrills and horrors, not for eighteen years. Judy's aura of highly charged emotion may be influenced by her drug-taking on occasion, but it's only a small part of the story, I insist. Besides, my love for her pre-dates her excessive drug use. I know now that if you love someone who is addicted to narcotics you need to give him or her a kiss and walk quietly away or you will go under too. I can't watch Judy when she's obviously suffering in this way. I flatter myself that I can tell the difference.

I turn off the *Judy Speaks* recording, replace the CD in its box, wrap it in an enormous silk handkerchief and slip it into the bottom of a large trunk, where it will be both safe and lost for ever, then I take myself off to bed.

Are
You a
Good Fan
or a
Bad Fan?

In the world of Judy Garland admirers there are only two types of fan: good and bad.* Good fans admire their Judy for her magnificent achievements: the 23 April 1961 Carnegie Hall performance, which was majestic, spectacular, devastating, candid and valiant. At Carnegie Hall Judy ensured, quite simply, that her powers of leadership and communication were to be the stuff of legend for ever. Good fans cherish the compelling 'Born in a Trunk' babyhood-to-fame musical within a musical from *A Star is Born*, which always impresses with its lavish theatrical sincerity. In that same film we love Garland's living-room recreation for her husband of the crazy production number she's been working on all day at the studio. Still in her rehearsal shirt and tights, she grabs a lamp, salt and pepper shakers and a serving trolley for props as soon as she's through the door. In this high-spirited yet tender performance of the rehearsal for a

*Or so I thought.
  Set within these pages are answers to a survey I sent to a hundred Judy fans worldwide.

performance, she both domesticates and ridicules her studio life, making it clear to her delicate husband that she is not taking any of it too seriously, pressing home to him, without saying a word, that he is her greatest love.

All good fans love the *Meet Me in St Louis* scene where Esther, fulsome, technicolored and fresh from her trolley-triumph, tells her sister at the dressing table looking-glass, 'Personally, I think I have a little too much bloom.' The pastry speech from *I Could Go On Singing*, where the pressures of performing are felt and communicated in a series of astonishingly wild outbursts, makes you feel as though you're in the room too, and then, of course, underscoring all these Judys there is Dorothy's blue-and-white yearning and ruby-coloured fortitude: that young woman's ability both to embody and transcend difficulties never disappoints.

Does your love of Judy affect any other aspects of your life, for example does it affect the way you treat people or handle situations?
Kindness

Have you ever hero-worshipped anyone else?
The Blessed Mother, St Francis, St Anthony, Marie Antoinette, Anne Frank

When do you feel closest to JG?
After a few drinks, when I'm having great cocktail conversation with extremely bright, funny people

Is there anything you know or have learned you would like to have shared with Judy?
No, I think she taught me a thing or two

Judy, to her good fans, is both the epitome of a very theatrical brand of glamour and an approachable, natural, hard-working champ. She is sophisticated and homely, humanity in its most dazzling incarnation, unassuming and captivating. It's an extraordinarily inviting combination. Who could ask for anything more?

Of course, most good fans cherish their own individual catalogue of details from Garland's life and performances over which they allow themselves a sort of proprietorial glee. When Garland promises Fred Astaire she can turn as many heads as any starlet as she walks down the street in *Easter Parade*, and achieves this by pulling a series of crazy faces that cause passers by to stop in their tracks, she taught this fan that entertainment was a species of beauty.

I love Judy in *Presenting Lily Mars*, as she unfurls the whole lovely, joyous, shimmering extent of herself: big sister, day-dreamer, romantic partner, tremulous Broadway star. It is a dewy pinnacle in Garland's beguiling early career for she is charm itself, as happy babysitting her six brothers and sisters as scaling a fence in a long evening dress to gatecrash a glamorous party. As Judy's fledgling glamour unleashes itself, reel by reel, she is unfailingly lovely, and in the nicest possible way she seems to know it too and her delight at her own considerable powers is plainly visible. This adds an extra

189

note of joy to the performance, for after years of being the girl next door/the plucky good sort/the stocky cousin, she's unarguably prime leading lady material now.

Judy Garland in Presenting Lily Mars

In my favourite scene she's at home, casually performing some scenes from *Macbeth* with her siblings when it just so happens that her – handy, this – Broadway producer neighbour comes to the house to see if she knows the whereabouts of the script she may have stolen to encourage his call.

To my mind, Judy's performance of 'I'm Nobody's Baby' at a swell party towards the close of *Andy Hardy Meets Debutante* is one of the greatest performances of her or anyone's career. Her beau has eyes for the sophisticated Daphne, cream of New York's high society but Judy's character Betsy is fairly sure that if Andy glimpses her best self – the person she is when she's singing – he will not be able to resist. In the song she will make it plain that she's no longer the obscure visiting-cousin type, homely and devoted, but a powerhouse of metropolitan allure.

When Betsy sings 'I'm Nobody's Baby', Betsy acts the song as Judy would, becoming a hapless, slightly wry girl made reckless through her unsuccessful search for love, but Judy also conveys, in a layer beneath this, Betsy's determination that her singing will win Andy Hardy over once and for all. 'I've got a song and if it doesn't wake Andy Hardy up he must be made of concrete.' Of course this whole tactical campaign is a terrible gamble. 'I'm Nobody's Baby' is all about the intricacies of being and feeling unwanted, and to wrest desire from an admirer with such a motif would be, you'd think, impossible. Wrong! It doesn't just win him over, it knocks him out. Throughout the song Betsy modulates and calculates (still with innocence) the full wattage of herself so that at times she is all brightness, but there are quieter moments, often on the more extravagant lines when she closes herself down a very little bit only to re-emerge all the more triumphant seconds later. Her singing both transforms and reveals Betsy. She presents herself as a rare discovery and, although she is belting her heart out in front of a large orchestra and a sophisticated ballroom audience, you see her strike Andy Hardy as though she's – miraculously – the most marvellous girl in the world, who is standing quietly and completely unattended in a deserted corner at a party and no one else knows it but him. By the time she sings, 'Won't someone hear my plea and take a chance on me . . .' well, he's hers all right. He begins pointing at himself, as if to say 'Me! Me! Me! I'll take the chance please. Me! Me over here!' In the second refrain of 'I'm Nobody's Baby' she positively smoulders, as much as a person in a frilly white dress with enormous puffed sleeves that are each bigger than the object of her affection's head *can* smoulder. The job is done but she cannot resist a little overtime.

The thoughts of some good fans may bend, with loyalty and discernment, towards Judy's less glamorous incarnations. Some good fans maintain that the *Pigskin Parade* performance is pure unadulterated Frances Gumm and feel a special bond with Little Miss Leather Lungs in her first full-length feature. Any fool can admire Judy Garland gliding down a staircase singing 'Who?' in yellow-gold silk satin surrounded by legions of admiring men in evening dress, but the stalwarts may prefer her in dungarees singing 'Down on Melody Farm' or in exaggerated tweed jodhpurs cavorting with cowboys and crooning 'Bidin' My Time' when her allure is more subtle but just as strong.

Good fans find her chubby *Summer Stock* incarnation very endearing. They like her more awkward shots, seeing, perhaps, in her later Hollywood gloss, an unnecessary anxiety to please, although unarguably pleasing she is too.

The hearts of good fans melt at the thought of Judy's lack of belief in her own powers. They're particularly drawn to her 'I know I'm no glamour girl' or her 'I know I'll never get a man let alone keep one' lines because they do invite one in. Good fans view Garland's modesty as monumental rather than pathological. Good fans don't need Judy to pander to Hollywood's superficialities; we like the unworldliness she displays in *For Me and My Gal* when she raises the hem of her utility skirt a good inch and a half the first time she sings 'Paree'! Good fans like Judy for the right reasons. They will speak of the injustice of cut scenes, like the tender episode in *Meet Me in St Louis* where Esther helps her mother prepare for an evening party. (One good fan recently invited me to sign a petition to have the cut scenes from the film of Lorna Luft's book *Me and My Shadows* restored. Where she intended to deliver this petition, I've no idea, she was extremely high-powered – the UN, I briefly wondered? – but I did sign.) A gathering of good fans will often rail at the cruel butchery of *A Star is Born*, which some believe cheated Judy of the Oscar she deserved. It's not great when you're lying in a hospital bed having just given birth and there are camera crews and lighting guys and make-up women waiting to film your acceptance speech and they call out Grace Kelly's name instead and the room empties quicker than you can say 'knife'. One very good and *bold* fan wrote to the Princess's heirs after her tragic accidental death in 1982, insisting that the hallowed statuette now be returned to the Garland family, where it truly belonged. I am told this man received no reply.

Good fans might, mysteriously and *sotto voce* admit that Garland's achievements have even more value *considering the difficulties she faced*: her depressions, her confusing upbringing, her bad treatment by authority figures, and her 'medication'. Good fans play down her difficulties in public as they would with a family member. Their feelings for Judy are most strongly characterised by a sensation of warmth. The most risqué Judy tale they will tell is,

LADY IN A POWDER ROOM: Oh, Judy, *never* forget the rainbow.

JG [*exiting grandly*]: Madam, how could I forget the rainbow? I've got rainbows up my ass.

If Judy Garland hadn't come into your life, what would you have missed?

I can't imagine not being a Judy fan! I'd have missed out on a hell of a lot. It'd be like my best friend not being around (sounds very corny I know) but she's very important to me, because when I'm down, I'll put on one of her torch songs and I always feel better! Or put on one of her movies. It's hard to explain, but to be able to listen to her songs and watch her films is just ... part of my daily diet!

Do you or close family suffer from problems with drugs or alcohol?
Well, my mother exaggerates a lot

Does Judy have any characteristics that you wish you had yourself?
Her innocence as a teenager. I don't have that at all

Does Judy have characteristics that you share?
We both sing, dance and act. She's so pretty and sweet

194

What attitude do you have to the parts of Judy that were difficult or less likeable?
We're only human. Judy may have been amazing but she wasn't perfect. I can be a right cow sometimes too!

Have you ever hero-worshipped anyone else?
I don't feel I hero-worship Judy, I just loved her being

Is there anything you know or have learned about life that you would like to have shared with Judy?
That there are other options apart from what you hate

When do you feel closest to JG?
When I'm defending her against people

Good fans like to go beyond the call of duty. One loyal fan I know met some sailors in New Orleans who boasted of having thrown food and a glass at Judy when she was on stage at the Talk of the Town in London, 1969. Incensed by their cruel behaviour, when the fellows went off to buy cigarettes this fan discreetly pissed in the main culprit's beer and watched him come back and drink it down.

One good fan, Scott Schechter, even went to the trouble of producing *Judy Garland: The Day-by-Day Chronicle of a Legend*, a book in which what Miss Garland did on each day of her life is catalogued. On the day I was born Judy and her soon-to-be-fifth husband Mickey Deans 'went to Caesar's Palace in Luton to see her friend Johnnie Ray in cabaret. Ray brought Judy on stage and they sang together. By the time Judy got to Talk of the Town for her show, she was fighting the flu, and had a fever; her doctor advised her to cancel the show but she went on anyway.' Judy in Luton! It's almost impossible to countenance. On the day my mother was born Judy, aged thirteen, sang at a party for Mr and Mrs Schennck given by Louis B. Mayer at the Trocadero in West Los Angeles, California. On the day my father turned twenty-one Judy Garland (herself twenty-one-and-a-half) filmed, from ten until five-fifty-five, an exterior trolley scene from *Meet Me in St Louis*. Did either of them, I wonder, spare a thought to the fact that they would be shaking hands in another twelve or fourteen years' time?

Good fans try not to claim Judy was a saint, because this is to range themselves into the category of crazy-good fans. Besides, no one's a saint, wrote one good fan, not even the saints. Yet good fans locate a moral imperative in Judy, an immaculacy of sentiment, many claiming that Judy taught them aspects of their best behaviour; above all, to respond and communicate openly and in a deeply feeling manner. In his biography, Vincente Minnelli wrote of his former wife's performance style as a natural extension of her character: 'She believed every word and her sincerity made believers of us all . . . whatever her personal tragedies – Judy's essential purity always remained. Her whole being was suffused with emotion.'

Judy teaches us to be unpretentious and to laugh at ourselves, to be like the lady in 'The Lady is a Tramp' who has no truck with graces and airs. Good fans always say, 'I always say I learned my manners from the musicals of MGM.' One lifelong ultra-good fan confided,

I think part of it is the immediacy. With Judy it's just – boom – and the connection is there. Judy has certainly taught me to extend my hand first and say, 'Hi, I'm John,' and I am painfully attuned to what people think of me or what I'm afraid people think of me and I think I operate too much on the wanting people to like me principle but along the way what I've learned is that everybody is shy, everybody is afraid to say hello first and that if you can be the one to break the ice it happens. I just shoot myself out of the cannon – it doesn't mean I'm not dripping wet with wanting everything to go well and wanting everyone to have a good time.

And then there are the crazy-good fans. Crazy-good fans will not hear a word against their heroine and are also sometimes known as sycophans, although they are not to be confused with the sicko- or even psycho-fans who range themselves in the bad fan *camp*. Crazy-good fans are so protective of Judy Garland's memory they will not actually let you speak about her for fear of what you'll say. So anxious are they that you'll slip in a 'Poor Judy' or shake your head or use the words 'sad' or 'waste' or 'pill' that they would prefer that you simply listened to the truth as they speak it. Crazy-good fans go to elaborate lengths to deter people from talking about Judy in the wrong, or indeed any, way. They police Judy's memory with passion and force. Crazy-good fans preface their Internet forums with all sorts of rules and regulations about how Judy's discussions must be structured and administered, and threaten punishments if these rules are not observed. One discussion website allocates each member with a 'warn' panel where infringements – repeat postings or the wrong kind of comments, say – are punished by a percentage points system that can lead to expulsion!

Although there are many gay people among their number, some crazy-good fans fear that the gay men and women who champion Judy Garland and claim her solely for their own do her a great disservice by marginalising her appeal to the rest of the population. They want Garland's star to be returned to the mainstream and

197

believe her appropriation by (other) gay men does her no favours in the world's marketplace. Some gay crazy and non-crazy good fans – and some bad fans – resent this view enormously. To have their devotion questioned and rejected by others who claim to know better and to know Judy better strikes them as a pitiful example of homosexual self-hatred. It's a bitter battle whose climax occurred when an enraged fan, who could no longer tolerate being corrected and criticised by Garland's staunchest defenders, sabotaged a Judy website by automatically posting blank messages every few seconds until its system was jammed and the site became inoperable. Not content with making such a statement, this angered fan also deliberately gave the site's director false clues leading to the identity of the perpetrator, which led to an incorrect accusation followed by a swift retraction and then, in a context of hovering legal action and fear of further retaliation, including an anxiety about a mail bomb attack, the site was forced to close. But do let other pens dwell on guilt and misery.

What do you think that you get from your relationship with Judy that you don't get from so-called 'real life' relationships?
Courage and bravery

Can you describe what it felt like?
It's hard to explain love! I feel smoother when I'm watching Judy. She's so adorable I feel I can touch her! She didn't die, in my opinion, because I feel near her especially when I'm watching movies or the *Judy Garland Show*. It seems like she is in front of me, in my house!

Is there anything in your nature or in your background that makes you feel particularly susceptible to loving Judy Garland?
Romanticism. A sense of isolation and pain during childhood, which JG seemed at once to embody and transcend

Have you ever hero-worshipped anyone else?
Not like JUDY. I have portraits of her tattooed on me, actually

Have you ever felt rivalry with other fans?
No, because she belongs just to me!

If you could have been a friend or partner to Judy what would you have done for her or said to her?
I would have found ways to move mountains for her if she wanted it so

Almost all crazy-good fans believe that speaking about Judy Garland's difficulties *in any way* can still do her harm. Crazy-good fans experience similar lapses of rationale when evaluating Judy's life choices. They will say that Judy Garland was a good mother because when a child of hers was ill she would sit up at his or her bedside all night, weeping. I'm not saying that she wasn't a good mother – I think she was most certainly a very interesting one, and she undoubtedly adored her children – but this episode does not prove it. The extremely heightened attitude of crazy-good fans to their heroine can sometimes echo the surge and crisis of love feelings that naturally occur in the mother of a newborn infant.

199

Bad fans savour Judy Garland's difficulties: they pile up her hospital visits and her psychiatrist rosters as children build towers with blocks. Good fans term this activity 'wallowing' and berate bad fans for it in person, on websites, across the street if necessary. 'I get so tired of people who are unhappy or miserable using Judy's unhappy or miserable moments to justify their own behaviour,' nineteen separate good fans told me. Interestingly, these good fans don't object to one using Judy's miserable or unhappy moments as catharsis, as a means of recovery or emotional support or fellow feeling when it is linked to self-improvement or an acceptable version of emotional honesty. Phew!

Bad fans memorise Garland's suicide notes, make collections of prescriptions and like to think of her as some sort of trench colleague 'in the wars'. For bad fans this is Judy Garland's supreme achievement; it is the quality of her suffering and not her vocal and communicative powers that really distinguishes her. T. S. Eliot wrote that Tennyson's poem 'In Memoriam' was a deeply religious work because of the quality of its doubt. In a similar way, bad fans see the failures in Judy Garland's life as bigger, bolder and brighter than her successes. She is most beautiful to them when viewed through a lens of pain. It is Garland's suffering that inspires and moves them, her mistreatment, her bad decisions and her instabilities that dazzle. Frequently spurred on by their own inner disarray, bad fans take heart in the fact that Judy Garland's difficulties were lived out in public, on a brightly lit stage. Bad fans like Judy Garland for what she couldn't do more than for what she could. They fetishise and elevate her disasters. A bad fan might declare Judy's 1964 concert at the Festival Hall, Melbourne, to be the pinnacle of her career, for she arrived on stage more than an hour late (after a twelve-hour train journey from Sydney), was booed, sang 'By Myself' then walked off the stage. Bad fans love the will-she won't-she factor in Judy's later performances. Bad fans prize embarrassment and feelings of excruciation above all other sensations because these are the kinds of strong feelings they prefer. Judy is, to them, the world's most glamorous ruin, a failure shrine. They compare her to their own on-off lovers, kind one moment, cruel the next. But Oh! The tension this creates!

To a bad fan contrast is everything. Almost all bad fans are on bad terms with their fathers. They feel Judy embodies and condones their worst excesses. 'Judy drank, Judy took drugs, so I can too!' their motto proclaims. Their favourite anecdote – from a friend of a friend of a friend, who used to be so . . . but now he's really lost his . . . 'I was in a lesbian night club in New York in 1968–9 and Judy came in and sang a few songs, totally out of it. Afterwards she passed round a paper bag for people's loose change and later on as I was leaving I saw a woman crouched on the stairs in a little heap, and when I peered at her closely it was Dorothy!' Their favourite Judy Garland quote is, 'Isn't it remarkable that with all the horror, with all that I've been through, I never drifted into booze or pills.' Their favourite item of Judy-related press is,

> Miss G is a talented young famous star. She is also a confirmed dope addict. Her smiling face has turned to a wet one. Her beautiful figure is now a thin shadow. King Dope has decided her fate; she has a habit which is almost incurable. Who struck Miss G down? Who failed to pick her up? What Studio officials have profited by millions of dollars due to her talent . . . pimps to the great whore, Dope.

Bad fans scour eBay for items such as Miss Garland's mortuary toe tag. A good-fan friend of mine was actually offered this not long ago by a cold caller who knew of his affiliation, but he replaced the receiver firmly when the vendor declared his purpose. Bad fans make wholly unsubstantiated claims, for example that Liza Minnelli, as a child, had a stomach pump on hand for family emergencies. Wrong! Good fans consider that bad fans seek to denigrate Judy Garland's achievements by dwelling first and foremost on her personal suffering. Feminist good fans say that this is something men have always done to women. 'What about Frank Sinatra?' one commented. 'He threw people through windows, he cancelled shows, he wasn't always around for his children. No one mentions *that*.' Some good-fan Garland historians have appendices to their books that pour disdain on those who speak of the life rather than the career.

As in any sort of arena of obsession that is beset with factions, the vocabulary chosen by individuals to discuss their Judy feelings is instantly revealing. Word order is important and so is sentence structure and body language. Instant exclamations such as 'What a shame! Poor Judy! What a tragic life!' indicate insufficient understanding and any self-respecting good fan will instantly counter this view with a sunnier one, drawing perhaps on the remarks made on the telephone by Kay Thompson to her goddaughter Liza Minnelli when Liza informed the old family friend of her mother's death: 'Let me tell you something before I hang up: she had one of the most wonderful lives that anybody ever could ask for. She had everything she ever wanted. There was nothing that, if she wanted it, she wouldn't go after . . . No matter what her complaints and tragedies and all that—'

'Yes,' said Liza.

The nearest comparison I can think of to this Judy word-sensitivity is the extra antennae new mothers have for those whose infant care beliefs veer from their own. Personally, I can't stand it when people make any sort of derogatory remark about their babies or children. I don't even like it, if I'm honest, when people say, 'She's not the world's best sleeper,' or refer without compassion to a female infant's chubby folds.

A friend of mine remarked to me yesterday, 'I put the baby down

202

at half-past six.' I hated her saying this, but I didn't quite object. To me, putting down at best means issuing insults, at worst administering poison. I know neither of these practices falls within my friend's range of babycare, but even still.

Judy Garland signing autographs in London, 1951

This spring I went to my first meeting of the Judy Garland Club. It was held in a building that is part of London University and proudly labelled SCHOOL OF PHARMACY. When I saw this sign I didn't know whether to laugh or cry. Under B in Judy Garland's address book the BEDFORD PRESCRIPTION PHARMACY is listed twice, once in type and again a page later (although the number hasn't changed) in extremely clear handwritten-by-Judy capitals. Next to each entry is the winning name BABE PEARL. Was she the world's most obliging chemist?

Although the club members were arranged in rows rather than a circle or a horseshoe shape, the gathering resembled to me a twelve-step meeting; but perhaps any group of amassed and seated random strangers on a Sunday afternoon, under bad lights in a hired hall, does. Like such meetings there was even a literature table, stacked with pamphlets and books and films. I rather hoped that someone would begin by sharing a Judy Story, how he or she first got hooked – the 'gotcha moment', as some fans describe it, when Judy gets you and that's just it for life. I wanted to hear about the joy she had brought my fellow devotees, the lengths they had gone to on her behalf. I had arrived late from the country and it was already the first

If Judy Garland hadn't come into your life, what would you have missed?
A certain soundtrack that can pull me through some of life's darker moments

Do you think you experienced many of your strongest feelings in life before you were ten years old?
Definitely. I think everyone does, although many people either forget or suppress them

Does Judy have any characteristics that you wish you had yourself?
Yes, laugh in front of miserable facts and be happier. I think I need to laugh more and more like Judy did, instead of keeping crying and blaming myself about everything. Judy loved to laugh: I wish I could enjoy more about life too

*If Judy was still alive today and in her eighties which designers
do you think should dress her?*
Hopefully she'd be able to dress herself! Just kidding ...
no designers, but whomever dresses Lauren Bacall, you
know, classy. Stylish

How would you define Judy's brand of glamour?
I think Judy's glamour was not only with her. Her era
was the Golden Age, when stars didn't show their
underwear or their genitals in public. There isn't any
glamour anymore. To me Judy's own glamour was on
stage and on screen. She was unique

What is your attitude to JG's children?
Liza Minnelli is a li'l goofy

refreshment break. On another table there was a wine box and some
tall drums of potato crisps. Suddenly I rather wished I'd brought a
tray of buns iced with *Judy* or *JG* in an indulgent pink font because
I could hardly imagine a setting that seemed less festive. The room
was quiet, the mood almost sombre. I wanted to communicate to
the assembled members that the things that occupied their hearts
also lodged in mine, but I did not know how. An odd sort of para-
lysis set in, the awkward new girl's anxiety about seeming too *this* or
not *that* enough. I mouthed the words, 'Isn't she just great!' but such
a phrase didn't seem to catch at the crisis of love feelings I wanted to
show that I shared.

It seemed to me that the fans at this meeting were so thoroughly
well-versed in Judy that there was hardly anything left to say. Their
relationship with her was all-encompassing; it was a fact of their lives

they lived with as best they could. It was too serious for casual talk. It meant too much. Any off-the-cuff pesky enquiries I might make were unsuited to the power of this 'condition'. It would be like a stranger requiring a mother to describe her feelings about her new-born child. It just wasn't speakable. You don't feel less strongly than the other people in the room, I said to myself, you're just chattier, that's all.

Saul Bellow's admiration for Berryman's treatment of his fellow alcoholics suddenly sprang into my mind. Berryman was 'grateful' and 'graceful' in accepting his co-sufferers' advice and criticisms and corrections. I thought of Berryman's AA life, and his rehab stints and sanatoria stays – conscientious in illness, almost pedantically so – he used to take taxis from his clinic to teach his seminars at the university, just as Judy would discharge herself from hospital to seize her stage.

I looked around the room and tried to feel grateful and graceful too. When you peered closely at the pattern in the carpet it spelled out, repeatedly, the word ILL.

A film show was about to start. I took a seat next to an enormous man who smiled at me warmly. 'Wake me up if I snore,' he said. I looked round for a face that appealed but the lights went down before my eyes could reap any fellow feeling.

Judy and Sid Luft attended two twelve-step meetings in California following the release of *A Star is Born*: once in Pasadena where coffee and cake were served in someone's house, and then a subsequent meeting of Drugs Anonymous in the San Fernando Valley. They did not like what they saw: 'Inside the house it was like a Frankenstein movie: low-keyed green lighting, men and women standing up to announce, "I am a user of drugs."' They left after twenty minutes and drove to Romanoff's for drinks.

Everything changes when Judy appears on a huge screen. Instantly a lighter kind of air flies into the room and there's an audible rush of excitement, a collective surge of devotion. As a group somehow, we rise to meet her. And the people sitting around me who seemed cast down or unreachable suddenly swell and bloom. We're all, it transpires, rather promising. The young girl next to me has eyes that brim and sparkle and her boyfriend tenderly kisses the side of her head. A woman behind me, it becomes clear, is astonishingly beautiful and hasn't realised. Judy, on screen, is singing 'I Can't Give You Anything But Love', wearing a long column dress covered with pictures of poppies encrusted with shiny beads and paillettes. It's a crazy dress I'm very familiar with, a little Andy Warhol-ish in style, and the intensity of the blooms is very unsettling for they are not delicate flowers but large and brash and slightly threatening up on the screen,

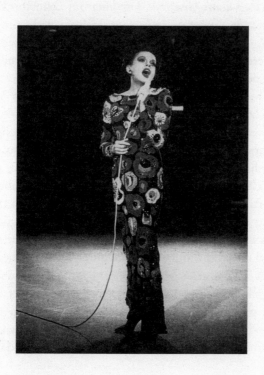

where they resemble bodily organs. Judy wore this dress on the twenty-first episode of her television series and there is a picture of her wearing it to dinner with her third husband, Mark Herron, at the opening of the Jack Jones show at the Cocoanut Grove in 1965. It makes me think of the gown Elizabeth I wears in a portrait that I saw on a school trip to a stately home, in which the fabric is covered with small eyes and ears. It's called, I remember with a wry smile, the Rainbow Portrait. The eyes and ears acknowledge the fact that Queen Elizabeth knew everything that was going on in her kingdom, the guide told us. The poppies on Judy's dress, gaudy and garish as sliced hearts, represent to me her power to feel everything in hers.

I listen to 'I Can't Give You Anything But Love' thinking how original and fresh it seems. Judy sings the lyrics with such seriousness. If it's delivered in a chirpy way this song can seem like a charmer's excuse for being a skinflint. 'Hey, I didn't get you nothing, but I sure do love ya!' A forgetful cad's quick-thinking excuse or a bounder's back-pedalling plea; the shopper's equivalent of 'You Were Always on My Mind'. What does it mean to be always on someone's mind if he can't quite treat you nicely? Nothing, is what it means.

Judy sings with melancholy warmth, a startling hymn of love and regret combined. She invests the words with a weight of meaning that would have taken their author by surprise. It would mean more to her than anything to be able to lavish luxury gifts on the song's object, and it's a failure she fully recognises in the languor of the lines. She's so sorry about the lack of things, and perhaps the muddle that caused the lack, and she takes the blame squarely. She won't go into details – it's your birthday! – but she recognises and acknowledges that she has let you down and about this she's sadder and more apologetic than she can say. However, there'll be other years when the gifts will be more than fine, and can you possibly just hang on a little until then? Can you trust me? Can you let my need of you be the present this year? And, do you know, there's no one anywhere in the universe more loved than you are now? I find myself remembering how my mother, feeling the pinch, used to 'give' us bits of furniture in the house on our birthdays when we were children. It was a bit abstract – what would my thirteen-year-old brother do with the large gilt mirror in our yellow sitting room, the only grand thing in our house? But it still felt oddly exciting.

Why do you think Judy became a gay icon?
Gay people are attracted to Judy because she didn't shun them, probably because of her involvement w/them, her marriages, etc. and to us gays, she's a symbol of surviving people's disapproval. Who knows ... she was dramatic, she was witty, she appeared strong

Why do you think Judy became a gay icon?
For the same reason she became an icon to anybody regardless of sexuality – the combination of strength and flexibility and also the talent

Why do you think Judy became a gay icon?
She could sing, dance and truly act like nobody's business, was a major film star fallen from grace at an early age, and she was often seen as the underdog, the disenfranchised, but she kept on going. That struggle, that battle every gay person can relate to

The flashes of love that I feel in my plastic chair at the School of Pharmacy as I watch aren't hard to describe. It's a small epiphany. I feel as though I am gazing at the faces of the people I adore at the happiest and most triumphant moments of their lives while glimpsing my own self – baby, child, adolescent, woman – in the most flattering and ecstatic light. The amount of pride I take in Judy's performances still surprises me. I admire her from afar but at the same time there's a familiarity that has the quality of an embrace, a distinct sensation that her magic is somehow a collaboration between us, as if she's in some way my own creation, a dream born of my own responsibilities. When I met Liza Minnelli I found myself saying, 'If I was your mother I'd be insane with pride.' To her credit she took this well. She even told me I was sweet. Well, when I watch Judy I feel this shared glow of triumph twenty times as strongly and in the texture of my admiration is woven all the pride I've ever taken in other people and all that others have taken in me.

I sang 'I Can't Give You Anything But Love' at one of my sisters' birthdays. I was so sad at that time I sometimes forgot if I was female or male. I had come down to her party from Oxford,

bringing with me the handsomest boy in college as a sort of deco-
ration, for I had literally bumped into him in the street on the way
to the bus.

'Don't suppose you want to come to a party in London?' I asked.
'Should be good.' I issued the invitation in the most casual way I
knew. It worked! 'All right,' he said. It was a small miracle. In his
jacket pocket was a half-bottle of whisky, which we shared. On the
bus he talked very romantically about a girl called Chloe I had been
at school with and referred to her as the nicest girl he knew. I could
hardly agree. He told me that in the summer he hoped to come to
London and take a lot of drugs. I looked at him severely. 'You are the
sort of person who shouldn't take aspirin two days running.' We
stopped off at my flat and I washed my hair and changed into a
velvet dress and then we took a bus to my sister's where I stood up
in front of about forty people and sang,

> Now that it's your birthday,
> I don't know what to do.
> Can't give you a Thunderbird,
> Or a penthouse with a view.
> Can't even buy a little present,
> I'm much too broke, I find.
> But there is a way
> I can save the day,
> And I sure hope you don't mind.

My date, who was lying on the floor by this point, flexed his limbs
and closed his eyes. Perhaps this is the most embarrassing moment
of his life, I thought. My sister took it very well. And I had bought
her a present; not a huge one, but a lipstick and matching nail polish
in a good cherry colour named Très très Dior. I prefer the shade
called Rouge de Fête now.

211

Judy herself attended a meeting of the Judy Garland Club on 29 November 1964. She was tremulous at first, as though unsure about the sort of reception she would receive from a room filled with . . . her sincerest admirers. It's an extraordinarily touching image. When she left after singing 'Make Someone Happy' and 'I Wish You Love' she addressed the club with a brief speech: 'Goodbye and God bless you all. I thank you so much. I couldn't have imagined a sweeter or a nicer thing than today and I'm terribly and eternally grateful.'

After the screening the people in the room at the Judy Garland Club seem just about the nicest that I've ever met. An extremely elegant gent shows me the drawing he did of Judy on stage at the Talk of the Town in 1957, which she signed for him. 'Do I really look like a Chinaman?' she asked. Another tells me how Judy often borrowed his back when writing autographs for fans at the stage door after shows. 'You may touch it if you like!' he grins. There is much talk of spending one's last shillings on flowers for Judy, then walking home twelve miles after concerts in the rain, flying, on cloud nine. Someone tells me that a taxi-driver friend of his described how Judy sometimes used to go and sit in the green wooden shelter in Belgrave Square in the middle of the night when she couldn't sleep, and play cards and entertain the cabbies. 'My nanny took me to see *The Wizard of Oz* when I was a boy,' another offers, 'and from that moment on I knew I would marry her, I just couldn't decide many children we should have.' Some of the younger fans ask me how I came to Judy and I mention that as a child her sensitivity seemed both to mirror and elevate my own. 'When you say that,' a young girl tells me in a tiny voice, 'I feel as though you're talking about me.' Her eyes begin to fill, as do mine. We speak animatedly, now that Judy has given us, in some way, a sort of permission. And we speak freely because we know there isn't a need to be wary.

When at a crossroads in life do you ever ask yourself, 'What would Dorothy do?'
No, Dorothy was a character. 'What would Judy do?' Well, I might look at reality a little different, but I doubt I'd solve my problems by downing speed, barbiturates and alcohol

How would you define Judy's brand of glamour?
Even in her 60s overly beaded pants suits, she exuded an iconic fashion sense

What do you think that you get from your relationship with Judy that you don't get from so-called 'real life' relationships?
Judy doesn't tell me what to do

Does Judy have any characteristics that you share?
We both don't let anyone get in our face. We both will tell u what we think weather u like it or not

The fans I am most drawn to, good, crazy-good or even bad, are those who consider that their ordinary personal development has been greatly aided by their love of Judy Garland, as mine was. I hear this again and again. I like people who believe that Judy has improved them in some way. I like the people for whom Judy was a beacon of hope in dark days because of the way she seemed both

213

> *What is the best thing that JG has brought into your life?*
> The feeling that it is ok to be upset

> Oh I did not know that you ask me that lots of questions ... you have to know I am a German man ... I love the movie the wizard of oz ... and I like her music ... her voice ... but I am not fanatic fan ... you understand ... ?? ... thank you ...

to embody and transcend pain. 'Judy provides a certain soundtrack that can pull me through some of life's darker moments' is what many of us feel. I'm delighted by those who tell me she helped to mend a hole in a heart or she made a large heart even bigger by lodging in it. I love it when people say, 'My love of Judy makes me my best self.'

The people who feel this way about Judy sense they owe her an enormous amount in return, but what to do with this feeling? If you had been a partner or friend to Judy Garland what would you have said or done, I've asked of every devotee I've met. Most have finely honed their fantasy care-taking roles. We would expect nothing from her, we all agree; we would have made everything easy for her, taken away the stresses and strains of everyday life so that she could feel as free and calm and happy as possible and *only sing when she wanted to.*

But what if she never wanted to sing again? Would you stand for that, I never quite ask. Would we stand for it, we good fans? Oh, but that's not what *she* would have wanted, we answer ourselves, perhaps.

For those who talk about their fantasy of working for her,

being part of her daily rituals, I sometimes say, 'But what would that have consisted of exactly in terms of, you know, day-to-day things?'

I would have died for her! I would, for her, have gone to the ends of the earth!

Dying and fleeing! Perfect! Of course!

The tenderest reply to this question came from a young Brazilian girl: 'If I were Judy's friend or related I would take care of her. I would put her in my home to live with my family, give her food, warm bed, treat her as a doll. I would give her the treatment she needed to leave the alcohol and pills without confine or mistreat her. I would brush her hair, wash her clothes, cook her food. And of course, leave the house clean of drinks or any other product with alcohol. I would do anything to keep her safe and alive.'

My friend Brian, a devoted fan, came very close to fulfilling his dream (my dream) of working for Judy Garland, of being with her regularly, at her side, attending to anything and everything, of *helping*. A friend of his, the costume designer Bumble Dawson, who had worked with Judy Garland on *I Could Go On Singing*, mentioned to Judy that Brian would be a good person to have around. Some days later a card arrived at his home:

Thank you for your letter which I told Judy about and she was pleased. She is supposed to go to New York on Thursday next but will be back . . . ring her up at Belgravia 7843 or write to 4 Cadogan Lane and I'm sure something could be arranged. Tell her that I spoke to her about you. Yours, Bumble Dawson.

Brian telephoned Judy and talked about the possibility of becoming her personal assistant. The conversation went very well. Towards the close of the call, he said, 'You know I've loved you all my life.'

'Well dear,' she said. 'It's getting terribly late . . .'

You *never* say that in a job interview, friends scolded him afterwards, shaking their heads. *Really!* Brian sent her flowers to thank her for the conversation. They had arranged to meet the following week. All the signs were good, but five days later Judy Garland died. The flowers arrived too late but they travelled back with her, with Brian's love, in the aeroplane to New York.

Knowing I am of the fold, fans from all over the world contact me regularly. One man, Marc Charbonnet, a flamboyant and distinguished interior designer from New York, with a very tender heart and excellent manners, wrote to me of his Judy love. He is now my Judy-best-friend.

Dear Susie,

My father, we were never close, was on the advisory board of the Salvation Army, I attended a sale and found an old album named (prophetically) *Forever Judy*, 75 cents. I saw that 'Over The Rainbow' was the first song and bought it for my friend's little sister. She never got it. In the car on the way home my father asked what I purchased. As a kid I used to get backhand remarks from him over many decisions I'd made. Never physical, but sometimes very bruising verbally. I thought I was going to get a ripe rant from him on this instance. I sheepishly showed him the album cover, expecting some caustic remark, and his face kind of lit up, with him saying, 'Ahh . . . Judy. Dear Judy, poor Judy.' Surprised, I asked him why. He explained to me that in World War II, stationed in different places, he would hear the recording of 'Over the Rainbow', and it made him and the boys think of home. He fondly remembered a friend of his, a roommate in one of his stations during his service in the Air Force, who had been crazy about Judy Garland. Most people had pin-ups of Betty Grable, Hedy Lamarr or Lana

Turner. But this guy had a cute picture of Judy Garland and swore that, one day, he'd meet her. Later it was announced she had married the composer David Rose, and this young man's heart was broken. (I would later learn how Judy would find out that her friend Lana Turner had married Judy's love, Artie Shaw, and her heart was broken – I wondered if Judy realized that hearts were broken when she married David Rose.) My father told me more, and I listened. It was an unusual connection between my father and me.

I also vaguely remembered my mother and father watching *The Judy Garland Show* on Sunday nights. I feel guilty to this day, remembering that I acted like I really wanted to change the channel and watch *Bonanza*. I didn't. Cowboys were the thing to be, but Judy Garland was the thing I really wanted to know. I remember, on the show, her crying at the end of her runway with the light bulbs and the wobbling vibrato and all of the emotion – it was like a kind of supreme voltage reaching out of the television set and grabbing me by the eyes and ears. While I would sit there, pretending not to be transfixed, my father would begin talking about Judy again. He told me how it was so sad that such a talent had withered, and we discussed it. These were the first conversations that I had with my father about something outside of our lives. It wasn't something about school not being right, or older siblings complaining about the way I had treated them, or that I had been mistreated by them. It wasn't about nuns calling on the phone to talk about things that hadn't shown up at school, or priests complaining that I had been late with my altar services. I would never have guessed it could happen, and still find it remarkable. Judy talk ended up being the familial glue between my father and me, in place of the sports talk that is for other dads and sons. It took something that excited us both in different ways, something sparkling, amazing and legendary. It took Judy. Judy was a real person, which shows in her performances. But she was big enough, strong enough, vulnerable enough, kind enough, cross enough, down-and-out enough, chic enough and even androgynous enough – to touch all hearts.

Later, I learned that a woman named Joyce, who worked at the pharmacy that filled my family's prescriptions, adored Judy Garland. She saw an album under my arm one day when I was there picking up a package, and glowingly reminisced to me about how she would save her money to go to Judy's films, and would watch her on television many years later. I asked her if she'd like me to play Judy over the telephone for her. She thought it would be wonderful. So I would actually telephone the pharmacy and she would get on the line, and I would leave the receiver next to a stack of albums that could drop automatically on to my turntable. I let her know that she could stay on the line as long as she wanted and listen all she liked. Sometimes I'd pick up the phone and realize that after three or four sides of album she was still there, waiting for more. There were obviously no phone orders at this pharmacy when Judy was playing. Within a year I owned over forty albums and a lot of other Garland paraphernalia.

I talk Judy with Marc at least twice a week. He alerts me to her best work for he knows much more than I. We'll fire off messages to each other in the insomniac portions of the night when the tips of one's dilemmas always seem enormously sharp.

SUSIE: When Judy sings, 'Remember neighbors, when you work for Mother Nature, You get paid by Father Time' in *Summer Stock*, what do you think she means?

MARC: I always presumed those lines meant if you toil on the
    land you'll live to a ripe old age, fresh air and physical labour
    being health-giving etc. etc.
SUSIE: Oh, OK.

I am a good fan. Of course I am, but there is a little part of me that's very
bad. I admire Judy for a quality I don't possess, and don't quite wish
to, and that is her incaution. I am a cautious person, sensible and
controlled, *defended* – modern metropolitan life to a certain extent
demands this – but what gigantic personal cost goes into maintain-
ing the defence budget every single day.

I have a little caution prescription that requires continual
acknowledgement and ticks and renewing:

> Keep yourself to yourself.
> Do not show vulnerability.
> Don't let people know what you think.
> Don't rely on anyone but yourself.
> Try not to be so intense.
> BE CAREFUL!
> Don't be any trouble.
> Hide your feelings for they may be used against you.
> Cover your needs.
> Be jolly but not outlandish.
> Be cheery but not inane.
> Be thoughtful but not anxious.
> Make the smallest amount of demands possible.
> Be intelligent but not too clever by half.
> Don't be angry.
> Don't keep people waiting.

Judy Garland adhered to none of the above and I love her for it, yet I know this is wrong, for the word *incautious* actually features in the coroner's report on her death.

Incaution has a monumental allure for me. It's something I love and require in all my heroes. But why do I want those I love to be in danger? Surely that's the antithesis of love. Have I got it wrong? Am I far more bad than good?

At a concert Liza Minnelli gave at the Opéra Garnier in Paris in 2006, the audience was far from prepossessing.* As we lingered under chandelier light on the broad steps of the Garnier's impressive marble horseshoe staircase, waiting to go in, hysteria gleaming on our faces, we did not like what we could see. There were terrible men in business suits whose emerging hands and faces were suntanned to a colour beyond human belief. Their mouths were so hard-looking that no joke or pleasantry could penetrate. Some of these men, I believed, had not laughed for years, except perhaps at the severe financial or romantic misfortunes of their friends. The women in dark clothes with gilt buttons who accompanied them had faces stunned by repeated cosmetic procedures, the skin eerily smooth as though freshly pressed, the noses pointy and chiselled, the mouths flat and taut from the cutting and sewing, the pumping and filling. Even their hairstyles, heated and stretched and rolled to perfection, lacked any human connotations. I turned to my friend Alex and inhaled sharply – we were each six months pregnant and it was to be our last crazy spree – 'I don't know what Liza is going to do with this audience.' They not only appeared to be wholly without feelings; they looked like the feeling of a feeling would be physiologically disastrous. 'It will be like trying to get blood into a stone.'

We took our seats and found a small enclave of fans who were more likeable. A high-spirited woman in a pink-and-white bouclé

*It was a charity event so it was not a typical Liza Minnelli crowd.

220

suit and a very dressy ponytail that had been inserted by a hairdresser declared that she'd driven all day and night from Seville to see Liza. Two men had fled Brooklyn for Paris to celebrate their anniversary. They owned the bowler hat from *Cabaret*, which they had bought at auction and installed in a glass case in their living room as a conversation point. 'That dreadful man made her sell it,' they said. 'So disgusting, but we got it for next to nothing!'

If you could have been a friend or partner to Judy what would you have done for her or said to her?
Made her feel important, and try to help her fight for her rights as a person and just give her love and care like she deserved and never got

If Judy Garland hadn't come into your life, what would you have missed?
A great talent and the love for the era that the most incredible woman lived in (my granny not Judy)

What is the single thing about JG you most admire?
She had a naughty, wicked humor

Does Judy have characteristics that you share?
A sense of propriety

221

At eight o'clock sharp Liza Minnelli came on stage to a standing
ovation, resplendent and gracious under the opera house's extravagant Chagall ceiling, with its rainbow-coloured ballerinas. 'It's the
best thing he ever did, if you ask me,' I murmur. Liza looks healthy,
which is an enormous relief. The cheers last for an age, then we all
sit down, perching on the edge of our *fauteuils*, guiltily sipping
champagne from plastic cups.

Liza begins with 'Bonjour Paris' from *Funny Face*, a song that's
extremely difficult to sing because it has masses of words, no powerful melody and is really a song for three voices. It is performed in
the film next to assorted Paris landmarks by bookshop-assistant-
turned-fashion model (it happens) Audrey Hepburn, photographer
Fred Astaire and Liza's godmother, the editor of fictional *Quality
Magazine*, Kay Thompson. It is a valiant effort but not altogether
successful. Liza is short of breath and it is hard to give a song your
all when it is taking so much out of you. She continues singing the
next few numbers without a great deal of distinction until suddenly,
in the middle of 'Alexander's Ragtime Band', something happens.

The old Liza is back, she's in her element and the entire audience leaps out of its seats spontaneously, both in the middle of the song and again at the end. It's a stunning moment, an extreme meeting point where a great weight of expectation collides with an extremely high-calibre performance, forcing hysteria to bloom. I thought it wasn't going to happen. Even the baby kicks wildly beneath my artfully draped grey velvet dress. During the rest of the performance, in 'Maybe This Time', in 'Who Cares So What?' from the stage version of *Cabaret* and in 'New York, New York' similar high moments are glimpsed.

I love Liza. I love her faith in faith and her hope in hope. At her last concert at the Albert Hall in London I was so caught up with watching her, with feeling with her, with wanting to protect and celebrate her, that I slipped my diamond engagement ring off my finger and it was only the fear of taking out her eye (I was very near the stage) and endless domestic repercussions that stopped me from flinging it at her there and then. Liza is completely unafraid of embarrassment. Who else on earth could sing a very long song about a woman who falls in love with a deaf mute with whom she must communicate through sign language, only to find that it's one of the best kinds of connection she has ever known? This song about tremulous and fledgling silent love is accompanied by Liza's own rough sign language interpretation of what she is singing, so that her hands make abrupt and complicated dancing and soaring movements every now and then as her voice explains the intricacies of an affair conducted without any conventional speech. Who else could pronounce with a straight face that, 'Everything I know in life I learned from Charles Aznavour!' Can this really be true? For the next few weeks this becomes my catchphrase too, causing many confused looks among family and friends.

It's not how I operate, but Liza's slightly surreal life philosophy cannot be denied. 'If you don't like your memories rewrite 'em,' she said to me when I met her. It was a very exciting thing to be told. Of course! Yet I left this truism, this falsism, out of the interview I was writing for a newspaper at that time, for she had a nasty court case pending and my fear was that a clever lawyer might just be able to make something of it.

Liza doesn't seem vulnerable on stage in Paris tonight. She doesn't need us, her audience; our applause is great – and hooray for it, honey! – but its not feeding her, it is in no way a matter of life and death. She's *working*. It's a job she obviously loves, one at which she excels, but it is a job in a way I don't quite think it was for her mother. She shows her lack of airs and graces by kicking off her high shoes and ripping out false eyelashes. This is a signal that we have the real person before us. She says that the MAC make-up people are darlings to sponsor her because she sweats so much all her cosmetics really enhance is her towel. She says this is the best night of her life as she said when I saw her at the Albert Hall in 1991 and 2002 and at the London Palladium in 1986.* The baby is kicking so hard my eyes begin to water. Does she know something I don't? Liza performs three spectacular encores and bids us adieu. We are hers. Even the stiff French audience, who had earlier slightly failed to convince as people, are screaming endearments and waving and beaming.

Afterwards we eat expensive salads in the Café de la Paix and curse our heartburn. I feel very flat and I don't quite understand why. Of course, being in Liza's presence is so exhilarating that the Liza-less hours that follow always feel relentlessly drab, but it's more than that. I'm trying to suppress something in myself. In previous concerts Liza has struck me as more unhinged, fluttering wildly at her extremities, all sorts of complex battles appearing to go on inside her and the tension and pull between health and ambition and the slight possibility

*She also said this at her concert at the London Coliseum last Thursday. Then she looked out into the audience and told us, 'You're my family now.' YIPPEE.

of disaster that was audible in the occasional catch in her throat added something. There was something at the Garnier concert that made me feel excluded. It was Liza's control. She was presenting a particular version of herself: Liza the indomitable showman who socks it to us. Life is good! Life is great! Say yes! Where her mother's heart trembled bravely before us in the face of unspeakably bad times and spectacularly good ones, Liza sometimes dazzles her audience with an elaborate sequin-studded shrug. Yet it's not indifference. It's philosophy. So what? Maybe next time? The world goes around. Liza's stage personality is a curious mixture, for there's an outpouring of undoubtedly strong emotion and at the same time a loud shriek of 'You know, I really don't care!' It's all obviously keenly meant, keenly felt, but despite

Does Judy have any characteristics that you wish you had yourself?
I'm fine with myself. I just wish I had her

Is there anything you know or have learned about life that you would like to have shared with Judy?
Not really ... if I were ever to meet a really famous person that I admire, I wouldn't have anything to say to them ... just either jump up and down and scream, or just stand there and then fall over, speechless :o)

Does Judy have any characteristics that you wish you had yourself?
I wish that I had her beauty. Unbeknownst to her, she was a truly beautiful woman

Does Judy have any characteristics that you share?
We're both short with brown hair and we're both very musical people

Does Judy have any characteristics that you wish you had yourself?
The voice, obviously, and, in many of her screen performances and in what I know of her private life, a greater ability to trust others no matter how often she has been hurt and betrayed, and a degree of innocence

Do you think you experienced many of your strongest feelings in life before you were ten years old?
Some before 10 but definitely before 12

When you find yourself at a crossroads do you ever ask yourself, 'What would Dorothy do?'
Hahaha. No

this it's hard on occasion to know exactly where the sincerity lies. Yet this doesn't result in any sort of tension. Her performance in Paris was remarkably smooth and even. Yet for a member of the audience this can be almost frustrating. Where's your way in with 'So what?'

My most excruciating experience with a Judy Garland fan (a very good one) occurred in the gift shop of the Judy Garland Birthplace Museum in Grand Rapids, Minnesota, on what would have been Judy's eighty-fifth birthday. Cakes are baked and iced blue and white, and candles are lit. The hairdresser in the local strip mall has a special offer. The Saw Mill Inn, adjacent to the museum, is filled with the devoted. A free basket of popovers arrives with every meal. The museum gift shop is freshly stocked with Dorothy cookie jars and assorted Oz bric-à-brac. Real life Dorothys, both tiny and gigantic, gambol about to honour their heroine. A scarecrow frightens the children a little too vehemently. Fourteen of Garland's costumes are displayed on stackable boy-sized mannequins, including her Blackglama mink. A munchkin or two, guests of honour, are gracious in their reminiscences. In the bar the night before the unselfconscious hard-core fans downed soft drinks and belted out 'Swannee' while another cooler, sharper Judy crew (these things are relative) shook their heads and smoked and almost mocked.

I linger in the gift shop of the Judy Garland House, where some of Judy's disciples are discussing her. The place is a little altar to Judyism: there are ruby slippers and blue gingham as far as the eye can see. I finger an alarm clock on which Glinda floats magisterially and stroke a Tin Man lunch pail. One woman is eating a piece of the Judy birthday cake baked by the Judy museum. It has a marbled interior and a pale buttercream filling. The woman is also celebrating an anniversary. It is exactly twenty-one years since she last drank or drugged. I eavesdrop, jiggling the baby who is now eight months old. The woman's voice halts and starts with emotion.

'I was so marked by her. My life was. I was deeply marked when she died. A part of me died. My parents didn't know what to do. My aunt wrote me a condolence card. I remember. I was so shocked. I grieved so hard. I couldn't stop crying. My parents bought me a car to try and cheer me up. It was only junk, but they didn't know what to do. My whole experience of college was different to what it would have been if Judy had lived. If she could have only lasted another twenty years until the insights were there. Until Betty Ford. They could have understood everything from the addiction to the co-dependency to the depression. The insights are there now . . . If the TV show could have been a success and sustained her a bit longer, turned a profit. Because we only saw one half of what she could do.

There was so much more to her. Directing, producing, writing – she could have done it all. She could have had a production company with her children instead of . . . she could be here with us today. They could all have been directing and producing.

'Imagine a healthy Judy. If she could have lived until her eighties. The day she died, I mean when she was ill in Hong Kong, I sneaked out of school every afternoon to telephone my mother and see if she was OK. Then when she died, I just couldn't believe it. I had to be told three times, I—' her face is suddenly twisted and creased with grief.

It is then I realise that Judy's son Joe Luft, a man I heard introduced the previous evening as one of the 'most loved children in history', is standing within hearing, taking some photographs on his mobile phone, oddly, of a Glinda, Good Witch of the North clutch bag. I think of his sister Lorna saying to me fiercely, 'She was everyone's legend but she was *our mom.*'

With a sharp anxiety flash I try to indicate wordlessly to the woman that it is not quite right to be talking of her grief in this way when Judy's actual son can hear, but she has tears dripping down her. Her pain is real and I want to attend to her and to Joe and to the baby in my arms who is beginning to cry, but I can't manage the situation so I move away smiling at everyone, bowing slightly, apologising. Later, when I recount this almost unbearable situation, I'm told by all and sundry, 'It's not something he hasn't heard a million times before . . .'

That's neither here or there, is what I think.

Joe Luft is certainly one of the most gracious men in history. Quiet and self-contained, often shielded by a baseball cap, he thanks everyone personally for coming to the event, taking photographs of us all. He even serenades the baby with the Simon and Garfunkel song 'Cecilia' (her name) one evening and tells me repeatedly how lovely she is. The meaningful glances of some of my Judy friends, full of wonderment and congratulation, say, 'Oh my God! Judy Garland's son is singing to your child!' All the Judy fans at the convention seem to adore my baby. Is it because she's not much younger than Frances Gumm was when she made her stage debut?

Once I sat next to Joe Luft as a twenty-minute reel of movie clips was being shown, a collage of some of his mother's best work. At the end of the film I saw him mouthing along to some of the words from 'Over the Rainbow', his soft eyes marvelling, full of love, for the creature on the screen. It was, for me, a very overwhelming sight.

'Very overwhelming,' I said to him clumsily. 'Does it feel all right?'

'It's fine,' he says quietly, and then, 'it's good.'

*

I like the thought of Judy owning a profitable production company and being in charge for a change. The idea that we had only seen a fraction of what she could do was wildly stimulating until I thought that the last thing she needed in her life was more work. More food, more money, more stability, more holidays, more rest and better clothes most certainly, more *me*, but not more to do.

I think of something Mickey Rooney wrote in his autobiography *Life is Too Short* (does he still think that at eighty-seven, I ask when we meet. He does.) 'Judy always had a lot of takers around her and few givers. "Are you still alive, Judy? Are you still breathing Judy? Just sign this contract. Now sing."'

Later I look up the Betty Ford Center on the Internet. It was founded in 1982, thirteen years after Judy's death. Thirteen years is an awfully long time to hold on. The prices are impressive. They even treat children between seven and twelve.

I leave the shop with a mountain of Judy merchandise for my nieces tucked under my arm. If you want someone to be well so they can give you more of themselves, is that all right?

That night, when the museum is closed, my new friend Marc, who owns one of the largest collections of Garlandia in the world, is allowed an hour alone in the new exhibition as a thank-you for the hundreds of items he has given and loaned. He invites me to join him in a little dressing-up party. *He has keys to all the cabinets.* We slide open the doors one by one. Unlocking a display case in a museum and taking things out and handling them and trying them on seems wicked, and even though we have permission to be there I feel like one of the two bad mice. As the glass door yields the cabinet's contents I draw out a leopardskin hat and muffler that Judy wore in the nineteen-forties and put them on.

Instantly I feel giddy in the extreme, a curious mix of anxiety and delight. It's a lovely tension, like remembered stage fright after a smash-hit success, I imagine. I pose for some photographs. 'Do I look Judyish?' It's a long way from blue gingham. I pick up the white and gold microphone from the *Judy Garland Show,* open my mouth and thrust my hand up high in the air. If my friends could see me now.

We examine Judy Garland's make-up trunk, easing open all the drawers. Inspecting her large stash of health and beauty aids feels almost too intimate, like reading private letters or a diary. As well as the usual lipsticks and eye shadows there is a wooden stick for fluffing up her hair, there are black fine-tooth combs and a packet of aromatic ammonia – smelling salts, I presume – so that, feeling faint or drowsy, she could still make it on to the stage. I shake my head. Then there are Beauté Lift instant face-lifts, little skin-coloured elastic contraptions you attach to your head and ears and watch the lines disappear. There are toothpicks in a little sachet, one used. There's

231

a faded four-leaf clover encased in a disc of glass. I am in awe in the presence of these relics. I sense a feeling I used to have as a child, that I mustn't look at or go into things too closely and never ask. Let her rest, I tell myself.

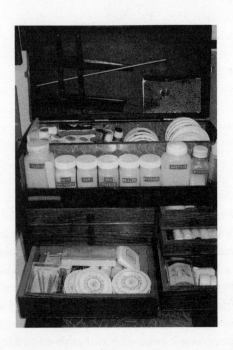

I close the drawers very carefully, and without deciding to do so mouth the word goodbye. I'd like to slip a little message in there, some words of appreciation from one friend to another through the years. I have a faded baby-sized envelope from the museum's gift shop that came with a three-inch Glinda card. In my best copper-plate writing I will compose a note to her and insert the envelope into the trunk to stiffen and yellow. What a pleasing reworking of history that would be. To Dear Judy, I'd write, To Dearest Judy . . .

and then what? I think of the best notes I've received from my father over the years, things that sit at the bottom of my jewellery box even now. I think of the love letters my older daughter Mary writes me, but nothing's quite right. If I could only think up some sort of final, saving maxim in which love, hope and encouragement mingle with startling jokes. Dear Judy, Please know how much I—. My thoughts grow wilder until they're almost blasphemy. Dear Judy, Remember this: The show doesn't have to go on! All best love, Susie. I've never signed off a letter with 'all best love' before. Ought I to add the word forever? What was it James Mason said at Judy's funeral about her enormous capacity to give love only being equalled by her vast need of it? Isn't that true of almost anyone?

I brush a bead of sweat from my brow. The leopardskin hat is roasting my scalp. Dear Judy, whose loving kindness and – Dear Judy, Dear – Dear Judy, I hope . . . and then a barrage of song lines come to me, 'Together, wherever we go,' and 'If you're ever in a mess, SOS' and 'Won't someone hear my plea and take a chance on me?' and 'Once you've found him, build your world around him' and then snippets from the tributes of her friends and admirers float about in my brain. John Carlyle: 'You know I miss Judy so much. The laughter: the laughter! Judy would laugh. It would come from the bottom of her feet. Why do they make such a big deal of the fact that she took forty Ritalin a day?' 'When you were with her she made you feel like the only person in the world,' my Judy-friend Brian says; his eyes brimming with love are vivid, even over the telephone. Lucille Ball once commented to distinguished Garland historian John Fricke that Judy was the funniest woman in Hollywood, that she made *her* look like a mortician. This story has always made me smile because I've met a few morticians in my time, all of whom have come equipped with a genuinely startling line of ultra-black humour. In *Party of One* the writer Clifton Fadiman pronounced that Garland's legs were as 'beautifully and smoothly turned as a couplet by Alexander Pope'!

I've often gazed at the possessions of the famous: James Joyce's pipe and candle snuffer in Dublin, for example; Cardinal Wolsey's hat in Oxford; Giuseppe Verdi's slender conducting baton in a Milanese museum; and none of it has meant very much. Yet these things in Judy's make-up trunk are astonishingly moving, the little sticks and pots and tubes and tricks she regularly used. Marc suddenly whisks a small cake of sky-blue eye shadow out of one of the drawers and presses it into my hand.

'No!' I say.

'Yes!'

If you could have been a friend or partner to Judy, what would you have done for her or said to her?
That it is most important to love yourself and if you can't do that then, at least, don't hate yourself

When did you first discover your Judy feelings?
I was 15. My Dorothy feelings, when I was 4

When and how did you first discover your Judy feelings?
I fell in love with her at the age of 3 when I was taken to *The Wizard of Oz* – my first film – in 1939

Is there anything you know or have learned about life that you would like to have shared with Judy?
As a Christian, I would've liked for her to meet my Lord and Savior Jesus Christ

Is there anything in your nature or in your background that makes you feel particularly susceptible to loving Judy Garland?
I feel like her singing came from her soul. That's what her songs do to me – they affect my soul whether they are happy or sad songs. When I was a baby one of the only things that would make me stop crying was the song 'Somewhere Over the Rainbow'

Your questions are really creepy and you are assuming that everyone loves and is infatuated with her. It is rare to find a die-hard Judy Garland fan and you would have an easier time trying to find a Latino man that speaks 7 languages fluently. Before you send this questionnaire out to any more people I would seriously rethink your questions

I squirrel it into my bag before he has a chance to change his mind. I glance up at the CCTV camera above our heads. Marc does actually own the trunk, but even still.

Later, another important collector approaches me, 'The trouble with buying Judy's dresses is that they require so much effort. It's like having a child: you have to store it exactly in the right conditions, look after it really carefully. Like a baby it's constant, like a handicapped child.'

'Does it require continual maintenance, then?' I am intrigued. 'I mean, once you get the Smithsonian or wherever to advise on storage do you have to treat it in a special way every day, or weekly or make sure it's upkeep is . . . steam it regularly and stuff and empty the sleeves and—'

235

'Well no, not exactly. You just have to store it in a careful way that . . .' his voice trails off. I was fairly sure before, but now I am certain this fellow has no children.

Some of my favourite Judy Garland dresses

Some of her uglier gowns

On the morning of Judy Garland's eighty-fifth birthday I attend a screening of *The Wizard of Oz* in a cinema that is a few hundred yards from the house where she was born in Grand Rapids. It's a bright house, white-framed like a childish drawing, filled with light. On the ground floor are four interconnecting square rooms simply furnished. I lift a saucepan at the fancy green-and-white enamel stove

236

in the kitchen, whistling 'Life is Just a Bowl of Cherries'. In the sitting room I brush my fingers on the black keys of the baby grand. I linger on the staircase where the Gumm sisters often rehearsed their numbers: 'When My Sugar Walks Down the Street'; 'You're the Cream in my Coffee'; 'But What do I Care?' I lean over the banister as Esther Smith does when singing to John Truett in *Meet Me in St Louis*, shortly after which he says her violet scent reminds him of his grandmother.

I feel romantic and madcap. When prying eyes are averted I even climb into Judy's bath, which is in a little tiled room at the top of the stairs. It's tiny and makes me feel like a big baby! For a second I wonder about removing my clothes, but I'm not insane. In her parents' bedroom I toy with Judy's little pink doll in its broderie anglaise dress. In the girls' bedrooms I perch for a moment on the edge of the bed. Frank Gumm used to sing his daughter 'Danny Boy' before she went to sleep, as my husband does to our older daughter Mary, accompanying himself on her quarter-sized guitar. The Gumm family's former nanny said that Judy's bedtime-resistance ploys would often involve begging for another piece of bread with Mrs Gumm's delicious peach conserve thickly spread on it, which she'd eat walking from one end of the kitchen cabinets to the other. 'She was so intelligent. She wasn't spoiled at all. She just wanted to sing. I didn't think she could ever get any better than when she was small, but she did.' Could Mrs Gumm have been such a terrible stage mother if she took the trouble to make her family jam?

Over the road, next to the strip mall, the cinema is packed with Judy fans and their descendents. The aisles are strewn with baby carriages. Advertisements for Christian bookshops fill the screen. Rumour has it that Ruth Duccini, a genuine munchkin, is in the audience, but if she is I can't make her out. An elderly munchkin and a little old lady look remarkably similar. Everyone says that when you actually meet the munchkins they are always bigger than you think! I met Ruth after the film, a woman who joined the Harvey Williams Midget Troupe in 1937, driving to Culver City from Minnesota to be one of the munchkins of Oz at Judy Garland's side. 'I'm proud I was a munchkin,' she told me sweetly, 'but I can't be one all the time, dear.'

'Well, of course!' I agree.

The auditorium darkens and the credits roll. The baby is sitting squarely on my knee, cooing. It's her first time. I brace myself for an avalanche of emotion.

As 'Over The Rainbow' begins I am struck by how attentively Toto listens to his mistress's voice. It's the closest I have seen a dog

What attitude do you have to the parts of Judy that were difficult or less likeable?
She was a complete human being. No one is a saint (including the saints)

Not to give up, to not let people put you down, or make you feel inferior, to realise that men aren't the be-all and end-all, and to know your own self-worth!

Do you think you experienced many of your strongest feelings in life before you were ten years old?
Nope. All kids experience strong feelings, that's mostly what they're all about. Kids are very emotional. They're kids!

What is the best thing that JG has brought into your life?
Answer: To love people, to be sweet and romantic ever And the most important thing: to start thinking in what's wrong with me and try to find a solution to my problems

come to tears. If you watch, it is clear that Toto, or rather the canine actor Terry (whose fee for the film was higher than each munchkin's), is genuinely moved, her head is inclined, her breaths controlled and her ears cocked for maximum listening. The same is true of my infant daughter.

On the screen Dorothy and her cohorts are skipping down the yellow brick road. In later life Judy claimed the trio of Bert Lahr, Jack Haley and Ray Bolger kept trying to edge her out of the shot. In a classic Judy anecdote she even has one of the film's many directors, Victor Fleming, shouting at the seasoned vaudevillians, 'Hold it you three dirty hams, let the little girl in there.' Ray Bolger – the Scarecrow – heard her tell this story on the *Jack Paar Show* with dismay; he was stung by this tale and shouted at the screen: 'How could we have edged her out of a wide-angle shot? It's not true! It's not true!'

Yet today it is I who feels edged out. For all my approval of Dorothy's fine behaviour – there are many worse life approaches than a 'what would Dorothy do?' mantra – the antics of the ging-hammed one today simply do not move me very far. I observe the film reasonably coolly and it feels in no way, as it usually does, like a collaboration wrought out of the fabric of our hearts. For some reason we aren't quite in it together and this lack of fellow feeling seems like a failure on my part. I had been certain that viewing *The Wizard of Oz* in this place on this day would feel ultra-involving, that I'd be watching the film with so much emphasis, my current reactions steeped in layers and layers of remembered joy and grieving, an italicised version in bold producing an obscene number of feelings, but today I don't seem to want to be involved. The baby is vexed and noisy and I am forced to leave the cinema in my non-mood, and I just don't feel that sorry. I have been watching *The Wizard of Oz*, it dawns on me, half incredulous, as though it were just, well, *a film*.

Sometimes my Judy feelings just don't materialise and today is one of those days. Very occasionally I immerse myself in her world and nothing occurs. What she says and does and represents doesn't catch at my heart; we don't connect and the force of her powers of communication, her lovely rendering of all that is bright and worrying and true, does not stun me. I watch with a limp smile and a sigh. My responses are mild. I may look away and turn again to her rapidly, newly and acutely in the hope of a better angle, like a knowing photographic model aping a fresh mood, but this just adds a forced intensity to the proceedings that doesn't exactly help. Sometimes the waves of pleasure and recognition don't arrive. My resistance is high. Once Judy Garland gets you she has got you for life – at least five people suggest I should call this book *Gotcha* – but just now I can only conclude that Judy Garland likes to appear to me and won't always be summoned. The conditions were too contrived, perhaps. Things that happen by chance are so often more powerful than those that are the result of design. If I aim to switch on my feelings or dress myself in her colours she sometimes resists, or I do. Is it because there's something insincere about me at these moments? Is it presumption or laziness or simulated emotion that threatens or flattens or dilutes?

On the anniversary of the death of a loved one or some other catastrophe, the given day may be harsher and crueller than the preceding one, the feelings like swords, all your limbs and even your joints weighted with loss, but sometimes on that given day you will feel fine and with the fineness will come relief, huge relief, and, to a degree, disappointment. The feelings may arrive a week or three days later. Your head may register the significance of the anniversary date and try to coordinate with your heart, but hearts don't work that way. They feel, at least I think they do, that anniversaries are manmade and artificial. They will send the feelings through when the time is right. You can't legislate about these things.

The
End of
the Road

Today I went to Judy Garland's tomb. It was a bright spring noon, lavish with blossom. Even a beggar by the side of the expressway was witty and upbeat. 'I'll tell the truth, I just want a cold beer' was his stylish manifesto, scrawled in brown felt tip on a cream fabric banner. One after another I saw cars stop for him. Flushed with experience and perhaps cold beer he knew it was easier for people to give money to satisfy another's whim rather than his need.

My best Judy friend Marc and I carry two bags packed with provisions to take to the grave: props, offerings, mementoes, for we had it in mind to build a little altar to our idol. We had a bowler hat, which had belonged to Wallace Beery, that Judy often wore on stage to sing 'We're a Couple of Swells'; we had a nineteen-forties gold bracelet and necklace that she liked; we had the photo of her in stripes, age twenty-four or so, looking anxious and brave holding on to an even more anxious-looking infant Liza Minnelli. We also had a silver christening cup that a young Judy had bought and given to her niece Judaline, on which it was inscribed, *To Judaline may you be as beautiful a woman as you are a little girl.* The birth of Judaline was such a happy event in the family, a breath of hope after Frank Gumm's death, Marc says. Judy was so excited.

Always this pesky emphasis on beauty, I thought to myself. Judy didn't believe she had the 'feminine strength' of other MGM stars. I look again at the inscription on the christening cup. Beauty never saved anyone, did it? Did it? Lana Turner once said to Judy Garland, 'You know, I'd give all the beauty I have for your talent, the expression in your face, your singing.'

Some people!

Lana and Judy in a scene from Ziegfeld Girl

We stopped the hire car at a corner grocer opposite the UN, near Marc's apartment, where insurance premiums are sky-high because it counts as the 'triangle of terror'. I bought pink and custard-yellow roses, and a packet of Benson and Hedges menthol cigarettes, Judy's favourite smokes. 'Do you want matches?' the assistant asked. I didn't know what to say.

There had been talk, earlier, of bringing a bottle of Blue Nun or some vodka and grapefruit, but I just wasn't sure. 'I don't really want to take her anything unhealthy.' We stop for vodka anyway, but they have no juice so Marc buys a large grapefruit. Back in the car I read out the directions carefully.

We listen to two different versions of Judy singing 'I Wish I Were in Love Again', one a charming informal rehearsal track which is boisterous and girlish and the other a fully fledged Judy Garland *performance,* full of passionate sophistication, from *Words and Music.* In this film Judy Garland appears at Lorenz Hart's party as herself while Mickey Rooney, rather oddly, plays Lorenz Hart. The scene doesn't quite work, for you expect the two old friends to start reminiscing about their 'Babes' or 'Andy Hardy' days, but they can't very well. In the car, Judy is listing the things she misses about not being in love. When she mentions 'the conversation with the flying plates', I mime a frisbee-style flick of the wrist towards Marc's head and he ducks and the car wildly swerves. TWO DIE ON GARLAND GRAVE VIGIL, the headline flashes before me. In the corner of the accompanying photograph, inside the car cracked and split, there are instant-memorial roses and a coroner-baffling gleaming yellow grapefruit.

Although commonly acknowledged as a health salve, grapefruit have always been as much of a memento mori for me as the skull beloved of the Old Masters. I was nearly killed by one once. On a bus travelling from London to Oxford one grim night I carefully removed the skin and pith from a whole grapefruit and popped a segment into my mouth. Immediately I started to choke. I could not dislodge the fruit, which was stuck at the back of my throat, and it was so large that there was no space left to breathe. I stood in my seat coughing and retching and sobbing and thumping myself on the

244

back and attempting to self-administer the Heimlich manoeuvre. No one came to my aid. There was a clock on the bus and it was horrifying, but oddly captivating, to watch two minutes pass. I tried to catch the attention of my fellow passengers, flailing and waving, but loud music was playing and besides I had turned into some sort of embarrassment and all heads were fenced from me by large pages of newsprint or learned journals or plugged, unreachably, into headphones. I am going to die, thought half my brain. Never mind, the other side cheerily rejoined. My head felt clamped and forced from all the violent heaving and lights were switching on and off and my blocked throat stung and strings of grapefruit juice were bleaching, in a natty lattice pattern, the navy gabardine of my coat. Another half-minute passed. Finally I flung my chest yet again into the back of the seat in front, and then repeatedly until a near-perfect two-inch missile of translucent fibrous fruit flew out of my mouth and hurtled through the air, landing next to the driver's seat. Of course everyone swung round to stare at me then.

'I was wondering about Judy's claim to be in the sympathy business,' I think out loud as Marc is driving. 'Sympathy can be such a limp thing, banal or ineffectual or somehow irrelevant. But in Judy's hands it's a powerful instrument of defiance. It's anarchic. Almost a weapon.'

'I know,' Marc says.

Ordinarily, I approach any new situation having already anticipated every possible thought or feeling I might have because I lack the constitution for surprises. Often I over-prepare for shocks that just don't come and with my relief there sometimes arrives a species of disappointment, yet for this visit I am completely unbraced. I have no idea what I'll feel. I've not long known my escort, although I've termed him my Judy-*frère*, and for all the printed pages of directions I'm clutching I'm not even really sure where it is we're going. (Westchester, a prosperous suburb of New York City, it transpires.) But it strikes me now and then that the only really bad outcome would be if I couldn't run to any feelings at the grave. That would be unbearable, a failure of gigantic proportions, and not just a failure but an indictment of my fidelity too. I prepare myself for how I might feel if no feelings materialise, my head blank, my heart uncontracted. Judy Garland communicated undiluted feeling better than any other performer in living memory. To fail to feel at her final . . . Well, that would be a feeling in itself, I suppose. As a human person you cannot always always summon the correct responses at exactly the right time, I pre-console.

I give one or two geographical pointers when necessary and, amazingly, it is the only time in my life where directions I've given have in any way helped. The journey, according to the route planner, should take thirty-five minutes and forty-seven seconds from midtown Manhattan. It does!

Marc is speaking as we turn into the lane that leads up to the Ferncliff Cemetery, and suddenly we see the sun dazzling on acres of bright lawn. 'Everyone else I know who likes Judy came to her through me,' Marc says. 'I introduced them. And it still counts but, you know—'

'Converts,' I say.

He nods. 'It's not the same.'

This sort of comment makes me thrill, but both of us proceed with caution. It seems to happen naturally. If you strike up a strong friendship with someone because you share a lifelong obsession for a highly obsessive third party, isn't it almost guaranteed to end in tears?

'I'm paranoid,' Marc tells me.

'Are you paranoid or are you wary?' I quiz him. 'Because that's just sensible.'

'Ever the mother,' he replies.

No one's ever said that to me before. We leave it there.

'Is she in or outside?' I ask.

'She's in one of the mausoleums.' We park neatly, but in the flurry of bits of paper and bags and necklaces and bowler hats the bottle of vodka smashes on the steps of Judy's building.

'Oh no!'

We pick up the pieces and enter the lobby inelegantly; our smart clothes have wilted rather and now we reek of alcohol. I am carefully dressed in a voluminous coral-coloured blouse with a gold stripe running through it and an enormous bow. Beneath I am sporting a tight Prince of Wales check pencil skirt and high gold peep-toe shoes. My hair was curled that morning by a softly spoken grandmother at Filles et Garçons named Maureen. Damp and crumpled now I feel like a louche flight attendant. Coffee, tea, me?

The mausoleum is more beautiful than I could possibly have imagined. Built in 1928 in the classical style, it is flooded with light and lined with sheets of pale marble and everywhere there are bright flowers – banks of lilies, raspberry ripple azaleas, roses – and one or two enormous picture windows giving on to ancient trees. Our shoes make loud noises on the floor. We mount a broad staircase and pass a dim standard lamp decorated with marble cherubs. The building is spotlessly clean and gleams, reminding me of one of those alluring convent hospitals in Italy or Spain. That, crossed with a cathedral. Once, before going on stage at the Palladium, Judy said to Father Peter Delaney, the man who would preside at her funeral, 'When I stand in the wings before a concert and look up into the darkness above the stage, the whole place becomes my church, the lights and wires become arches and I feel I am in my cathedral . . .'

I am overjoyed that Judy is somewhere so splendid. 'I don't mean to be rude, but I didn't know Americans were so good at this sort of thing,' I say. It is a low-key luxury: there's nothing hysterical about it. I sometimes feel sad that Judy didn't have more luxury in her life; I've even felt a sort of grief on learning that a necklace she liked

247

wasn't made of real gold, even though much of the fashionable jewellery of the era was costume. I don't, if I'm honest, even like to think
of her eating a hamburger. There is something irreproachable about
Ferncliff. It is a dignified place, grand, elegant and peaceful, the only
sound a very faint rustling of leaves.

Inside there are many many high white walls made up of large rec-
tangular marble panels; grave stones, I suppose. These banks of
graves extend up to eighteen feet or so, like a cultured giant's chest
of drawers. At the end of some of these rows of tombs there are
squares of red and purple stained glass, or long windows.

It takes several minutes to find Judy as we make some wrong
turns. I feel the feelings peeping through, a stab of sadness followed
by relief that the sadness has come, then a sort of jolt of recognition
as I brace myself against some old familiar non-specific ladder of loss.
We pass a row of twin memorials to married couples and I stop in
front of a pair of prim Wedgwood-blue urns and shake my head. It's
meant to be cosy and tender but it makes me feel desperate, this
little, pretty, brutal image of extinction. I am startled at my reaction.
Did you forget, I ask myself gently, that you were coming to a place
full of the dead?

I *had* forgotten. I thought it would feel like a party just being near
her. We dressed up! We brought hats! We had vodka! It was going to
be a carnival. I wasn't prepared for . . .

Then round a corner, finally, Judy!

She has one of the littlest headstones in the entire mausoleum,
perhaps three foot by two. 'I'm so glad she's somewhere so lovely,' I
say, but Marc is quiet. After a moment I see there are matters of
status to confront.

'Do you think it's a bit too modest?' I ask, for it isn't a star's grave
by any means, more the grave of a refined and prosperous professional, or the wife of one.

Reluctantly he says, 'I do.' To many fans this final placing of Judy in a position that does not distinguish her from the general crowd is a source of further grief. It seems wrong to at least one biographer that 'the name Judy Garland is in smaller characters than many of the inscriptions on the other tombs, and that her grave is the smallest in the lowest row of six rows of otherwise unknown names'.

To me it feels right. It is humble, but being buried in the limelight isn't what I'd ask for Judy. It is discreet, but that seems stylish to me, understated, holy. She doesn't, to my mind, need the trappings of a fancy monument, intricate carving and pillars and marble doves. She will always, always have top billing with her fans. This setting would certainly be a good resting place for anybody's loved one, but I do see that it doesn't redress in any way the injustices of her life. Virtually penniless when she died despite four and a half decades of hard work, living in a small rented house with a man she only slenderly knew who was out of his depth, choked with debt, plagued by ill health, estranged from family and running out of friends – Judy Garland's simple memorial at Ferncliff doesn't make up for any of that. How could it?

I read once of a solemn young boy in shorts among the crowds telling a policeman supervising Judy's journey from the Frank E. Campbell Funeral Home in New York City to Ferncliff Cemetery, 'I don't think I'm dressed respectful enough.' The officer lifted him up so he could see better and said, 'Respect is from the heart, son.' I think of the nine-year-old girl who mounted a poem on cardboard and offered it up to Judy:

> To one . . . who shares my joys.
> Who cheers when sad.
> The greatest friend I ever had.

Tears come, unexpectedly. I cast my head down. The greatest friend I never had, I think. What is it you are actually feeling? I ask myself.

Loss specific? Loss unknown? My lazy heart wants to mourn all those who haven't loved me in the ways I've wished, but I want to be disciplined about it. You can't just build a tower of everything that's ever gone wrong and drag it over to Judy Garland's grave, because that means nothing – that's insulting. Was it not enough that in her life strangers repeatedly heaped their fantasies of shared disappointment on her as though she were some kind of all-knowing, all-feeling disaster scene? Did the sheer weight of the worries of the world and his wife (and his husband) crush her? And you're doing it to her still? Can she have no rest? 'Who needs a happy Judy Garland?' she often wryly asked. I do. I really do. I pull myself up sharply. I can be quite strict at times.

'The first time you come is very overwhelming,' Marc says as though he's reading my mind. 'Perhaps we can come again some time in a lighter vein.'

Marc fetches vases and we put the flowers in water next to the headstone. I tuck the cigarettes and the grapefruit out of sight behind the blooms. I don't want to be outlandish in any way. I look scathingly on our bags of assorted bric-à-brac. To parade that stuff around the grave feels now completely wrong, stagey, insincere, *garish*. I had thought we might sing at the graveside but singing seems wronger than anything. And what would we have sung? 'After You've Gone'? 'The Man that Got Away'? I can smell the vodka fumes rising from us. I'm soaking wet from tears. My hem has come down. I'm a disgrace. It's almost funny. An image of young nuns I once saw wolfing éclairs in a café in Lourdes flashes through my head, the dark chocolate icing gleaming on their colourless lips, the granular piped cream.

We sit and stare at the headstone: JUDY GARLAND 1922–1969. There *is* something a little wrong with the scale. For although the lettering is smaller than that on the other graves, the width of the words JUDY GARLAND is still bigger than her shoulder measurement would have been. Wouldn't a large grave have been a burden for a person of such tiny dimensions? Marc uses the remains of the vodka, which has puddled in the plastic bag, to wash down the engraving of her name. 'The first time I came I did it with my tears,' he says. More tears are streaming down my face now. My heart swells with Judy, the immense pleasure she has brought me, the iron cheer. I inhale and exhale her.

'Wasn't it lovely, the letter of condolence that the waiter from the Por Favor restaurant sent to John Carlyle?' I say to Marc. I have it by heart: 'In this time of deep sorrow, may I take the opportunity to say that I cannot thank you enough for sharing with me in some small way your close relationship with the Mightiest Lady of our time. There are no words.' We are silent for a while.

Marc is speaking: 'Judy sometimes said a rosary on planes. Shall we say a Hail Mary?' Our hands reach for each other. I hear our shaky voices whisper, 'Blessed art thee amongst women.'

'Thank you for Judy,' I say afterwards.

'And for friendship,' Marc kindly adds.

'When I think of God, I don't really think of someone all powerful and all good. Well, sometimes I do, but mostly I think of someone all good doing his absolute best against impossible odds,' I hear my voice wavering slightly.

We take three photographs.

Our grocery store roses, surprisingly rich with scent, make me think of my friend Robert's death. The day after he died we made a bed of flowers in the street in Oxford; even strangers did, on the pavement just where he fell. We cut open water bottles to make vases.

'May I ask how he passed away?' Marc enquires.

'He climbed a university building. It was ancient, seventeenth century or something, and although he was a very experienced climber he used a bit of ornamental masonry for a foothold and it gave way under him. It was only about forty foot down, the kind of fall you could survive, but . . . I went to the inquest. Everyone told me not to go. A witness said, I'll never forget it, that she thought she saw a heavy coat being thrown from the roof. But there were no coats because it was midsummer's day, the longest day of the year.

'He liked to climb things when he was in a very good mood,' I explain. 'It was just something that he did. A way he liked to celebrate. He'd just finished his final exams that morning. We had lunch together – it was weird because all these priests and cardinals came in to the restaurant in red and purple robes and it was very surreal, and one of them knew him and came over and said hello. His spirits were very high that day and generally. He said how happy he was, that he had everything he wanted in life. It was very flattering. The college was fenced off because they were having a big ball and it was all locked up to guard against gatecrashers. He was coming to see me that afternoon to meet me from my exam and didn't want to go all the way round. So it was a sort of short cut, the climbing . . . and he just never arrived. I waited and waited. I went to the hospital. I rang his parents from a payphone. I'd never spoken to them before. I had to introduce myself. It was a terrible way of meeting and I couldn't make them understand at first. For an awful moment I thought they didn't speak English. They were four hours' drive away. The doctors thought they could do something at first, but . . . we sat in this terrible room while they tried . . . but then they found that they couldn't. It was the internal bleeding. There was red dye in his hair, so he didn't look himself. I don't know why. Somebody said it was iodine. I sat and held his hand for hours until his family came. Afterwards, my friend Alex drove up from London to collect me from the hospital and she took me back to college. It was exactly twenty years to the day that Judy died and there had been a celebration of her on the radio the day before that she had taped and we listened to it all night, playing it over and over again until it got light, just talking and crying. And then, and this is *really* bad, the next morning the university made me do my exams. Can you believe it?

'I think they said it was accidental death, by misadventure. The coroners I mean, at the inquest. Everyone told me not to go, but I wanted to be there. I didn't speak to any of the press and as a result they put the name of his old girlfriend in all the newspaper reports. The night after he died some of us met at his house and she arrived later on, really beautiful she was, and she went straight upstairs to the bedroom and didn't come down for forty minutes, while I just sat downstairs. Suddenly everything in my life was so extreme.'

Marc shakes his head very kindly. The coroner at Judy's inquest decreed that Judy had 'died accidentally from barbiturate poisoning due to an incautious self over-dosage'. The incaution I so admired had actually killed her. 'I think one should bring it out publicly there

253

was no question of alcoholism,' the coroner added. And what did the Oz coroner, played by Meinhardt Raabe (now ninety) sing when reporting on the body of the Wicked Witch of the East, forever stilled by Dorothy Gale's flying house?

> As Coroner I must aver,
> I thoroughly examined her,
> And she's not only merely dead,
> But really most sincerely dead.

It is, as Raabe accurately claims, the most repeatable, unbeatable death announcement ever recorded. Marc and I are both silent for a while. I like the idea of someone being sincerely dead. I suppose it isn't any sort of time for pretence, but even still.

As a bereavement counsellor I am often struck by my long-term clients' ambivalence. They find the pain of mourning excruciating, but they are also unwilling to give it up as they fear that the less acutely they mourn, the further from the lost object they will feel and the more truly apart and away their loved one will become. This is an idea that is intolerable.

So there is much to-ing and fro-ing. The promise of reinvesting in life without a missing loved one has to seem not only possible but also more alluring than the prospect of carrying on a life lived at the crux of loss, otherwise why make the transition?

This is not a matter of self-indulgence, it is simply a case of emotional economics, supply and demand. If we cling to our losses in life, encase ourselves in them, like a uniform, they may seem less like losses. Our intense relationship with them forms such a strong part of our lives that our losses become a vital and vivid aspect of our daily existence, allowing for an almost sacred dialogue.

If I engage daily and heartily with my losses, conjure them up, emphasise them to myself, examine and write and rewrite them end-lessly in my mind, I counteract, in some ways, the fact of them. Thus I can lessen my sense of loss by immersing myself in it, providing myself with a lively and stimulating exchange that seems to deny the very lostness of the missing objects. The relationship I live out with my losses, nursing them and feeding them with memory and insights, with words and pictures and sensations recalled from the past, to a certain extent replaces what I have lost. It is a new phase and I may, if it suits me, begin to love my losses as I have loved the lost person.

I may bring the same verve and creativity, the attentiveness and my own peculiar talents to the relationship with my losses as I did to the relationship with the lost person – I may even surpass myself! My losses may appreciate me for my fidelity, for my strength of char-acter, more than the absent person ever did. The loss itself may come to seem a form of epiphany, something that defines my life and my personality in the most intricate and accurate ways. This is the best part of mourning. It is also the most dangerous.

I'm not exactly sure how – I hope to be so soon – but I know all these feelings are involved in my love of Judy Garland.

I don't long or pine for Judy Garland. In fact, I'm not sure what I'd do with her if she appeared to me (a beautiful conundrum!) although of course I have numerous ideas. Nor do I mourn her, but the longing, pining, mourning feelings operate fully in me when I listen to her sing. They are abstract sensations, which Judy's voice awakens, but the enormity of them dazzles. For these are vast unspecified human losses and universal super-joys that Judy's voice summons in me then authenticates, promotes and champions until their status is as high as heaven's. With Judy singing in the room the longing, pining, mourning side of me is omnipresent and omni-potent. When Judy's around my longing suits me to the ground, it's cut on the bias and sparkles, glossy and sequinned under lights pink and amber. Listening to Judy's voice, part of me is bathed in grief but it is grief of the highest order, triumphant grief that has a transforming potential, challenging grief, mountain-moving grief, grief as a heroic spur. It's grief as love with all the glory and the degradation entwined.

Many seasoned Judy fans say they don't have to play Judy Garland's records to hear her sing any more. Can you blame them?

My eyes stray to Judy's neighbour's memorial. It is named for a Mae and Leo Mintzer; Leo died in 1969 and his wife followed twenty-one years later. I imagine them cosy, prosperous golfers in bright intarsia knitwear and tailored shorts, his arm draped uxoriously over hers. Were they fans? Did they know their luck? Were they anxious about being positioned next to a well-known hell-raiser, or did they love the idea? I wondered if their surviving relatives, their 'loving son' who had supplied them with the pot of yellow chrysanthemum I was gazing at, boasted of this connection or whether it seemed to him too random, this final enduring closeness that they did not choose. Did he hang his head in dark bar rooms, drowning his sorrows on winter nights, staring at ruin and regaling anyone who'd listen with 'And to top it all my mother's next to Judy Garland!'? Besides, could one actually get a wink of peace in a grave next to JG? The four a.m. calls to the dawn patrol, the high jinks and horseplay, the 'we'll stay all night and I'll sing 'em all!'

'There's something so hackneyed now about the phrase Rest in Peace,' Marc says.

'It's almost dismissive.' I agree: 'You might as well put Shut up or Fuck Off.' My eyes dart round the building and I spy a memorial to a Sadie McGradie.

On the other side of Judy, it gradually occurs to me, there is a large oblong of smooth grey marble with no lettering at all. My pulse quickens; it looks exactly like – well – a vacant plot! 'Oh my God, look! Marc! There's a space on her other side!' I tot up, in dribs and drabs, my life savings to date. It's not impressive. But I would have so much time to accumulate the sum. If I live another fifty years . . . I do elaborate calculations and in place of my eyeballs I do not see the ker-ching of dollars but the leaden clang of ruby-coloured cartoon tombs. If I could just secure the sum . . . And perhaps it wouldn't even hurt to ask – because this is really a once in a lifetime, once in a deathtime opportun—

Marc looks at me wisely. 'The first time I came here, I saw the plot empty and although I don't like enclosed spaces and I definitely want to be cremated, no question, I thought about it and then I thought, don't be crazy, but before I knew it I was tearing round, calling for the attendant, and I said, "Excuse me! Excuse me, Miss." I could hardly speak, "The grave next to Judy! Is it free? I want it! I need it! I have to have it! I want to buy it. Can you please tell me how much I . . . what I need to . . . where I apply for the . . .?"'

The lady looked at him squarely, then rolled her tiny eyes. 'You know, Sir, we must put a Not for Sale sign up over there. That plot was reserved. Years and years ago.'

I put on the 'We're a Couple of Swells' bowler hat and Judy's gold necklace, and feel comfort from them.

I knew her journey to this place was more eventful than you would wish for a loved one. Her interment was complicated, her burial delayed for over a year while she lay in a temporary vault – a drawer, really – until money was found for a proper memorial. She died in London but when her coffin arrived at JFK three days later she was already in bad shape. She had to be re-embalmed, re-dressed, a new casket had to be found and sprayed white and she was powdered and rouged by a Hollywood make-up artist who painted her face as she liked it. I've heard an account of these processes from one of the undertakers involved, a nineteen-year-old who was a stranger to Judy at the time. The part he played in her final journey made a lifelong fan of him. I heard his story with trepidation, because I couldn't bear the idea that her very last arrangements were made without respect, but I had nothing to fear. All he could be accused of was squirrelling away the handles of her London casket as a keepsake. From the awe and concern with which he spoke you could tell that his role in Judy's funeral arrangements was one of the most meaningful episodes of his life.

Over twenty-two thousand people paraded past the glass-lidded coffin in the little chapel at Campbell's funeral parlour to pay their final respects to Judy Garland on 26 and 27 June. Those who knew her best said she would have loathed this, but it was the wish of her fifth husband, Mickey Deans. He thought it fitting for a star. Fifth and Madison Avenues were closed as the streets bulged with fans, queuing devotedly for hours to file past Judy's body on its bed of yellow roses. 'There were the young and the old, rich and poor, there were people on crutches, and people with afflictions, there were nuns and priests, hippies and housewives, service men on leave and the veterans who Judy entertained so many years ago . . .'

And Andy Warhol. He wrote,

I took Ondine and Candy up to the round-the-block line for Judy Garland at Frank Campbell's Funeral Home on 82nd and Madison. I wanted to tape-record them as they were waiting to go past the casket . . . I had it in my head that this would make a great play – Ondine and Candy in a line stretching across the stage with criers and laughers all over the place, and everybody telling each other what'd brought them there . . . But being with Ondine that day was really strange; it was like being with a normal person. He hadn't been coming around the Factory much. He had a steady lover now, he said he was totally off speed, and he was sort of settled down, working as a mailman in Brooklyn . . . For weeks I couldn't stop thinking about this new nonpersonality of Ondine's. Talking to him now was like talking to your Aunt Tillie. Sure, it was good he was off drugs (I supposed), and I was glad for him (I supposed), but he was so boring: there was no getting around that. The brilliance was gone.

James Mason's eulogy in the church two days later was grand and momentous:

I travelled in her orbit only for a while but it was an exciting while and one during which it seemed that the joys in her life outbalanced the miseries. The little girl whom I knew, who had a curl right in the middle of her forehead; when she was good she was not only very, very good, she was the most sympathetic, the funniest, the sharpest and the most stimulating woman I ever knew. She was a lady who gave so much and richly, both to the vast audiences whom she entertained, and to the friends around her whom she loved, that there was no currency in which to repay her.

Marc and I pack up our things. We both feel weak and overwhelmed and we head back to the city where we share a gigantic lunch at Sparks Steak House, sitting, he tells me, at the mafia table where he once dined with the dainty daughter of Olivia de Havilland. 'She was a big collector of Dior, wasn't she,' I remark absently.

'I believe she was,' comes his reply. 'I spoke to her on the telephone once.'

How could Judy have been properly repaid, we wonder. If she'd had the requisite cash to take every other year off work, to build up her strength so she only worked when well? If she'd married that mythical sensible but gregarious doctor with a large private income and no other patients? If her life had been arranged for her so that she only had to sing *when she wanted to*? If she'd had me to look after her with levels of care designed to stun?

After her death Mickey Rooney wrote, 'If they could have taken her to their hearts a little sooner she might have been alive today.' Although I was just five months old at the time I've always experienced this comment as a personal reproach.

When I met Lorna Luft for tea last year at the Lowell Hotel in New York to interview her about her *Songs My Mother Taught Me* album, I asked her if she felt that there was anything anyone could have done to save Judy.

If she had had more of a grounding in her childhood, if her mother cared more about her as a daughter as a person as a human being rather than a commodity her whole entire life. I think that's what it goes back to, it goes back to what did her mom do to her and that's why I am so fiercely protective of my children, what they do, how they feel . . . There is just something so not right about little children on the stage . . . But I've never known another story and/or type of human being where their talent was too big for their person. The overwhelming sheer and

260

utter talent, I would imagine the only other person would be Michelangelo. When people are that overwhelmingly gifted that's the only thing people will see, they won't see the human being, they just see that talent.

Marc and I finish our steaks and our spinach. We're too tired now to speak at all. A bereavement counselling colleague of mine said she once heard Judy sing at a party in London in the late fifties. Noel Coward was there too, just at someone's piano in someone's spacious drawing room. 'I won't forget it till the day I die,' she said.

'What did she sing?' I ask her.

'Oh I can't remember that!'

Please don't waste my time, I do not say.

JUDY'S PEOPLE DIDN'T FORGET proclaimed the early edition of the *New York Daily News* on the day of Judy Garland's funeral.

We never ever will.

Encore,
Encore

On the second floor of the wardrobe department at MGM in the nineteen-thirties there was a spraying room with a galvanised interior. There was another long room with huge tables where bolts of fabric could be stretched and dried, and then there was an area with an enormous vat for water dying.

> Vera Mordaunt – head of MGM's dye department – thought that dying the shoes for *The Wizard of Oz* was the most boring job in the world. 'You have to tape the soles out, stuff the insides of each pair. And there were boxes of shoes! Satin shoes, dance shoes, things that had been used in other pictures and were left over. I had this new girl and I thought, "Well, she's new so she can do it." I brought her the spray gun and showed her how to mix the dye. She worked along and along on that thing, and about two days later somebody said, "Aren't you getting bored to death with those shoes?" She looked up, so surprised and said, "I was just thinking how wonderful it was. To be doing this and getting paid for it."'

Sometimes, when I'm sitting at a leather-topped table in the library with Judy as my work, I begin to feel a little sad and sorry for the other people near me: the gaunt military historian yawning and stretching; the young biographer who accosted me in the corridor, with outrage, to say that a critic who told him in person that his book was 'really terrific' merely described it as 'juicily entertaining' and 'exceptional' in print; the narrow poet whose face looks stricken when in repose; the pinstriped journalist who once opined that religion was only for children, bored housewives and homosexuals. The librarians seem cheerful, or at least stoic. But regarding all these people and overhearing their dry remarks it's clear they just don't love their work as I do and if they do they don't feel intensely proud to be doing it and even privileged, and from time to time properly ecstatic. It doesn't look as though they are having the time of their lives.

One evening I stage in my mind a meeting between Judy Garland and John Berryman. They are both sporting institutional pyjamas, striped white and cornflower blue. 'I feel half *nn* . . . clown half *nn* . . . convict,' she says. Both agree they have been very, very bad and it is almost funny. The nursing home is severe. It is a little like the clinic Norman Maine visits in the last half-hour of *A Star is Born*, yet in their meeting is the dim suggestion of spring. What a pair! How they wish that their setting were otherwise, for the etiquette of sanatorium flirtation has yet to be devised. He has read of her collapse and can see in her eyes that his has registered with her. The place, of course, is a *big* clue. They're equals, a couple of genuine swells now. There is little to lose, little worth losing. I'm not fit to be seen, both believe, but it's not what the other sees. Her courage sends arrows to his heart. He longs for a disreputable bar room, he always longs for that, and powerful drinks and chunks of lethally strong cheese. She's so tiny!

They sit, fascinating each other squarely. At the fringes of the room a handful of derelicts totter and leer. A woman glides by with a trolley. It's six now, the room darkens slightly. The singing dame would fit inside a cocktail glass.

How ambitious are they? She sees she's high in his estimation, not high enough but it's only been minutes. He's gruff and so clever it hurts but he's kind of nice. Can they let themselves be maudlin for a moment? Do they dare? I just can't do it any more, is what they feel. ENOUGH OF THAT! The sky is heavy and withholds its rain to scold these citizens. Both have exactly what the other doesn't need. It's seven now. Lights out is eight-thirty in this sterile heaven, this immaculate hellhole, and no talking. Yes, that does go for singing too. The doctors think they know everything about bonhomie. The mattresses are very stiff, no give. Visitors will come in the morning and drink tea. There's progress, say the docs, of sorts.

'Read me a poem,' she asks him.

He is pink with the flattery. Some dame, this bluebird lady! 'You want a good one or a bad one?'

'Oh I like 'em very bad.'

Nodding, he looks in his memory, dark, long, craggy, delving. Rainbows anywhere? Can't see one. For someone cast down her spirits are fine and high. They say she hungers, greedy for love, like a starving man. Sounds ordinary to me. He chooses the Dream Song everyone likes, monsieur number 29. He clears his throat, fingering his chin like a poet. She is actually lovely.

'If you can't close on the consonants you can raise your hand,' she says, showing him.

He bows.

'Hit it, Mort,' she barks, cackling. She is all ears, he can see. All ears and legs. He speaks softly so she might lean in.

> There sat down, once, a thing on Henry's heart
> So heavy, if he had a hundred years
> & more, & weeping, sleepless, in all them time
> Henry could not make good.
> Starts again always in Henry's ears
> The little cough somewhere, an odour, a chime.
>
> And there is another thing he has in mind
> Like a grave Siennese face a thousand years
> Would fail to blur the still profiled reproach of. Ghastly,
> With open eyes, he attends, blind.
> All the bells say: too late. This is not for tears;
> Thinking.
>
> But never did Henry, as he thought he did,
> End anyone and hacks her body up

And hide the pieces, where they may be found.
He knows: he went over everyone, & nobody's missing.
Often he reckons, in the dawn, them up.
Nobody is ever missing.

She looks at him, nodding. She cackles, startling the room. 'Nobody is ever . . . nnn . . . goddam fucking missing, are they?' She agrees as if it's a grave source of regret. It is in a way. Thanks God & his shy Son that the crime doesn't fit the punishment, he mutters. She agrees that the punishment stinks. No one's been *that* bad.

He softens. She's still got it, she notes, smoothing the folds of her crazy-wear. The room empties. Nurses come and go, some of them are fourteen. He's not going to ask her to sing is he?

It's late. He is so tall she could be his baby boy. How ambitious do they feel? The signs are good. She's much more feminine than he imagined. Older-looking than she is & miniscule and a wreck, of course, but a very, very good one & promisingly, still blue-and-white checked at heart, but you're a fine one to talk, he remembers. He never could resist anything. He feels hungry for the first time in eleven weeks. That good?

'Bedtime!' the blonde nurse carols; the brunette breezes through with hot milk. Milk! She can't keep anything down, or up. They won't keep still, these child-nurses. They are kittenish with her, shaky. One crept into her room last night, snapped on the lamp. 'You know I've loved you all my life,' she says, sort of tremulous.

'Well dear,' she begins brightly, 'you know it is *terribly* . . . nnn . . . late.'

'I'm so sorry,' the girl says and tears spring. It's all rather *odd.* They talk for an hour about the nurse's rat of a boyfriend. A mechanic with a taste for all sorts of awful—

Me, you're asking?

'*Bed time Miss Garland.*' The blonde one holds out her hand to help her up. She stands, creaking a little. The pyjamas flop and crinkle. 'I feel like I'm swimming in . . . nn . . . toothpaste,' she says. It's nice to be in costume again. All her life people have been trying to force her to sleep. These nurses have no patience, they're really terribly . . . Oh. That . . . nnn . . . *poet* is stirring again. His eyes flash and yearn and he's . . .

'Tomorrow?' he says and she walks away, but at the door she turns. She stumbles slightly then her legs scissor and she trips up, falling flat on her behind, and he springs to his feet, rapidly, but there's a lovely smile spreading and it's a *prank*! And it's only the fact of the nurses and the seven other patients that stops him from leaping on her there and then. She has such a nervous grace and she's looking up at him, looking up *to* him & all from her little coiled huddle on the floor. Then she stands up and dusts down the pieces, this spry, exhausted, beautiful, feeling, vaudeville Madonna-&-child. She drops an elaborate bow, flings out her arms and races up the stairs pursued by a nurse. He cheers vehemently & really she's the most— He is heavy impressed!

Of Berryman's last days Saul Bellow wrote,

> Out of affection and goodwill he made gestures of normalcy. He was a husband, a citizen, a father, a householder, he went on the wagon, he fell off, he joined AA. He knocked himself out to be like everyone else – he liked, he loved, he cared, but he was aware that there was something peculiarly comical in all this.
>
> And at last it must have seemed that he had used up all his resources. Faith against despair, love versus nihilism had been the themes of his struggles and his poems. What he needed for his art had been supplied by his own person, by his mind, his wit. He drew it out of his vital organs, out of his very skin. At last there was no more. Reinforcements failed to arrive. Forces were not

joined. The cycle of resolution, reform and relapse had become a bad joke which could not continue.

When I picture Berryman speeding in a taxi from the Golden Valley Clinic to address his humanities class at the university, and watch Judy climbing off a stretcher and straight on to the stage, I'm not sure what it proves: tenacity, I suppose, loyalty, courage and a certain crazy conscientiousness I can't help but admire. I'm not sure what you gain if you never give up, but I know it's almost everything.

One spring afternoon I invite my mother to watch *The Concert Years* with me. We sit and I know my tears are very close for it takes me back immediately to the terrible time when I saw it every day. When you are living on the edge of yourself, at the very brink of what you can bear, other people who are living extreme lives also are the only ones who really count, but these are the last companions you need. At these times chalk needs cheese and not more chalk. Judy Garland provided this sort of companionship for me without increasing my sense of ruin. She came to the awful places with me, but we didn't pool our resources and double or quadruple our trouble as I might have done with a flesh and blood co-sufferer. There was a degree of emotional economy at the heart of our connection, perhaps.

I think about how I will manage the moment with my mother. Will I talk about that time? We've scarcely discussed it before. In my imagination I compose a little scene that surprises me.

MY MOTHER: Why are you crying?
ME: Because when I used to watch this before I was so sad and lonely
MY MOTHER: Do you miss those days rather?
I nod

Judy sings 'Get Happy' wearing a fedora and a black dress whose skirt is slit into ribbons. It's beautifully directed: the movement of her dress, the play of light against the curtain. The white arms that peek from her half-sleeves are so long and expressive and they move with such wild, angular fluidity that they seem to belong to someone who lurks behind her, a person made on quite a different scale who has lent a pair of ultra-long limbs for the performance. To the right of the screen her shadow nimbly copies her movements. It is a startling performance, witty and full of celebration and love of life. A mammoth spotlight shines down on her, its middle darkened like an eyeball. I'd like to watch my mother watching but I didn't arrange the seating very well.

'Isn't she great!' we say to each other.

We listen to Judy sing 'Ol' Man River' and there's so much neat sincerity in her voice and she inhabits the character and the lyric so completely that when the song ends and she smiles and bobs a curtsey in her black cocktail dress, you can't believe she's not a struggling elderly black slave any more. How does she do that?

Judy is singing 'Who' from *Till the Clouds Roll By*, descending a moving staircase resplendent in a yellow gold gown and accompanied by many, many men in evening dress and top hats, the picture of MGM musical glamour. Soon, Judy is singing on screen to an audience of 108,000 on Boston Common and being thanked by Boston's stolid mayor, who says, 'We all love you.'

'Would you have liked to be Judy Garland?' my mother asks me.

'No.' I say without thinking. 'If I were her I wouldn't be able to feel about her the way that I do.'

'I mean a big star,' she presses. 'Of course you *are* a big star,' she says, remembering she's my mother.

'No, I don't think so. I'd like to be a small star, a quietly appreciated character actress or in the chorus on Broadway shows. Or I'd like to have been her dresser, standing by with a wrap and a hairdryer. Or her sister, perhaps.' One of her sisters was known as Suzy. It is my mother's name too. 'If I'd been Judy Garland, I'd have to have done things very differently. I wouldn't have done it nearly so well, I guess.'

Judy on screen sings a love song to her son and another to her youngest daughter. I think of her children sitting in the front row at concerts, tiny, late at night, hearing their mother's valentines sung straight into their hearts. Could any other expression of love match that if you lived to be a hundred years old?

Judy is singing 'The Man that Got Away' now and it is a more harrowing version than the one from *A Star is Born*. It is, in fact, such a paroxysm of longing and loss that it is impossible to listen to it and stay in one piece. I daren't look at my mother, but when I do she is crying. It strikes me I have been very selfish, subjecting her to this, what is it? An experiment? An ordeal?

'I'm so sorry,' I say. 'Perhaps it *is* a bit much.'

'That's all right,' she counters bravely, 'it's probably good, really.'

We compose ourselves. 'I suppose because your life is so nice now – you can afford to let yourself have such strong things . . .' she begins.

I've scaled myself down, reined myself in, I try to explain. My heart is no longer allowed the sort of freakish surges and dips that are constitutional to it, that perhaps are constitutional to all hearts. But when Judy's around I give it free play. For a moment now and then I will admit that life is more intensely terrible and also far, far greater than anyone ever says. At these times I feel more alive than is possibly wise, all my nerves jangling wildly and a sense that absolutely everything is possible, desirable, attainable, losable and in desperate need of protracted mourning.

'Oh,' she says, thinking, thinking. 'I see!'

Briefly I glimpse my reflection in the mirror, see my mother catch me looking at myself and watch it register with her that I know she can see me. There's nothing to do but roll our eyes.

We ease ourselves from Judy and the screen and eat a hearty lunch. I put on a recording of 'Stormy Weather' by a singer called Turner Layton, whose restrained and elegant tones make you think he is actually lamenting the bore of continually turbulent meteorological conditions. It's very reviving.

Next, after eighteen conversations with his agent in New Jersey, I arrange to have breakfast with Mickey Rooney in the chocolate-coloured lounge of a fancy London hotel. 'Everyone expected so much from Judy, it was such a pressure, it was impossible for her to live up to that,' he says when pressed. 'It makes me too sad to speak about it,' he snaps.

Mickey's wife Jan sits at his side, 'Number eight!' she tells me with jollity. Her extreme softness is a lovely foil to his grumpy lapses. I regard her with awe as she tends to her husband, protective, respectful and adoring. Like the most perfect old-school department store, you feel in her presence you have absolutely everything you need. I wish suddenly that Judy had had a partner like Jan to love and protect her. I suspect Mickey Rooney will live to be at least 108 because Jan is the sort of wife who just wouldn't stand for him dying.

I try to pose a question to Mickey about the difficulties of being a child star. Two weeks after he was born, he was on the road with his father, a comic, and his mother, a chorus girl. His parents separated when he was three. There was dire poverty and in his autobiography Rooney describes his mother in absolute desperation entertaining men for money in their tiny apartment; he would overhear and cover his head with a pillow. I imagine that the contrast between the highly wholesome world painted by the Andy Hardy films and the one Mickey inhabited, being the main wage earner from five in a struggling single-parent family, was not lost on him. In some years with MGM he made as many as nine films. There can't have been much in the way of childhood, I suggest.

'It was very hard for him,' his wife says. 'Who knows what damage was done.'

Mickey looks both angry and dismissive. He doesn't want to talk about it and why should he? In a recent interview, when asked if MGM over-worked him, he said, 'I wish they had worked me more. I loved it. They were my family.' I appreciate there is an element of humiliation for most people in the suggestion they were maltreated. Besides, I rather admire people who don't complain.

In the past I've often felt touched that Mickey telephoned Judy at the end of 1968, suggesting that they set up a chain of Mickey and Judy stage schools across America and make themselves a bit of money in the process. He'd do all the legwork, he offered, and she could sit back and count the dough! I find this cheering not because it would have succeeded but because it shows Rooney's utter fidelity, after all he went through, to the notion that putting on a show is the proper answer to life's troubles. I hope with all my heart that this is true.

'Do you think "let's put on a show" is almost always a good response when the chips are down in life?' I enquire. 'I sometimes think the idea of putting on a show can be a solution to most problems. It does almost have a moral basis, making the best of things, looking for the colour and the music in life, distracting one-self from difficulties, making something out of nothing, being a good host and everything?' my voice trails off.

Mickey won't indulge me. It's very understandable. We all chat a little longer and Mickey grows wistful. He's not keen to reminisce but every now and then he moulds a stunning rhetorical flourish such as, 'Susan, who today swashbuckles like Errol?' It's one of the best questions I've ever been asked. If I squint I can still see that Andy Hardy twinkle in his eyes. We shouldn't be sitting in the modish chocolate wooden nook of a luxury hotel, we should be on high stools in a drugstore, or in a diner booth sipping through straws.

'Could we sing something?' I ask him, 'Could we sing "Our Love Affair"?' From *Girl Crazy*, I almost add, that you sang with Judy, but it's lucky I don't because it's actually from *Strike Up the Band*.

After a few false starts because I can't quite believe he's agreed to it and then we're not quite singing the same verse, our song echoes through this fashionable West End enclave where businessmen are talking mergers and disdainful French waiters raise one then two high, slanted eyebrows. I don't care.

> Here we are, two very bewildered people.
> Here we are, two babes that are lost in the wood.
> We're not quite certain what has happened to us,
> This lovely thing that's so marvelous,
> But right from here, the future looks awfully good.

His wife makes to join in but he tells her roughly to stop singing, and it's true, our two voices do complement each other rather nicely, it seems to me. If my friends could see me now, I whisper out loud. Jan giggles.

> Our love affair was meant to be.
> It's me for you dear, and you for me.
> We'll fuss and quarrel
> And tears start to brew,
> But after the tears, our love will smile through.

At this point I begin, 'I'm sure that I could never hide/The joy I get when you're by my side.' But Mickey is singing the song's ending, 'When youth has had its merry fling/We'll spend the evenings remembering', but we come together at the end,

> Two happy people who said, on the square,
> Wasn't ours a lovely love affair?

There's a tear in my eye but we're all smiles. I think this is the most Judy-ish I have ever felt. Aglow, frank, passionate, thoroughly 'on the square' and with a sort of madcap cheer that makes me two feet taller. I can almost feel the dew on my brows. Afterwards I hand over a big envelope bulging with cash. For such life pleasures do *not* come free. I put it into Mickey's own hands to make sure he gets it. Judy didn't get her money, Mickey will, my smug little maxim goes.

Mickey Rooney insists on seeing me out, although both his wife and his stepson Chris offer to do the job. He shoos them away and they both stand back, amused. 'I'm not quite sure what's happening,' I say to Chris as Mickey and I, locked at the shoulder, pass by. 'I know what you mean,' he agrees. If you invite someone to sing a love song with you, I mildly panic, is it a given that you are – that you might? Although in medium heels I am a good eight inches taller than he is, Mickey Rooney somehow hoists me up and holds my arm in such a way that it is as though he is throwing me off the premises for a serious infringement rather than showing old world courtesy, but it's curiously intimate nonetheless. When we get to the double doors he leans in, his face against my face, squeezes me slightly and says, 'Never, ever forget this.' I gasp. He's going to tell me something that makes sense of everything, I can tell: the MGM days, Judy, what really went on and what he learned from it, and then suddenly I brace myself for my fear is that it will be sad news he'll impart.

Mickey Rooney pauses, squeezes my arm for emphasis, for drama, and then he whispers in my ear with a sort of forced theatrical intensity and a very strong look . . . something so quiet that I don't hear a word. Oh no! I ask him to repeat it but suddenly he's on the other side of the foyer waving me off sweetly in his brown knitted shirt.

I scold myself severely. Some detective! You had it in the palm of your hand, maybe, the answer, the pinnacle of . . . maybe and what did you do? You fluffed it. Why do you always always, always . . .

But afterwards I wondered whether, ever the prankster, this is Mickey Rooney's habitual slapstick farewell.

In every novel I've written I've felt a strange, binding responsibility to my characters, a sort of moral obligation to leave them in a better place than I find them. Though I write about people who are in extreme states, there is only so much I can put them through. I cannot be needlessly cruel for it would feel like a betrayal. I could no more kill a child in a book than I could in real life, I think. Although little may really be learned during the course of a novel – however much the arc of the story wishes otherwise – everyone has good days and bad days and I never unhand a character on a very bad day. I suspect I couldn't do it, even if I wanted to, although I know someday soon I must at least try.

Yet it's different here. My image of Judy now is stronger, brighter and sharper than ever. Everything that first drew me to her is magnified, more extraordinary, more triumphant, funnier, darker and more affecting too. I still don't completely understand her, yet this doesn't feel like a failure. I'm too keen to understand people in life, perhaps. I always thought it was a strength that every character I've created has had a carefully charted psychoanalytic map going back for generations which, when closely examined – perhaps by an expert – would add up exactly to today's pressing travails. I thought this was subtle and complex but I see now it's too simplistic. You have to allow that things may be richer and more compelling when they don't add up; you need to make space for the idea that unknowable things may contribute as much to a person's character and history as the facts that lie before you.

And then something marvellous happens.

I'm standing under the spotlight on a sliver of stage in a New York restaurant, my arm draped over the lid of a baby grand, in my best black satin dress with the three tiers of ruffles and the bracelet sleeves. I am clinging to the microphone with proper love and singing my heart out. My whole life has been a preparation for this moment, which in itself is a rehearsal for a moment that will take place in half an hour. I think of the description Judy once made of stage fright as 'a lovely tension'.

I had to read the message seven or eight times when it came through, to understand:

Dear Susie, I have taken the liberty of (tentatively) booking you as the special guest on Monday, October 22nd for 'Debra and Mary's Night on the Town'. They are Debra Barsha (author of *Radiant Baby*, a musical about Keith Haring) and Mary Cleere Haran, cabaret star, who's about to start her show at Feinstein's. They do a little show every Monday night in Brooklyn called (see above) – it's a combination cabaret/talk show, and they always have a special guest. Mary is fascinated by Judy and they really want you on.

'You do realise Brooklyn isn't the same as Broadway?' my husband says very, very tenderly when I slide down the banisters to read him this astonishing note. I don't care. I don't even care that the venue, which was pitched to me originally as a moody little French place called Night and Day, is actually a meat-feast destination called Biscuit BBQ. I should be choosy? I don't think so.

Debra, an appealing woman who looks like Liza Minnelli, takes the microphone, jams it in to the holder then wrenches it out to show me how. 'You have to snap it in, then snap it out.' The words fix in my head like a fabulous showbusiness talisman and I murmur them over and over again.

I hold the mic tenderly right under my chin and wander up and down the room, trying to take in all the details: the forty chairs arranged around little tables, the bar with its slender bottles of Austrian wine, the pink and white lights. On the wall adjacent to the stage it is quite clear that there once was some sort of sign or mural that has been painted over. My eyes close.

I am enjoying even the rehearsal so much I don't want it ever to end. Debra runs through my song again, which is a short Judy number called 'Do I Love You, Do I?' My voice seems to disagree with the piano over some of the notes and Debra adjusts the score accordingly, which is high courtesy. She is all grins and encouragement. We do the song five times and then Mary arrives. She is glamorous in a burgundy bias-cut floor-length silk gown and pale cropped hair.

'Put some acting into it!' she yells after hearing me sing.

'She's a writer!' Debra defends.

'So what! Think of Judy! Think of anyone!'

I try the song again. 'Does it sound too sad . . .?

'Well, it's kind of a sad song,' Mary says.

'I guess you don't really feel that it's going to work out. When you listen to the words, I mean,' I say. It is a song I sometimes used to sing when my father was painting me. I always chose comfortable, even lazy poses where I could lie down and possibly sleep and when I was awake I used to sing.

Judy Garland sitting for her portrait

Debra rehearses 'The Boy Next Door' from *Meet Me in St Louis,* as it's to be a Judy-themed night. It's instantly clear that she will not only sing me right off the stage (who doesn't?) but her wonderful vocal ability will lash me back to JFK or even Newark and right through the skies to foggy London, or wherever it is I crawled from, where there are no pink lights waiting, and no patient and indulgent (possibly bribed?) cabaret stars willing to perform enormous acts of human charity.

Mary, Debra and I slip into the green room, which is a small office under the stairs, and I drink a glass of wine. I congratulate Mary on the wonderful reviews of her much-lauded Doris Day show at Feinstein's at the Regency.

Mary begins talking with a great deal of enthusiasm about next week's star attraction who she says is 'just great!' I have a flash of the sensation you get when you arrive a little early and glimpse another patient leave the consulting room. You have to believe, at certain times in life, that you're the only one.

'Is it quite right,' I question, with confidence that astounds, 'to discuss your future guests in front of this week's?' They grudgingly agree with me about this. Mary is severe. She is also a huddle of needs – it's nerves, I expect. She wants Diet Coke urgently and cigarettes and her boyfriend, who is quickly found. I am an irritant to her, I'm not quite sure why, but I decide to take it as a compliment.

Suddenly it is showtime. After a witty introduction about the particularities of the Park Slope neighbourhood and its larger-than-life characters in song form, I am called up to sit between Debra and Mary on the stage. Debra has brought a large Dorothy doll belonging to her girlfriend, which stands on the piano. 'She's really tough so I was very touched when she told me as a girl she wanted to take care of Judy Garland,' she says.

I am introduced by the august ladies, welcomed on to my bar stool and then quizzed about what Judy means to me, how I first came to her and how, to a certain extent, I have navigated my life under her star. I am all heartfelt anecdotes and jolly repartee. I am fluent but not rambling. The 175 millilitres of Austrian wine was obviously the perfect amount. And the odd thing is I have never quite felt this comfortable anywhere in my whole life. The audience is laughing very regularly and looking touched when they're not laughing. I think of John Berryman's line – I often do – 'I may have heard better news but I can't think when.' I wish all the people I love were in the audience to see me: my parents and siblings and sisters-in-law and best friends, and other people too, a curly haired girl called Natalie who taunted me repeatedly with a nasty song about my size when I was eight that made me so miserable I used to tear my hair. I'm always touched by the passage in *The Catcher in the Rye* where Holden Caulfield confesses that he kind of misses the boy who used to rough him up in the lift. I wonder what Natalie is doing now? Does she ever think of me?

I tell the audience that when I saw quite how strong Judy's feelings were I felt both enormous respect and a sort of wonderful validation. I love the notion I get from her that people with very strong feelings are the world's best citizens and that very painful feelings and very jubilant ones are absolutely as good as each other. These ideas made sense to me, I say, made sense of life to me when nothing else did very much.

Then I sing. I sing the song quickly, straight at my husband who is beaming at me wildly from the front row. It is very much a writer's performance rather than a singer's and it isn't at all great but it's sincere and it is, I'm told afterwards, very respectable.

Then more questions. I tell Mary that I longed with all my heart for a stage mother who'd say to me every morning, 'Until you've played the Palace/You might as well be dead,' and she bristles slightly, regarding me as though I am an idiot who is trying and failing to be cute. Afterwards it transpires that she had a real-life stage mother, and it was no picnic. My wide-eyed enthusiasm for total showbusiness immersion would grate on a person with that history, wouldn't it? I quickly see I have committed some sort of offence. I'll learn a lesson from this.

Towards the end of the interview, when Mary tells me as an aside that I have beautiful skin I thank her and tell her she can have it.

'But I have *talent*,' she says tartly.

'Wow, you showpeople are harsh,' I murmur and the audience roars with laughter. They are, I believe, utterly on my side and I adore them for it just as they adore me.

Then it's Mary's turn to sing 'On the Atchison, Topeka and the Santa Fe', Judy's Oscar-winning song from *The Harvey Girls*, a song known in the trade, I am delighted to learn, as 'Atchison'. It is a show-stopping performance, dynamic, spectacular and full of feeling. She even manages to convey with a great deal of poignancy quite how much all her life she has adored trains. She makes this seem something that any right-thinking person feels.

> Back in Ohio where I come from
> I've done a lot of dreamin' and I've traveled some
> But I never thought I'd see the day
> When I ever took a ride on the Santa Fe.

'Acting' a song sounds so easy, but it isn't. Even if I were a massive train fancier I don't think I could ever get across, as Mary did, how an intense passion for this form of transport can really overwhelm a person. I am minded to ask Mary, later on, if she really likes trains, but I don't wish to plague her with any more pesky questions. She must love trains, mustn't she? I quiz my husband later that night after he has fallen asleep.

In a tribute he wrote for the Judy Garland Club in London, after Judy died, John Meyer compared his former love to a train:

Being with Judy – it was like you were shivery cold from snow and fatigue, and maybe hunger, and you're waiting in Queens on a dim, deserted subway platform; waiting for the local – and suddenly, before you know it, the express is rushing through the station, from out of nowhere, filling your head for an endless, suspended instant, and all you know or feel or hear or see is the sharp taste of that bright, dark, speeding train, the express, and you forget about the cold and the fatigue, and about getting up for the dentist tomorrow, or buying your sisters birthday present, you forget it all, because there's no room to concentrate on anything but that incredible train – that beautiful, dark, rushing incredible train.

Before I'm ready, the show's over. People are packing up and leaving. I wanted it to last for ever. What about the show must go on? I don't ever want to go home.

'Was it OK for you?' Debra and Mary ask me. Mary is mildly curious as to whether I am offended. 'No, no, no, no, no!' I say, for I too am a trouper. 'Come on! I loved it. It was better even than a journey on the Santa Fe,' I tell them. A dream come true. A miracle. Afterwards several kind souls congratulate me, 'You were so completely this!', 'You were so utterly that!' an accountant who also writes musicals tells me, but I hardly hear because the fact that the show is over is already making my heart sink in sharp, angular thuds. 'Goodbye then,' I mouth to the Dorothy doll perched on the piano. Back in London I watch the film my husband made of my performance, repeatedly. You know, it holds up.

It's almost Christmas. The centenary of Judy's birth is 2022. Can I keep going until then? I still don't have my finale. I'd like a new beginning. I have thousands of discarded paragraphs that may be better, brighter and more acute than the ones I've used. I feel I've said too much and not enough. I don't want to put Judy away.

We've been in this small, high room together now for twenty-two months and every surface of it smarts with Judy: books about her tower and loom, pictures of her delight or seem to seek consolation as they console. There are ruby slipper stickers and Glinda cut-outs and Dorothy dolls; there are letters from fans; publicity material; countless records and films; a treasure corner with a gold bracelet and the cake of blue eye-shadow and the coral-coloured lipstick that were hers. There's a fax from Christies about two rare Andy Warhols made with forties Garland images that are coming on to the market imminently, estimate three million pounds the pair. There are two thank-you notes Judy wrote to my friend Brian and a letter to him from Marcus Rabwin, the Gumms' family doctor who saved her life when she was in the womb. He writes, 'I loved her from the time she was born, and as far as I was concerned she could do no wrong.' There are lyrics and sheets of Judy stamps and Liza tickets and Lorna tickets and the phone numbers of the caretaker who is protecting the London house in which Judy died and the business card of the man from the local dry cleaners who mourns his own film-star mother still. There's a photograph of Carnegie Hall and the words to 'Palace Montage' pinned on the wall. There are diminutive McDonald's Happy Meal toys of each of the important characters from *The Wizard of Oz*. There's a Dorothy figurine and some framed Judy dolls with fashion clothes. In fact it's no longer my room; it's hers. Photographs of my relatives peep from behind ranks of Minnellis and Lufts and Gumms. I know I will need to clear this room at some point for there's a novel to finish and another brewing and she doesn't quite belong, physically, in either of those spaces. But it's still too soon. When you decide to dismantle, even a little, the person that helps you meet your losses you do an enormous thing. The end of mourning can be the hardest part.

A friend sends me a handkerchief by the artist Louise Bourgeois that states, 'I've been to Hell and back and let me tell you it was wonderful.' Should I order one for Liza for Christmas? One for Lorna who is in town to promote her record *Songs My Mother Taught Me*? One for Joey too?

Downstairs the doorbell's ringing. There's a neighbour with a wrongly delivered parcel from New York. It's Judy's CBS TV show episodes 7 and 9 (vol. 5). *You must watch this now* says the note. I slide the disc into the machine and forward to the chapter specified. Judy is singing with Donald O'Connor songs made famous by other people. 'I'm always remembered for this song,' Judy says, then starts with a long mock serious '*If* . . .' and then clapping her hands and waving her head, she bounces in to . . . 'If You Knew Susie'!

> If you knew Susie
> Like I know Susie,
> Oh, oh, oh what a girl . . .

Judy sings, capering about wildly and flapping her little white handkerchief at Donald O'Connor. I didn't know she had ever sung this song, although it's less than a whole verse and she misses out my favourite bit that goes, 'She wears long tresses and nice tight dresses/Oh, oh, what a future she possesses.' I've always loved the idea of possessing a future.

As I listen to Judy singing my name it strikes me that it's one of the few times in my life where it *doesn't* feel as though she's singing just to me. It's a joke, that's all. Horseplay, high jinks, a gas. There's no weight of feeling to it. But afterwards, in a button-through white bugle-beaded column gown, she looks straight at me and starts to sing 'Fly Me to the Moon'. I am completely captivated. It's like the beginning all over again as she closes the song down with the full, frank focus of her all-seeing eyes, her whole person suffused with feelings of the highest calibre as she fills my room with the final lustrous phrase, 'In other words, I love you.'

>I love you too.
>Goodnight Judy.
>Goodnight.

Notes

How It All Began

I am indebted to T. S. Eliot's indebtedness to Laforgue in this chapter.
T. S. Eliot, *Inventions of the March Hare*, pp. 399, 400.

p. 4 *'Put him in the basket, Henry,'*: This is what Aunt Em says when she realises that the Gale family cannot save Toto from the mean-spirited authority of Elvira Gulch.

p. 5 'Friendship' music and lyrics by Cole Porter, from the 1939 show *Du Barry Was a Lady*.

World's Greatest Entertainer

p. 7 *The rapport Garland maintained with her audiences is unequalled in history.* 'Almost everyone in the theatre was crying and for days afterwards people around Broadway talked of it as if they had beheld a miracle.' Article in *Life* magazine following the Palace concerts of 1951, quoted in David Shipman, *Judy Garland*, p. 284.

Reviewing *A Star Is Born*, Virginia Graham wrote in the *Spectator*, 'After hearing her sing "The Man that Got Away" and "Born in a Trunk" I felt she had seized the torch I carry for her from my hand and scorched my soul with it.' Ibid., p. 326.

In *Good Housekeeping* in 1962, Rosalind Barber wrote of the concert in Forest Hills, New York, July 1961: 'When she makes contact with an audience, small wonder that there's an explosion of exultant hysteria. Actually it's compounded of thousands of small explosions, of thousands of captive emotions – and in their wake, thousands of fleeting intimations of what love is like . . . let us be hopeful that more of us do to each other the wondrous thing that Judy does for us.' I am grateful to the *Judy Garland Review*, spring 2008, for this article.

p. 8 *'Bedlam superimposed upon bedlam'*: This is how *Holiday* magazine described Judy at the Palace in 1951. Gerald Clarke, *Get Happy*, p. 295.

p. 8 *the wild sorrow of the white-gloved ushers . . . the star-struck usherettes*: The ushers and usherettes are as described by John Carlyle in his memoir *Under The Rainbow*, for he was among their number

p. 8 *a hero to her accompanists*: Judy's pianist at the Palace in 1951, Hugh Martin, described the job as 'the greatest experience of my life, watching that woman She was such a genius.' John Fricke, *Judy Garland: World's Greatest Entertainer*, p. 137.

p. 8 *Scientific praise:* Clifton Fadiman in *Holiday* magazine wrote, following the Palace show in September 1956, 'Where lay the magic? Why did we grow silent, self-forgetting, our faces lit as with so many candles, our eyes glittering with unregarded tears? Why did we call her back again and again and again, not as if she had been giving a good performance, but as if she had been offering salvation?'

Love letter-style praise: Buddy Pepper, 'No Sad Songs for Judy', *Photoplay*, August 1951: 'She'll be back in pictures too. She'll be back anywhere she wants to be back, and she'll climb to even new heights if her miraculous transformation continues. And this is good news for all the people who love Judy Garland – and that's about all the people there are.'

Doctor-style advice: Joe Pasternak, in his memoir *Easy the Hard Way*, wrote, 'Wish her well, return her love, all you who cherish talent and genius and a great heart.' p. 176.

Sanford Lewis, 'The Sad Echo of a Distant Song', *TV Mirror* 1965: 'I don't want to watch the death of a star. And it doesn't have to be that way. She means too much to too many people BUT the important thing is she has to discover what she means to herself, then possibly the voice of Judy Garland will begin to live again.'

p. 10 *'I would like them to know that I have been in love with them all my life.'*: John Fricke, *Judy Garland: World's Greatest Entertainer*, p. 253.

p. 10 *a Robin Hood quality to it*: Judy's Robin Hood quality at work in Carnegie Hall is described by the critic Rex Reed, and quoted by John

Fricke: 'I've never seen an audience of more important, celebrated, influential, powerful, wealthy, jaded people in my life, grouped together in one setting, decimated to such as state of universal hysteria as I saw that night.' Ibid., pp. 183–4.

John Springer, Garland's publicist, commented, 'Leonard Bernstein, the tears running down his face, screaming . . . and Hank Fonda, normally an impassive man, "bravoing".' Ibid., p. 184.

p. 10 *Betty Hutton*: Hutton replaced Judy in *Annie Get Your Gun*, and it was she who followed Judy at the Palace in 1952. Hutton's head and neck remained intact. Gerald Clarke, *The Life of Judy Garland*, p. 296.

p. 12 'A Foggy Day' words by Ira Gershwin, music by George Gershwin.

p. 13 *'something of the forest'*: A comment by Joseph L. Mankiewicz. Gerold Frank, *Judy*, p. 57. The quotation is actually 'something out of a forest'.

p. 13 *Judy's imperial sway*: 'It was impossible to deny Judy anything [if you] wanted to remain in her circle.' Ibid., p. 217.

This is not true of me.

p. 14 The photograph is of Judy at Carnegie Hall in April 1961, reaching out with what was called her 'glad hand'.

p. 15 *my family had recently returned from its greatest adventure*: My sister Rose wrote beautifully and movingly about this episode in my family's history in her novel *Rose* (Chatto and Windus, 1991).

p. 22 *Annie Get Your Gun, from which Garland was ejected*: Garland was asked to leave *Annie Get Your Gun* on 10 May 1949 following two letters that day from Louis K. Sidney, vice-president of MGM, outlining her 'infractions'. Gerold Frank, *Judy*, pp. 249–52.

Judy's co-star Howard Keel said the studio should have waited for Judy: 'Letting her go was the only tacky think I knew MGM do.' David Shipman, *Judy Garland*, p. 236.

p. 22 *Lana says*: Lana Turner, *Lana: The Lady, The Legend, The Truth*, p. 287.

p. 22 *Judy's five husbands*: David Rose, married 1941; Vincente Minnelli, married 1945; Sid Luft, married 1952; Mark Herron, married 1965; Mickey Deans, married 1969.

p. 23 *I Could Go On Singing*, 1963, directed by Ronald Neame.

pp. 23–24 Accounts of the filming of *I Could Go on Singing* feature in Neame and Bogarde's autobiographies.

p. 25 *'Whoopee!'*: John Fricke, *Judy Garland: World's Greatest Entertainer*, p. 177.

p. 27 *Judy's CBS television series*: This aired for twenty-six weeks in 1963–4.

p. 29 *Meet Me In St Louis*, 1944, directed by Vincente Minnelli.

p. 30 *Dorothy's impeccable manners*: L. Frank Baum's original description of Dorothy: 'She was loving and usually sweet tempered, and had a round rosy face and earnest eyes. Life was a serious thing to Dorothy and a wonderful thing too . . .' L. Frank Baum, *The Wonderful Wizard of Oz*.

p. 31 *exiles*: The best account of *The Wizard of Oz's* appeal to exiles appears in Salman Rushdie's book, *The Wizard of Oz*, published by the British Film Institute in 1992.

p. 36 *Judy and Noel Coward*: Their conversation was recorded and this transcript was printed in *Redbook* magazine in 1961.

p. 37 *singing 'Over the Rainbow'*: This description of Judy singing to the Boston police appears in John Meyer's book, *Heartbreaker: My Life with Judy Garland*. The event occurred on 5 December 1968.

p. 37 *clown make-up*: Judy's clown make-up is described by Gerold Frank in the introduction to *Judy*.

p. 38 *Little Miss Leatherlungs*: This nickname and the names of Judy's childhood friends occur in *Young Judy* by David Dahl and Barry Kehoe.

Stage Struck

p. 39 *"Deep below the glitter, it's all solid tinsel"*: This comment is attributed to Sam Goldwyn.

p. 40 *the make-up lady*: Dorothy (Dottie) Ponedel was Judy's make-up artist on *Meet Me In St Louis* and became a great favourite.

p. 50 Accounts of the MGM stage school appear in *Young Judy* by David Dahl and Barry Kehoe, *Life Is Too Short* by Mickey Rooney and *Lana: The Lady, The Legend, The Truth* by Lana Turner.

p. 54 *child star*: Sybil Jason did not have a stage mother but a stage sister who was ten years older. Sybil describes with wonder what it felt like to look round the Warner Brothers studios for the first time: 'It was like walking into a fairytale book and becoming one of its characters.' Sybil Jason, *My Fifteen Minutes*, p. 23.

p. 55 The descriptions of Judy and Lana are taken from *Life Is Too Short* by Mickey Rooney.

p. 60 *the following exercise.* This exercise was described in one of the many excellent books by Geneen Roth, the best of which is *When Food is Love.*

p. 60 *A Star Is Born*, 1954, directed by George Cukor, produced by Sidney Luft.

p. 62 *A Star is Born*, 1937, directed by William A. Wellman, produced by David O. Selznick.

p. 62 I met Liza Minnelli in 2006 when the *Observer* newspaper asked me to interview her to coincide with the release of *Liza with a 'Z'* on DVD.

p. 63 Judy filmed this interview for NBC's *Today* show with Barbara Walters from her suite at the St Regis Hotel in New York, with Lorna and Joe at her side. Judy was wearing a blue outfit of Lorna's, according to Scott Schechter, *Judy Garland: The Day by Day Chronicle of a Legend*, p. 324.

pp. 63–4 'Palace Montage' or 'Palace Medley' music and lyrics by Roger Edens. The version I know comes from Judy's television series, which I first saw in the excellent PBS documentary, *Judy Garland: The Concert Years.*

The Rescuers

p. 68 *lemon meringue pie.* It is important to bake the pastry shell blind before you add the filling.

p. 69 The Margaret story comes from John Meyer's book about the weeks he spent with Judy in late 1968, published as *Heartbreaker: My Life with Judy Garland* in 1983, and subsequently republished as *Heartbreaker* in 2006.

p. 70 *'I'd Like to Hate Myself in the Morning'*: Judy Garland performed this song for the Merv Griffin Show. The programme was filmed on 19 December 1968 and aired on 2 January 1969.

p. 75 *'You demand a great deal of satisfaction for the little you give'*: A line spoken by Kate Croy to her father in the first chapter of *The Wings of the Dove* by Henry James.

p. 75 *Her television series recorded its final show.* This account of the end of

Judy Garland's CBS show comes from Coyne Steven Sanders' excellent book, *Rainbow's End: The Judy Garland Show*, pp. 357–74.

p. 76 This version of 'Call Me Irresponsible' is called, by Coyne Steven Sanders, 'a Garland–Schlatter–Bradford parody of the original'. Ibid., p. 69. The line 'Rainbows I'm inclined to pursue' comes from the original version by Sammy Cahn and Jimmy Van Heusen.

p. 77 *Her life could be comfortable*: 'David Begelman told me there was no reason I shouldn't have a steady home with by children, be very rich and do a weekly TV show – that I should have been very rich a long time ago like Bob Hope or Como.' From 'I'm Judy Garland and This is my Story', *New York Journal-American*, 28 February 1964, quoted by Gerald Clarke in *Get Happy*, p. 371.

p. 81 'Me and My Shadow' music by Al Jolson and Dave Dreyer, lyrics by Billy Rose. The recording I listen to is from the *Judy Alone* album, which was released in 1957 and again in 1989.

p. 82 *Judy Garland: The Concert Years*, a 1985 PBS documentary directed by David Heeley and presented by Lorna Luft.

p. 84 *a sort of ecstatic collapse*: This point about the public's collapse at the thought that Judy was happy was first made by the journalist James Goode. John Fricke, *Judy Garland: World's Greatest Entertainer*, p. 183.

p. 85 *One night, when the chips were down*: Tony Bennett told this story on the A & E Biography programme *Judy Garland: Beyond the Rainbow* and it also features, slightly differently, in Bennett's 1998 autobiography, *The Good Life*, where there are 'nine hundred cops downstairs and five lawyers in my room'.

p. 89 *Fred Finklehoffe*: Fincklehoffe was the Hollywood writer responsible for several of Judy's films. He was the writer on *Words and Music*, and wrote screenplays for *Meet Me In St Louis*, *Girl Crazy*, *For Me and My Gal*, *Babes on Broadway* and *Strike Up the Band*.

p. 91 This story about Paulette Goddard comes from Hedda Hopper, *Under My Hat*, p. 246.

p. 93 *The Pirate*, 1948, directed by Vincente Minnelli.

p. 95 *Ernst Simmel*: Simmel distinguished himself in Hollywood by being the first doctor to diagnose George Gershwin's blinding headaches as the symptom of a brain tumour.

p. 95 *'a gigantic mistake'*: 'America is a mistake; a gigantic mistake, it is true, but none the less a mistake.' This comes from the second volume of Ernest Jones's *The Life and Work of Sigmund Freud*. The remark was made to Jones.

Freud also considered America obsessed with money, a disease he termed Dollaria, and thought the nation was lacking in passion, that even its love affairs were fleeting.

p. 95 *'a blessed, a happy land'*: From Ernst Stern (ed.), *The Letters of Sigmund Freud*, p. 447.

p. 95 *people were obsessed with their mothers*: 'In their analyses, American patients tended to talk endlessly not of their fathers but of their mothers ... The differences in symptomatology called forth important modifications of psychoanalytic technique.' Nathan G. Hale, Jr., 'New Heads for Freud's Hydra: Psychoanalysis in Los Angeles'.

p. 95 *an essay written by Simmel*: 'Alcoholism and Addiction' was written in 1947 for *The Psychoanalytic Quarterly* at the instance of the editor.

pp. 96–8 This account of Judy's psychoanalysis with Augustus Rose is taken from *Judy* by Gerold Frank, pp. 253–7.

p. 101 *My father-in-law told me*: My father-in-law knew a great deal about the Freud family as he was a long-term patient of Anna Freud.

pp. 102–3 This account of Judy's 1969 Copenhagen tour comes from *Judy Garland* by Anne Edwards, pp. 294–8.

p. 102 *shocked at how frail his heroine was*: Hans Vangkilde said 'she looked like a slender bough, snapped in two and ready to break . . . she had the look of death camps'. Ibid., p. 295.

p. 104 Quotation from Promis website: www.promis.co.uk. Compulsive helping is sometimes a synonym for co-dependency.

p. 105 Quotation from John Meyer, *Heartbreaker: My Life with Judy Garland*, p. 314.

p. 106 *a plane that was blazing with flames*: 'Luft himself had almost burned to death when he was trapped in a Douglas plane he was testing during the war . . . He had ridden the flaming plane to the ground, followed by a screaming ambulance, was somehow extricated – he was hanging head down, burning – wrapped in a sheet and rushed to the hospital, severe burns on his left leg, the side of his face, his lower back . . . For a full minute, trapped in the plane, he knew he was going to be burned alive. It was an experience, he told Judy, against which no calamity in the future would compare.' Gerold Frank, *Judy*, p. 402.

The Things that Judy Taught Me

pp. 109–10 'It's All For You' words and music by John Meyer. Judy sang this song on *The Tonight Show* with Johnny Carson on 17 December 1968. The show aired that evening.

p. 110 'Make Someone Happy' music by Julie Styne, lyrics by Betty Comden and Adolph Green.

pp. 111–12 *'The Hero and Divinity*': Taken from *On Heroes and Hero Worship* by Thomas Carlyle.

p. 114 The photograph is a film still from *Ziegfeld Girl*, 1941, directed by Robert Z. Leonard and Busby Berkeley.

p. 115 The photograph is an MGM publicity shot from spring 1950 – Judy's final sittings – using the 'All For You' dress from *Summer Stock*.

p. 124 *I fancied myself a nineteen-fifties American poet-professor's wife*: this feeling was inspired and abetted by reading Eileen Simpson's wonderful memoir, *Poets in their Youth*, from which the information in this section comes.

p. 127 *Boy George*: The actual quotation is 'If nuclear wear did happen I'd be thinking, is Boy George safe?' Quoted on the jacket of *Starlust: The Secret Life of Fans* by Fred and Judy Vermorel.

p. 134 Lorna Luft's conversation with Rex Reed is quoted in *Rainbow* by Ethlie Anne Vare, p. 198.

p. 136 *Dolce Vita roses*: Dolce Vita roses have fat heads that are pinkish cream, with light and deep pink colouration at the edge of the petals.

p. 139 *Care must be taken; attention must be paid*: Judy referred to her liking for this line in *Death of a Salesman* in an article called 'The Plot Against Judy Garland' published in the *Ladies Home Journal* in August 1967: 'I don't approve of Arthur Miller as a person, because I don't think he understood Marilyn Monroe very well, but I do love his line from *Death of a Salesman* . . . Miller was talking about his aging salesman Willie Loman, but that's the way I feel about myself, too.'

p. 141 *What is there left to say?*: 'Do I have to talk about her any more? Why do they want me to be the keeper of the flame and the destroyer of the myth at the same time?' Interview with Barbra Grizzuti Harrison, *McCall's*, 1975.

The Disillusionment Stage

p. 146 *I stuck a ball of juicy bubblegum into my best friend's silky white-blonde hair*: Sorry Amy, it was very wrong of me.

p. 146 *the reviews from when she was a child*:

Variety, August 1932: '. . . Gumm sisters, harmony trio, socked with two numbers. Selling end of trio is the ten-year-old sister with a pip of a low-down voice. Kid stopped the show.'

Baby Gumm, in Maurice Kussell's *Juvenile Christmas Revue* at the Million Dollar Theater in Los Angeles, winter 1932–3, was 'astounding. Her singing all but knocks one for a loop, her dancing is snappy and clever. She handles herself onstage like a veteran pro.'

Variety, 'New Acts' column, 1934: 'Possessing a voice that, without a PA system is audible throughout a house as large as the Chinese, she handles ballades like a veteran, and gets every note and word over with a personality that hits audiences . . . Nothing slow about her on hot stuff and to top it, she hoofs . . . she never failed to stop the show.'

p. 146 *Francesca*: Francesca Simon is the author of the bestselling Horrid Henry books.

p. 153 *New Jersey*: The New Jersey concert was on 2 May 1961, and was reviewed in the *Newark Star Ledger*: 'Her hair falling over her eyes and perspiration streaming down her face, Judy obliged and obliged again, singing her last four encores to a standing room only audience that had to be forcibly restrained by police from rushing on stage.

'Even the dropping of the curtain failed to stop the cheers and Judy took her last bows to the chant of the crowd demanding "Come back to Newark!"

'"Come back?" Judy said in her final words. "Why, I'd love to play my entire tour right here!"'

p. 154 *'Over the Rainbow' a cappella*: In the last few lines of 'Over the Rainbow', in New Jersey that night, instead of rainbows and happy little bluebirds, it seemed to Mayo Simon that Judy sang 'Help me, love me,/I need you to love me,/If you don't love me/I . . . will . . . die.'

p. 156 *David Begelman*: David Begelman's reputation as a crook was sealed by the publication of *Indecent Exposure: A True Story of Hollwood and Wall Street* by David McClintick in 1982.

p. 159 *108,000 people in one night in Boston*: there are scenes of Judy singing on Boston Common in *Judy Garland: The Concert Years*. The date was 31 August 1967.

p. 159 *a manila envelope of printed matter*: these items are listed in *Heartbreaker* by John Meyer, p. 72.

p. 160 *Vincente Minnelli described the 'shocking confession'*: *I Remember It Well*, p. 248.

p. 161 Quotation from John Meyer, *Heartbreaker*, pp. 246–7.

pp. 161–2 Quotation from Dirk Bogarde, *Snakes and Ladders*, p. 296.

p. 162 *'I was afraid that she was no longer a survivor, and I had to be.'*: John Carlyle, *Under the Rainbow*, p. 224.

p. 163 *Artie Shaw*: This account of Artie Shaw and Judy Garland comes from Gerold Frank, *Judy*, p. 345.

pp. 163–4 Liza Minnelli told this anecdote most recently on *Parkinson*, broadcast in the UK in September 2006.

p. 164 *she pulled kitchen knives on people*: These incidents occur in Lorna Luft, *Me and My Shadows*, p. 210.

p. 164 *I have a voice that hurts people*: Judy said this to Dirk Bogarde, which he records in his autobiography *Snakes and Ladders*, p. 199.

p. 165 *she manipulated deliberately the emotions*: a newspaper review of Judy's 1957 triumph at the Dominion states that Judy Garland is 'as calculating as adding machine'. Who isn't?

p. 165 *Dick Cavett show*: from John Meyer, *Heartbreaker*, p. 240.

p. 165 *profligacy and extravagance*: In *Snakes and Ladders* (p. 198), Dirk Bogarde remarks that the food Judy served at home came, in the main, from Fortnum and Mason. GOOD.

p. 166 *'Frank Gumm's sad frailty'*: This expression appears in *Young Judy* by David Dahl and Barry Kehoe, p. 54.

p. 173 Sid Luft described in an interview given to the author in Grand Rapids, 2007.

p. 177 *Elizabeth Hardwick*: This obituary appeared in the *Guardian*, 6 December 2007.

p. 177 The Carnegie Hall album spent ninety-four weeks in the US charts, thirteen weeks at Number 1. It was the fastest-selling two-disc record of its era and garnered five Grammy Awards.

p. 179 Vincente Minnelli quotes this letter from 1944 written by his wife-to-be in *I Remember It Well*, p. 145.

p. 180 Artie Shaw, *The Trouble with Cinderella*, p. 222.

p. 181 *Judy's childhood was so wonderful*: The idea that the delightfulness of Garland's life was in some respects her undoing is one half of the thesis of the authors of *Young Judy*. For example: 'On stage in later years she would match the emotional richness and perfection of her childhood. In her private life she would search for the equivalent of her extraordinary early life . . . She had been shielded from the unhappiness and sorrow of the world, and had never even been to a funeral, and now suddenly, the golden years were over, the gallant years ahead.' David Dahl and Barry Kehoe, *Young Judy*, p. 223.

pp. 182–3 *moral hierarchy of drug taking*: this section owes a debt to an article written by John Lanchester in the *New Yorker* in 2003, entitled 'High Style: Writing Under the Influence'.

Are You a Good Fan or a Bad Fan?

p. 187 Some reviews of Judy at Carnegie Hall:
New York Herald Tribune: ' . . . ingenious warmth dominated the evening . . . Well, I can't give you anything but raves, Miss Garland.'
Variety: 'The audience couldn't resist anything she did.'
New York Times: 'The religious ritual of greeting, watching, and listening to Judy Garland took place last night at Carnegie Hall . . . What Billy Graham would have given for such a welcome from the faithful!'
Long Island Daily Press: 'If the building had caught fire, I think they'd have perished on the spot rather than leave her . . . She is full of fun and absolutely lovable. When she bends back and pulls those big notes up from her toes – well, forget about it – there is no other woman in show business.'
Hollywood Reporter: 'No other performer weaves that spell. Her fellow

pros have no rivalry where she is concerned. All of them agree that *she is the greatest.*'

p. 188 *'Personally, I think I have a little too much bloom.'*: Judy's character Esther Smith utters this phrase after her older sister informs her that she shouldn't kiss their neighbour because 'men don't like to see the bloom rubbed off'.

p. 189 *Easter Parade*, 1948, directed by Charles Walters.

p. 189 *Presenting Lily Mars*, 1943, directed by Norman Taurog.

p. 191 'I'm Nobody's Baby' words and music by Milton Ager, Benny Davis and Lester Santly.

p. 191 *Andy Hardy Meets Debutante*, 1940, directed by George B. Seitz.

p. 192 *Pigskin Parade*: The reviewer from the *New York Times* wrote, 'She's cute, not too pretty, but a pleasingly fetching personality.'

p. 192 'Who?' words by Otto Harback and Oscar Hammerstein II, music by Jerome Kern; sung by Judy in *Till The Clouds Roll By*, 1946, the biopic of Jerome Kern directed by Richard Whorf.

p. 192 'Down on Melody Farm' words by Gus Kahn, music by Bronislau Kaper and Walter Jurmann, from *Everybody Sing*, 1938, directed by Edwin L. Marin.

p. 192 'Bidin' My Time' words by Ira Gershwin, music by George Gershwin, from *Girl Crazy*, 1943, directed by Norman Taurog.

p. 193 *'Paree'*: the song is 'How 'Ya Gonna Keep 'em Down on the Farm (After They've Seen Paree?)'. I once heard this song sung by inmates of the UK drugs treatment centre Farm Place, to great effect.

p. 193 *like Judy for the right reasons*: good fans feel sick when we read old magazine articles that say, for example, 'For it is beyond dispute that Judy is not what Hollywood understands by the word glamorous.' W. H. Mooring writing in *Picturegoer*, in a 1943 called 'How Can Judy Cheat Crisis?'

p. 193 *One very good and bold fan*: I am grateful to John Fricke for this anecdote, which he told to me after I had visited, ruefully and with ambivalence, an exhibition of Princess Grace's gowns and assorted trinkets at Sotheby's in New York in 2007.

p. 194 *The most risqué tale*: Remembered by Liza Minnelli from when she was fourteen, in David Dahl and Barry Kehoe, *Young Judy*, p. xxi.

p. 198 *a bitter battle*: A full account of this extraordinary battle is given in Steven Cohan, *Incongruous Entertainment*.

p. 200 *Festival Hall, Melbourne*: Francis Wyndham pays attention to this concert in *The Theatre of Embarrassment*, p. 3.

p. 201 Quotation from Ethlie Ann Vare (ed.), *Rainbow*, p. xx. Attributed to 'muckraking' Jimmie Tarantino in *Hollywood Night Life*, 1948.

p. 202 Kay Thompson's remarks to Liza from Gerold Frank, *Judy*, p. 630.

p. 206 Saul Bellow's comments are from his introduction to John Berryman's novel, *Recovery*, reprinted in *It All Adds Up*.

p. 206 The visit to Drugs Anonymous comes from Gerold Frank, *Judy*, pp. 400–1.

p. 207 'I Can't Give You Anything but Love' words by Dorothy Fields, music by Jimmy McHugh.

p. 208 The Rainbow Portrait is on show at Hatfield House in Hertfordshire.

p. 212 *Judy herself attended a meeting*: I am grateful to Ken Sephton and Brian Glanvill for this story.

p. 212 'I Wish You Love' words and music by Charles Trenet, English translation by Albert A. Beach.

p. 215 *Bumble Dawson*: Beatrice 'Bumble' Dawson costume design credits include: *Dear Mr Prohack* (1949), *Svengali* (1955), *The Prince and the Showgirl* (1957), *A Tale of Two Cities* (1958), *Espresso Bongo* (1960), *The L-Shaped Room* (1962), *Life at the Top* (1965) and *Modesty Blaise* (1966).

p. 218 *'Remember neighbors, when you work for Mother Nature, You get paid by Father Time'*: 'Happy Harvest' from *Summer Stock*, 1950, directed by Charles Walters.

p. 222 *Funny Face*, 1957, directed by Stanley Donen.

p. 222 'Alexander's Ragtime Band' words and music by Irving Berlin

p. 223 *song about a woman who falls in love with a deaf mute*: The only other person I have heard sing this song is its lyricist, Mr Charles Aznavour. The song is called 'Quiet Love'.

p. 226 Information about the Judy Garland Birthplace Museum and its annual Judy festival in June can be found at www.judygarlandmuseum.com.

p. 227 *Fourteen of Garland's costumes*: This collection of Judy's dresses belongs to the collector Michael Siewart. His travelling exhibition is 'Judy Garland: The Dressing of a Legend'.

p. 228 *The day she died, I mean when she was ill in Hong Kong*: Judy was ill in Hong Kong in May 1964, and nearly died. In fact, it was announced on the radio on 28 May that she had died.

An apocryphal story has Judy on a gurney in a Hong Kong hospital and the doctor laying a sheet over her face, whereupon she sat bolt upright and shouted, 'Get your fucking hands off me!'

p. 233 'Together, Wherever We Go' words by Stephen Sondheim, music by Julie Styne.

p. 233 John Carlyle quotation from *Under the Rainbow*, p. 310.

p. 233 *Lucille Ball once commented*: Thanks to John Fricke for this anecdote.

p. 237 'Life is Just a Bowl of Cherries' words by Lew Brown, music by Ray Henderson.

p. 237 *their numbers*: These were all songs sung by the Gumm family in Grand Rapids, according to *Songs the Gumm Family Sang* by Michelle Russell.

p. 237 *The Gumm family's former nanny*: Wilma Hendricks Casper talked abut Judy in a documentary made by John Fricke at the Judy Garland Festival in 2007.

The End of the Road

p. 242 Judy Garland's tomb is at Ferncliff Cemetery, Westchester, New York. www.ferncliffcemetery.com.

p. 242 *Wallace Beery*: Wallace Beery was a film actor of the silent era. He later found work as a character actor in sound film. Credits include *Min and Bill*, *The Big House*, *The Champ*, *Billy the Kid*, *Tugboat Annie* and *The Mighty McGurk*.

p. 242 'We're a Couple of Swells' from *Easter Parade*. I taught both my children to walk to the chorus of this song.

p. 242 Judaline was born in May 1938 and christened Judy Gail, but always known as Judaline, which means 'little Judy'.

p. 244 *Words and Music*, 1948, directed by Norman Taurog.

p. 249 *I read once*: These children's tributes come from John Fricke, *Judy Garland: World's Greatest Entertainer*, p. 239.

p. 250 '*Who needs a happy Judy Garland?*': David Shipman describes how Judy asked this during the spectacular 1961 tour, pre Carnegie Hall, in *Judy Garland*, p. 401.

p. 251 *letter of condolence*: From John Carlyle, *Under the Rainbow*, p. 231.

p. 254 *Meinhardt Raabe*: www.wizardofozfestival.org/meinhardt-raabe

p. 256 *regaling anyone who'd listen*: These sort of antics are made very vivid in Mel Tormé's mean-spirited *The Other Side of the Rainbow: With Judy Garland on the Dawn Patrol*.

pp. 258–9 Quotation from Andy Warhol and Pat Hackett, *POPism: The Warhol Sixties*, p. 288.

p. 259 James Mason's eulogy is quoted in many biographies, including *Weep No More My Lady* by Garland's last husband, Mickey Deans (p. 236).

p. 261 In *Variety*, the memorial headline after Judy died was, simply, THE STARS HAVE LOST THEIR GLITTER – Ira Gershwin's phrase from 'The Man that Got Away'.

Encore, Encore

p. 262 Quotation from Aljean Harmetz, *The Making of the Wizard of Oz*, p. 236.

pp. 263–7 This meeting between Judy Garland and John Berryman is slightly inspired by the short story, 'Children are Bored on Sundays' by Jean Stafford. First published in the *New Yorker*, 21 February 1948, p. 23.

pp. 265–6 'Dream Song 29' from John Berryman, *The Dream Songs*.

pp. 267–8 Quotation from Saul Bellow's introduction to *Recovery* by John Berryman.

p. 269 'Get Happy' words by Ted Koehler, music by Harold Arlen.

p. 269 'Ol' Man River' music by Jerome Kern, music by Oscar Hammerstein II, from the 1936 musical *Show Boat*.

p. 271 'Stormy Weather' words by Ted Koehler, music by Harold Arlen.

p. 271 *Turner Layton*: Turner Layton was an American songwriter, singer and pianist who, working with the lyricist Henry Creamer, wrote numbers for various Broadway shows, including *Ziegfeld Follies*. He later performed as a cabaret artist in London and New York.

p. 272 *difficulties of being a child star*: from *Life Is Too Short* by Mickey Rooney.

p. 272 '*I wish they had worked me more*': Mickey Rooney made this comment to TCM's Robert Osborne in the bonus DVD that accompanies Warner Home Video's *The Mickey Rooney & Judy Garland Collection*.

p. 274 'Our Love Affair' words by Arthur Freed, music by Roger Edens.

p. 278 'Do I Love You?' words and music by Cole Porter.

p. 279 'The Boy Next Door' words and music by Hugh Martin and Ralph Blane.

p. 280 *I may have heard better news but I can't think when*: I have slightly misremembered the Berryman quotation. The actual line is 'I may have heard better news but I don't know when', from the poem 'Tea' in *Love and Fame*.

p. 281 'On the Atchison, Topeka and the Santa Fe' words by Johnny Mercer, music by Harry Warren.

p. 282 Quotation from John Meyer, writing in a memorial journal compiled, in tribute, by Lorna Smith on behalf of the Judy Garland Club, 1969.

p. 284 'If You Knew Susie' words by George 'Buddy' De Sylva, music by Joseph Meyer and Stephen W. Ballantine.

p. 284 'Fly Me to the Moon' words and music by Bart Howard.

Information about joining the Judy Garland Club can be found at www.judygarlandclub.org.

Bibliography

Judy

Clarke, Gerald, *Get Happy: The Life of Judy Garland* (London: Little, Brown, 2000)

Dahl, David and Barry Kehoe, *Young Judy* (New York: Mason/Charter, 1975)

Deans, Mickey and Ann Pinchot, *Weep No More My Lady: An Intimate Biography of Judy Garland* (London: W. H. Allen, 1972)

DiOrio, Al, Jr., *Little Girl Lost: The Life and Hard Times of Judy Garland* (New York: Arlington House, 1974)

Donnelley, Paul, *Judy Garland* (London: Haus, 2007)

Edwards, Anne, *Judy Garland* (New York: Simon and Schuster, 1975)

Frank, Gerold, *Judy* (London: W. H. Allen, 1975)

Finch, Christopher, *Rainbow: The Stormy Life of Judy Garland* (New York: Grossett & Dunlap, 1975)

Fricke, John, *Judy Garland: World's Greatest Entertainer – A Unique Photographic Tribute* (London: Little, Brown, 1992)

——, *Judy Garland: A Portrait in Art and Anecdote* (London: Bullfinch, 2003)

Harmetz, Aljean, *The Making of the Wizard of Oz* (London: Pavilion, 1989)

Haver, Ronald, *A Star is Born: The Making of the 1954 Movie and its 1983 Restoration* (New York: Alfred A. Knopf, 1988)

Meyer, John, *Heartbreaker: My Life with Judy Garland* (London: W. H. Allen, 1983)

Morella, Joe and Edward Epstein, *Judy: The Films and Career of Judy Garland* (London: Leslie Frewin, 1969)

302

Rushdie, Salman, *The Wizard of Oz* (London: British Film Institute, 1992)

Schechter, Scott, *Judy Garland: The Day-by-Day Chronicle of a Legend* (New York: Cooper Square Press, 2002)

Shipman, David, *Judy Garland* (London: Fourth Estate, 1992)

Smith, Lorna, *Judy with Love: The Story of Miss Showbusiness* (London: Robert Hale, 1975)

———, *My Life Over the Rainbow: Judy Garland's Life, as told to Lorna Smith* (New York: Vantage Press, 1987)

Spada, James, *Judy and Liza* (London: Sidgwick & Jackson, 1983)

Steiger, Brad, *Judy Garland* (New York: Ace Books, 1969)

Sanders, Coyne Steven, *Rainbow's End: The Judy Garland Show* (New York: Zebra Books, 1990)

Tormé, Mel, *The Other Side of the Rainbow: With Judy Garland on the Dawn Patrol* (New York: William Morrow, 1970)

Vare, Ethlie Ann (ed.), *Rainbow: A Star-Studded Tribute to Judy Garland* (New York: Boulevard Books, 1998)

The Wizard of Oz: 50th Anniversary Edition with Original Script and Songs (Limpsfield: Dragon's World, 1989)

I am extremely grateful to *The Rainbow Review*, especially those editions that appeared under the marvellous editorship of Gary Horrocks between 1998 and 2007.

Autobiography, biography and memoir

Allyson, June with Frances Spatz Leighton, *June Allyson* (New York: Putnam, 1982)

Bogarde, Dirk, *Snakes and Ladders* (London: Chatto and Windus, 1978)

Carlyle, John, *Under the Rainbow: An Intimate Memoir of Judy Garland, Rock Hudson and my Life in Old Hollywood* (New York: Carroll & Graf, 2006)

Cox, Stephen, *The Munchkins of Oz* (Nashville: Cumberland House, 1996)

Freedland, Michael, *Liza with a Z: The Traumas and Triumphs of Liza Minnelli* (London: Chrysalis, 1998)

Hopper, Hedda, *From Under My Hat* (n.p.: Frederick Muller, 1953)

Hopper, Hedda and James Brough, *The Whole Truth and Nothing But* (Garden City, NY: Doubleday, 1963)

Hyam, Hannah, *Fred and Ginger: The Astaire–Rogers Partnership, 1934–1938* (Brighton: Pen Press, 2007)

Jason, Sybil, *My Fifteen Minutes* (Albany, GA: BearManor Media, 2005)

Keel, Howard with Joyce Spizer, *Only Make Believe: My Life in Show Business* (Fort Lee, NJ: Barricade Books, 2005)

Lahr, John, *Notes on a Cowardly Lion: The Biography of Bert Lahr* (New York: Random House, 1969)

Luft, Lorna, *Me and My Shadows: A Family Memoir* (New York: Simon and Schuster, 1998)

Mason, James, *Before I Forget* (London: Sphere, 1981)

Mair, George, *Under the Rainbow: The Real Liza Minnelli* (London: Aurum, 1997)

Merman, Ethel with George Eells, *Merman, An Autobiography* (New York: Simon and Schuster 1978)

Minnelli, Vincente, *I Remember It Well* (Garden City, NY: Doubleday, 1974)

Neame, Ronald, *Straight from the Horse's Mouth* (Lanham, MD: Scarecrow Press, 2003)

Pasternak, Joe and David Chandler, *Easy the Hard Way: An Autobiography* (London: Allen, 1956)

Fauvre, Beverly Raffensperger, *Imagining Liza: Memoir of a Fan* (Carmel, IN: Hawthorne, 2000)

Rooney, Mickey, *Life Is Too Short* (New York: Random House, 1991)

Shaw, Artie, *The Trouble with Cinderella: An Outline of Identity* (New York: Farrar, Straus & Young, 1952)

Turner, Lana, *Lana: The Lady, The Legend, The Truth* (Sevenoaks: New English Library, 1983)

Hollywood

Breitbart, Andrew and Mark Ebner, *Hollywood Interruped: Insanity Chic in Babylon – The Case Against Celebrity* (Hoboken, NJ: Wiley, 2004)

Cohan, Steven, *Incongruous Entertainment: Camp, Cultural Value, and the*

MGM Musical (Durham, NC: Duke University Press, 2005)

McClintick, David, *Indecent Exposure: A True Story of Hollywood and Wall Street* (New York: Collins, 1982)

Gabler, Neal, *An Empire of their Own: How the Jews Invented Hollywood* (New York: Crown, 1988)

Wayne, Jane Ellen, *The Golden Girls of MGM: Greta Garbo, Lana Turner, Judy Garland, Ava Gardner, Grace Kelly, and Others* (New York: Carroll & Graf, 2003)

Wilk, Max, *They're Playing Our Song: The Truth Behind the Words and Music of Three Generations* (New York: Moyer Bell, 1991)

Zec, Donald, *Put the Knife in Gently: Memoirs of a Life with Legends* (London: Chrysalis, 2003)

Zierold, Norman J., *The Child Stars* (London: Macdonald, 1965)

Hero worship

Baker, Nicholson, *U & I: A True Story* (London: Granta, 1991)

Carlyle, Thomas, *On Heroes and Hero-Worship* (n.p., 1841)

Koestenbaum, Wayne, *Jackie Under My Skin: Interpreting an Icon* (New York: Farar, Straus & Giroux, 1995)

Maltby, John, James Houran, Rense Lange, Diane Ashe and Lynn E. McCutcheon, 'Thou Shalt Worship No Other Gods – Unless They Are Celebrities: The Relationship Between Celebrity Worship and Religious Orientation', *Personality and Individual Differences*, 32, 2002, pp. 1157–72

Vermorel, Fred and Judy, *Starlust: The Secret Life of Fans* (London: W. H. Allen, 1985)

Wecter, Dixon, *The Hero in America: A Chronicle of Hero-Worship* (New York: Charles Scribner's Sons, 1941)

Psychological

Edmundson, Mark, *The Death of Sigmund Freud: Fascism, Psychoanalysis and the Rise of Fundamentalism* (London: Bloomsbury, 2007)

——, 'Defender of the Faith?', *New York Times*, 9 September 2007

Freud, Ernst (ed., trans. Tania and James Stern), *Letters of Sigmund Freud* (New York: Basic Books, 1961)

Hale, Nathan G., Jr., *The Rise and Crisis of Psychoanalysis in the United States: Freud and the Americans, 1917–1985* (New York: Oxford University Press, 1995)

———, 'New Heads for Freud's Hydra: Psychoanalysis in Los Angeles', *Journal of the History of the Behavioural Sciences*, vol. 37(2), spring 2001, pp. 111–22

McDougall, Joyce, *Plea for a Measure of Abnormality* (London: Free Association Books, 1990)

Lanchester, John, 'High Style: Writing under the Influence', *The New Yorker*, 6 January 2003

Roth, Geneen, *When Food is Love: Exploring the Relationship Between Eating and Intimacy* (New York: Plume, 1992)

Simmel, Ernst, 'Alcoholism and Addiction' in Sandor Lorand (ed.) *Yearbook of Psychoanalysis*, vol. 5, 1949, p. 238

Other

Bellow, Saul, *It All Adds Up: From the Dim Past to the Uncertain Future – A Nonfiction Collection* (London: Penguin, 1995)

Berryman, John, *The Collected Poems of John Berryman, 1937–1971* (London: Faber, 1989)

———, *The Dream Songs* (London: Faber, 1969)

———, *Recovery* (London: Faber, 1973)

Fadiman, Clifton, *Party of One: The Selected Writings of Clifton Fadiman* (New York: The World Publishing Co., 1955)

James, Henry, *In the Cage* (n.p., 1898)

Lahr, John, *Coward the Playwright* (London: Methuen, 1999)

Ryman, Geoff, *Was* (New York: Penguin, 1972)

Simpson, Eileen, *Poets in their Youth: A Memoir* (London: Faber, 1982)

Stafford, Jean, *The Collected Stories of Jean Stafford* (New York: Farrar, Straus & Giroux, 1969)

Wyndham, Francis, *The Theatre of Embarrassment* (London: Chatto and Windus, 1991)

Acknowledgements

Thanks first and foremost to the one and only Mr Marc Charbonnet, the most elegant, swelligant Judy best-friend a person could hope to have. A true wizard indeed, with or without curtains.

Enormous thanks to Caroline Dawnay . . . because of the wonderful things she does.

Huge thanks to Lennie Goodings for her terrific heart, brain and nerve.

Thanks also to Kate Mackenzie Davey, John Fricke, Mayo Simon, Brian Glanvill, Gary Horrocks, John Haffenden, Frances Costelloe, Ann Rittenberg, John Haffenden, Alexander Boyt, Suzy Boyt, Christie Hickman, Fiona Harrold, the Judy Garland Club and the Judy Garland Birthplace Museum.

Thanks to everyone at Virago for their enthusiasm, high standards and dedication to keeping the blue stocking firmly inside the ruby slippers.

And thanks as ever to Tom and Mary and Cecilia who prove every day that there's no place like home.

Credits

Under the Rainbow: An Intimate Memoir of Judy Garland, Rock Hudson and My Life in Old Hollywood by John Carlyle, published by Da Capo Press. Used by permission of Perseus Books Group.

The Whole Truth and Nothing But by Hedda Hopper, published by Doubleday. Used by permission of Random House Inc.

A portion of the Liza Minnelli interview was previously published in *Observer Music Monthly* and is reproduced here with the newspaper's kind permission.

Parts of the interviews with Mickey Rooney and Lorna Luft, and a part of the section about Christmas in Chapter One were first published in the *Financial Times* and are reproduced here with the newspaper's kind permission.

PHOTOGRAPHS

© Rollie McKenna: 176

AFP/Getty Images: 44

Aquarius: plate 5

ARNI: 124

Author's collection: 2, 19, 21, 46, 50, 59, 136, 231, 232, 236, 251, plate 7, plate 8

British Film Institute: 29, 114

Christopher Holland: 278

Hulton Archive/Getty Images: 23 (David, Vincente, Mark and Mickey), 35, 56 (right), 67, 81, 129, 192 (right), 207, 240

Judy Garland Museum: 90

MGM/Kobal Collection: plate 1, plate 2

MGM: 3, 26, 52, 56 (left), 93, 97 (right), 115, 190, 243, 271, plate 3

Popperfoto/Getty Images: 23 (Sid), 310

Private collections: 6, 9, 14, 28, 36, 37, 40, 51, 78, 86, 88, 97 (left), 103, 107, 142, 148, 155, 158, 179, 192 (left), 203, 228, 264, 273, plate 4, plate 6

Still Images/Getty Images: 72

Time and Life Pictures/Getty Images: 94, 101, 121, 259

Timothy Taylor Gallery: 175

United Press International: 65

Just wanted you to know that I did read your letter.
Remember "Anything is possible"
Frances Gumm
Judy Garland